Want your practice **SAT essay**
scored and critiqued?

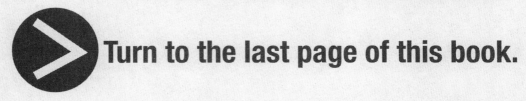 Turn to the last page of this book.

Peterson's
New SAT Writing
Workbook

Margaret Moran

THOMSON

PETERSON'S

Australia • Canada • Mexico • Singapore • Spain • United Kingdom • United States

About Thomson Peterson's

Thomson Peterson's (www.petersons.com) is a leading provider of education information and advice, with books and online resources focusing on education search, test preparation, and financial aid. Its Web site offers searchable databases and interactive tools for contacting educational institutions, online practice tests and instruction, and planning tools for securing financial aid. Thomson Peterson's serves 110 million education consumers annually.

Petersons.com/publishing

Check out our Web site at www.petersons.com/publishing to see if there is any new information regarding the test and any revisions or corrections to the content of this book. We've made sure the information in this book is accurate and up-to-date; however, the test format or content may have changed since the time of publication.

For more information, contact Thomson Peterson's, 2000 Lenox Drive, Lawrenceville, NJ 08648; 800-338-3282; or find us on the World Wide Web at www.petersons.com/about.

Editor: Wallie Walker Hammond; Production Editor: Teresina Jonkoski; Manufacturing Manager: Judy Coleman; Composition Manager: Linda M. Williams.

ISBN 0-7689-1714-X

Printed in the United States of America

10 9 8 7 6 5 4 3 2 1   06 05 04

First Edition

CONTENTS

CONTENTS

CONTENTS

CONTENTS

Introduction

ABOUT THE WRITING SECTION ON THE NEW SAT I

Beginning with the Spring 2005 administration of the SAT I, the College Board added a Writing section to the test. Along with changes to the Math section, the new Writing section is expected to provide a better assessment of how prepared students are for college. The basic facts about the new Writing section are the following:

The Writing section will consist of two parts:
- One student-produced essay
- Multiple-choice questions on grammar, usage, and word choice

The Writing section will be 50 minutes in length:
- 20 minutes for the essay
- 30 minutes for the multiple-choice questions

The scoring will be the same as the old SAT I and SAT II Writing Subject Test:
- 200 to 800 scale
- 1 to 6 scale for the essay
- Use of a holistic approach to scoring the essay

The essay prompt will require you to
- Write a persuasive essay

The multiple-choice questions will ask you to
- Identify sentence errors
- Improve sentences
- Improve paragraphs

USING *PETERSON'S NEW SAT WRITING WORKBOOK* TO IMPROVE YOUR SCORE

Peterson's New SAT Writing Workbook has been designed to give you concentrated practice in the skills you will need for both the essay and the multiple-choice questions on the Writing section of the SAT I. Employ the following steps to get the most from using this book:

- Apply the test-taking strategies as you practice writing the timed essays and answering the multiple-choice questions.

- Evaluate your essays against the rubric that is given. It is similar to the one used for the actual test.

- Compare your multiple-choice responses with the Answer and Explanations that follow the questions.

- Read all the answer explanations, even for questions you answered correctly. You will be reinforcing and extending what you know—and maybe learning something new.

- Use your practice sessions to pinpoint those areas that you need to spend more time reviewing.

- Make a list of weak areas for review. Check them off as you become more confident about each one.

If you take the time to read each chapter and complete each exercise, including the simulated writing sections, you will increase your test-taking skills and gain confidence for the real SAT I.

PETERSON'S SAT ESSAYEDGE

Peterson's SAT EssayEdge service will offer an edit and critique of your practice SAT essays. EssayEdge will tell you what score your essays would have received, as well as give you a critique that explains additional concepts and strategies needed to improve your score on test day. This service is available at www.petersons.com/satessayedge.

A WORD ABOUT THE FUTURE

The writing process, effective writing guidelines, and standard English conventions that you are learning in *Peterson's New SAT Writing Workbook* apply to whatever you write, whenever you write. The words *whatever* and *whenever* are important to remember. Using this book to improve your writing for the SAT I is one reason to buy it. It is equally important to use the writing process, strategies, and standard English discussed in this book FOREVER. You will be required to write once you are in college, and most likely, you will be required to write in your workplace. The goal of this book is to help you develop and practice your skills in writing clearly expressed, coherent, and well-developed prose. Practice for the SAT I by using the writing strategies and practice exercises in this book and you will be on your way to turning these strategies into life-long habits.

Part I
Practicing Your Essay Writing Skills

In Chapters 1 through 5, you will find

- Basic information about the writing section on the SAT I

- An explanation of the scoring rubric

- Strategies for understanding writing prompts with exercises for practice

- A review of the writing process

- Strategies for planning and writing the essay

- A sample writing guide to help you pace your writing

- Timed essays for practice

- 10 rules for effective writing, followed by exercises

Chapter 1

ABOUT THE ESSAY ON THE SAT I

Your goals for this chapter are to learn the
- Basic information about the Writing section on the SAT I
- Elements of the scoring rubric

The Writing section of the SAT I assesses

- How clearly you can express your ideas when writing "on demand"

- How well you know and can apply the rules of standard written English

"On demand," according to the College Board, is the kind of writing you will do in college on tests and in the workplace in memos, email messages, or letters—short pieces of writing done quickly.

The term *standard written English* refers to the rules of grammar, mechanics, and usage that you find in any English grammar textbook. On the SAT I, you will show your skills with the conventions of standard English by

- Writing your essay

- Recognizing and correcting errors

- Demonstrating an awareness of language through the revision of others' writing

The focus in Chapters 1 through 4 is on getting your ideas down on paper. Chapter 5 reviews some basic grammar, mechanics, and usage issues that can affect your writing. You will be reviewing and practicing the skills and test-taking tips for identifying errors and improving sentences and paragraphs in Chapters 6 through 9.

WHAT THE ESSAY ASSESSES

The essay question is included on the SAT I for an obvious reason—to test your writing skills. To do well, you need to

- Explain your thinking about the topic

- Support your thinking with facts, examples, and ideas

- Organize your writing in a logical, effective manner

- Communicate your ideas clearly, concisely, and effectively
- Prove your mastery of the conventions of standard written English while doing all of the above

In other words, you must show that you can write well enough to produce an essay that is acceptable to a college professor. Your writing must demonstrate that you can

- Express and support an opinion or defend a position
- Use facts and examples in expressing your opinion or defending your position

ESSAY TOPICS

The topic for the essay on the SAT I will require you to write a persuasive essay. You will be asked to take a position and use examples to support your position. The essay, however, will not require any special subject matter knowledge on your part. You will not be asked to write about whether global warming exists or whether the United States trade deficit is good or bad for the economy. The topic will be broad and general, such as agreeing or disagreeing with the statement that change is a constant in society.

   Because this is an essay, you will be asked to support your opinion with examples from literature, art, music, history, science and technology, current events, or your own experience and observation. As noted, you may use personal experience as evidence. However, the more information you can bring to your topic from outside yourself, the more well-rounded and knowledgeable you will appear to the readers. That is, do not only use personal observations like "I think . . . ," "I feel . . . ," "It seems to me . . ." to prop up your arguments. Use facts and data whenever you can.

THE LENGTH OF THE ESSAY

There is no required length for your essay. It is the quality, not the quantity, that is important to the readers. Realistically, however, a one-paragraph essay is unlikely to garner you a high mark because you probably cannot develop a well-reasoned opinion and effectively present it in one paragraph. An essay of three to five paragraphs with several sentences in each paragraph is a good goal for your writing. By following this model, you can set up your idea with an interesting introduction, develop a soundly reasoned body, and provide a solid conclusion. This means you will need to write between 200 and 250 words.

SCORING THE ESSAY

Your handwritten essays will be scanned and delivered to College Board-trained readers over the Internet. The readers will review each essay for its general, overall impression and score it using a scale from 1 to 6. There is no right or wrong answer to an essay topic. Each essay is read by two readers who are high school or college teachers. They will not mark grammar, spelling, or punctuation errors. However, they will consider such errors along with the organization of your essay, the logical development of your argument, your choice of words, and the consistency of your style—all the elements that go into writing a good essay.

Your essay score will be reported in two ways. It will be combined with the scaled score from the multiple-choice section and reported within a range from 200 to 800. You will also receive a subscore for your essay. As you know, each reader will give your essay a score on a scale from 1 to 6 (see below for a detailed description of this scale). These two scores are then added to give you your subscore. For example, if one reader gives your essay a 6, and the second reader gives it a 5, then your subscore will be 11. The subscore will use a scale from 2 to 12.

One more word about scoring: The College Board cautions its readers to ignore handwriting. However, if the reader can't read what you wrote, it is your loss, because the reader is *forced* to "ignore" your ideas. So, write legibly. Even if you are excited about the topic and hurry to get down all your ideas before the time is up, be careful. Write so that someone not familiar with your handwriting can read it.

THE SCORING RUBRIC

The readers for the SAT I essays are trained by the College Board to score essays holistically. This means that the scorers are looking at the overall impression that an essay makes on them. They do not expect you to write a perfect, polished composition in the 20 minutes you are allowed. However, the readers *do* consider how successfully a writer was able to

- Organize the essay

- Logically develop ideas

- Use evidence to support ideas

- Use appropriate diction or word choice

- Vary sentence structure

- Use correct grammar and punctuation

The readers award good scores to essays that are clear, interesting, and correct.

Let's take a closer look at what the scorers are looking for as they read the essays.

An essay that receives a 6 will have the following characteristics:

These characteristics deal with the **overall impression** your essay makes:

- Clarity and consistency throughout

- Virtually error-free (Notice that the scorers are not expecting you to write a perfect essay. An occasional error is acceptable.)

The readers are looking for your **thesis,** or the statement of your main idea, and how well you establish the **purpose** of your essay:

- Insightful and effective addressing of the topic

The **organization** of your essay and **development** of your ideas are basic elements that the scorers read for:

- Excellent organization

- Fully developed with appropriate examples, facts, and details supporting your thesis

Readers assess your use of **correct sentence structure** and a **variety of sentence structures:**

- Variety in sentence structure

This characteristic relates to your choice of words, or **diction,** to convey your ideas:

- Breadth in vocabulary

Your overall use of correct **grammar** and **usage** is also evaluated:

- Excellent facility in language usage

An essay that receives a 5 will have the following characteristics:

- Good clarity and consistency

- Few errors and lapses in quality

- Effective addressing of the topic

- Good organization
- Adequate development with examples, facts, and details supporting the thesis
- Some sentence variety
- Some breadth in vocabulary
- Facility in language usage

An essay that receives a 4 will have the following characteristics:

- Adequate clarity and consistency
- Some errors and lapses in quality
- Adequate addressing of the topic
- Adequate organization
- Some development with examples, facts, and details supporting the thesis
- Minimal variety in sentence structure
- Some errors in vocabulary
- Inconsistent facility in language usage; some errors in grammar

An essay that receives a 3 will have the following characteristics:

- Emerging competence
- Many errors
- Somewhat off the topic
- Insufficient organization
- Inadequate or insufficient support
- Errors in sentence structure
- Simplistic vocabulary; errors in diction
- Errors in grammar and other language usage

An essay that receives a 2 will have the following characteristics:

- Some incompetence
- Flaws throughout
- Inadequate treatment of the topic
- Poor organization

- Lack of adequate support; inappropriate support
- Many errors in sentence structure
- Frequent errors in diction
- Many errors in grammar and other language usage

An essay that receives a 1 will have the following characteristics:

- Incompetence
- Serious flaws throughout
- Very poor addressing of the topic
- Extremely insufficient organization
- Very inappropriate or insufficient support
- Serious errors in sentence structure
- Many errors in diction that affect understanding
- Errors in grammar and other language usage that cloud meaning

An essay receives a zero (0) if the writer did not write on the assigned topic. However, there is no penalty for an incomplete essay. But you do have to write enough to demonstrate your writing skills.

PLANNING YOUR TIME

What does all this mean? It means that you need to do some planning and practicing in order to do well on test day. The best way to write a good essay in 20 minutes is to write many essays within that time constraint. In other words, you must practice, practice, practice.

Since you have only 20 minutes to write your essay, you cannot spend 15 minutes planning and 5 minutes composing. When you practice, take only 20 minutes to plan, write, and edit your essays. Use the following timetable to help you develop a schedule that works for you.

Prewriting
- Allow 2–4 minutes for this step.
- Read and study the question in detail.
- Jot down ideas, facts, and examples.
- Develop your thesis.
- Order your ideas in a logical pattern to support your thesis.

Writing
- Allow approximately 12–16 minutes to shape your essay.
- Write your essay following the pattern you determined during the prewriting stage.
- Develop the ideas that support your thesis fully.
- Compose your paragraphs so that each one develops a single point.
- Choose effective words.
- Include transitional words and phrases to unify your work.

Revising and Editing
- Set aside 2–4 minutes for revising, editing, and proofreading.
- Revise for sense, making sure that everything you included helps achieve your purpose.
- Edit so that every word says what you mean.
- Revise sentences for clarity and variety.
- Correct grammar, spelling, punctuation, and capitalization.

By planning before you start writing, you can be confident that your clear, coherent, unified—and neatly written—essay will shine in each scorer's pile of vague, incoherent, fragmented, and illegible essays.

CHECK YOUR WRITING SKILLS

How does your writing right now measure up against the characteristics readers use to score your essay? Find the most recent piece of writing that you did for a class.

- Evaluate it against each of the six levels on the rubric given below.

- Write the number of the level that best indicates each aspect of your writing. For example, if you used a mix of sentence structures throughout your piece, give it a 6.

Title/topic of writing:

_____

SELF-EVALUATION

Each category is rated 6 (high) to 1 (low)
Overall Impression _____
Thesis and Purpose _____
Organization and Development _____
Use of Sentences _____
Word Choice _____
Grammar and Usage _____

TOTAL _____
    Divide by 6 for final score _____

How did you do? Where could your writing use some improvement? Organization? Statement of your thesis? Word choice? Begin your list for review by writing down those areas you want to work on.

WRITING AS THE ONLY PREPARATION

There is no way to prepare for the SAT I Writing test except by writing. After all, you cannot choose a topic and prepare a well-researched, well-organized, and clearly expressed essay ahead of time. You don't know the topic ahead of time. What you do know is that the writing prompt will require you to take a stand on an issue and support it with evidence. The only way to become skilled at this kind of writing is to practice. "Practice makes perfect," as the old saying goes. Continue on to Chapter 2 to begin practicing dissecting writing prompts.

PRACTICAL ADVICE

As you begin to practice for the essay, keep the following strategies in mind:

- Make sure that your essay is long enough to demonstrate your writing skills.

- Write approximately 200 to 250 words and more than one paragraph to ensure that your essay is well-developed.

- Write about the given prompt only.

- Write legibly.

CHECK OFF

Before you go on to the next chapter, can you

- Repeat the basic information about the writing section on the SAT I?

- List the characteristics that readers will be looking for as they score SAT I essays?

Chapter 2
DISSECTING THE WRITING PROMPT

Your goals for this chapter are to
- Learn how to determine what you are being asked to write about
- Practice pulling apart writing prompts to understand them
- Practice thinking of examples to use to support your opinion

The essay section of the writing test consists of a set of directions, a writing prompt or assignment, and blank lines. Your "assignment" is to fill in the blank lines with a coherent, unified, and interesting piece of writing that answers the question posed.

The typical format for the writing prompt will look much like the following:

Directions: Think carefully about the issue described in the excerpt below and about the assignment that follows it.

The role of advertising is to induce people to buy goods and services. Advertising is neither moral nor immoral. It is ethically neutral.

Assignment: What is your opinion of the idea that considerations of morality have no place in advertising? Plan and write an essay that develops your point of view on the issue. Support your opinion with reasoning and examples from your reading, your classwork, your personal experiences, or your observations.

THE DIRECTIONS

The directions are brief and straightforward.

> **Directions:** Think carefully about the issue described in the excerpt below and about the assignment that follows it.

That seems simple enough. All you have to do is read the excerpt, read the assignment, and start writing. Wrong! The directions say "think carefully about the issue." Ok, you say, you've read the excerpt—twice. Now, you can write. Wrong!

Before you tackle writing your essay or even planning it, you need to be sure that you know what the writing prompt—the excerpt and the assignment—is *really* asking you to write about. You have to dissect the prompt to decide what to write.

THE WRITING PROMPT

Topics for writing prompts tend to be broad, open-ended, and adaptable enough for any test-taker to find something to write about. Remember that you will not need any specific subject matter knowledge to answer the question. The excerpt in this sample is a typical example.

> The role of advertising is to induce people to buy goods and services. Advertising is neither moral nor immoral. It is ethically neutral.

The writing prompt will most likely be based on a statement or a quotation. In order to answer the question that follows, you must understand what the excerpt is about. However, if you can't figure out the meaning or aren't sure, don't worry. The test-writers tell you the issue in the assignment.

However, don't ignore the excerpt. You may find some phrases that you can use in your essay. Referring back to the excerpt by paraphrasing it or using some words from it can be an effective technique. For example, "Unlike the author, I do not think that advertising is ethically neutral" or "The purpose of advertising may be to get people to buy things, but . . ." are strong essay openers. After you read the assignment, reread the excerpt. Underline any key words or phrases that you might want to use in your essay.

THE ASSIGNMENT

The assignment gives you the issue, or point, of the excerpt. It also tells you what you need to write about.

Assignment: What is your opinion of the idea that considerations of morality have no place in advertising? Plan and write an essay that develops your point of view on the issue. Support your opinion with reasoning and examples from your reading, your classwork, your personal experiences, or your observations.
This assignment has multiple parts:

1. What is your opinion of the idea that considerations of morality have no place in advertising?

"What is your opinion of the idea" is the question that you have to answer. "Considerations of morality have no place in advertising" is the issue, or point, of the excerpt. By asking you to give your opinion, the test-writers are telling you to write a persuasive essay.

2. **Plan and write an essay that develops your point of view on the issue.**

   The phrase *your point of view* is another clue that you are to write a persuasive essay. Note that the assignment tells you to "plan and write." It doesn't say just "write." Because your time is limited, you won't be able to outline your ideas. But you should jot down ideas and number them in logical order. With a plan, your essay is guaranteed to be clearer and more logically organized than if you just begin to write without a plan. Chapters 3 and 4 will help you with the planning part of your essay writing.

3. **Support your opinion with reasoning and examples from your reading, your class work, your personal experiences, or your observations.**

   The last part of the assignment tells you that you need to support your opinion with reasoning and examples. By reasoning, the test-writers mean you need to develop a logical and well-thought-out piece of writing. You are also told that you need evidence in the form of examples to defend your point, or support your position. That evidence may come from

- Reading you have done for personal enjoyment or personal education
- Information you have learned in classes you have taken—from music and art to science and technology
- Personal experiences such as family relationships, friendships, jobs, and extracurricular activities
- Personal observations of self, family, friends, classmates, neighbors, and customers or employers in jobs that you have held

CHECK YOUR WRITING SKILLS

Read the writing prompts and answer the following questions.

Directions: Think carefully about the issue described in the excerpt below and about the assignment that follows it.

The role of advertising is to induce people to buy goods and services. Advertising is neither moral nor immoral. It is ethically neutral.

Assignment: What is your opinion of the idea that considerations of morality have no place in advertising? Plan and write an essay that develops your point of view on the issue. Support your opinion with reasoning and examples from your reading, your class work, your personal experiences, or your observations.

1. What is the issue of the excerpt as stated by the test-writer?

2. What are you supposed to write about the issue?

3. If you had to write an essay to answer this question, what would your opinion be? Write your opinion in one sentence.

4. What examples would you use? Jot down three of them; use single words or phrases for each.

5. Next to each example, write the source of the idea—for example, a book you read, a cable show you watched, etc.

ANALYZING MORE PROMPTS

Let's take a look at some more prompts and how you might answer them.

Directions: Think carefully about the issue described in the excerpt below and about the assignment that follows it.

Many people believe that what is important is playing or participating in sports, not winning.

Assignment: What is your opinion of the idea that playing is more important than winning? Plan and write an essay that develops your point of view on the issue. Support your opinion with reasoning and examples from your reading, your class work, your personal experiences, or your observations.

To answer a prompt that asks for your opinion, you first need to ask yourself if you agree with the issue or not. Do you think that people value participation more than victory? Or do you disagree, believing that triumph is more important?

In truth, your opinion about the issue is less important than the support that you bring to your essay. You need to cite specific examples from your life experience or your knowledge base to support your viewpoint. You will need to include more than one example to write an effective essay. You should plan on presenting at least three examples. Be specific and use details to describe each example. The more you use relevant details, the more interesting your essay will be. You will learn more about writing interesting essays in Chapter 3.

Take a look at another example.

Directions: Think carefully about the issue described in the excerpt below and about the assignment that follows it.

When good people in any country cease their vigilance and struggle, then evil men prevail.
—Pearl S. Buck

Assignment: What is your opinion of Buck's viewpoint that good people must always strive against evil? Plan and write an essay that develops your point of view on the issue. Support your opinion with reasoning and examples from your reading, your class work, your personal experiences, or your observations.

To answer this question, you need to decide your own viewpoint first. Do you think that Buck's idea is valid? Do you think that evil occurs when good takes no stand against it? Can you think of examples in present-day events or from history that support your thesis?

CHECK YOUR WRITING SKILLS

Read the following writing prompts and assignments. The directions are not repeated each time. State your opinion and list three examples that you could use to support your opinion. Try to vary your sources of evidence.

1. It is better to err on the side of daring than the side of caution.
   —Alvin Toffler

Assignment: What is your view of the idea that it is better to be daring than to be cautious in living one's life? Plan and write an essay that develops your point of view on the issue. Support your opinion with reasoning and examples from your reading, your class work, your personal experiences, or your observations.

Issue:_____

_____

My opinion:_____

_____

Some evidence I could use:_____

_____

_____

2. When you are right, you cannot be too radical; when you are wrong, you cannot be too conservative.
—Dr. Martin Luther King, Jr.

Assignment: What is your view of the idea that it is acceptable to be radical when pursuing something that is just and right, but conservative when in error? Plan and write an essay that develops your point of view on the issue. Support your opinion with reasoning and examples from your reading, your class work, your personal experiences, or your observations.

Issue:_____

_____

My opinion:_____

_____

Some evidence I could use:_____

_____

_____

3. Knowledge is capable of being its own end. Such is the constitution of the human mind, that any kind of knowledge, if it really be such, is its own reward.
—John, Cardinal Newman, *The Idea of a University*

Assignment: What is your view of the idea that knowledge is its own reward? Plan and write an essay that develops your point of view on the issue. Support your opinion with reasoning and examples from your reading, your class work, your personal experiences, or your observations.

Issue:_____

_____

My opinion:_____

_____

Some evidence I could use:_____

_____

_____

4. A good idea is one that turns you on rather than shuts you off. It keeps generating more ideas and they improve on one another. A bad idea is one that closes doors instead of opening them. It is confining and restrictive.
—Twyla Tharp, *The Creative Habit*

Assignment: What is your view of the opinion that good ideas generate more ideas, whereas bad ideas limit your creative thinking? Plan and write an essay that develops your point of view on the issue. Support your opinion with reasoning and examples from your reading, your class work, your personal experiences, or your observations.

Issue:_____

_____

My opinion:_____

_____

Some evidence I could use:_____

_____

_____

5. As we let our own light shine, we unconsciously give other people permission to do the same. As we are liberated from our own fears, our presence automatically liberates others.
—Nelson Mandela

Assignment: What is your view of the idea that in allowing ourselves the freedom to be and do our best, we aid others in being and doing their best? Plan and write an essay that develops your point of view on the issue. Support your opinion with reasoning and examples from your reading, your class work, your personal experiences, or your observations.

Issue:_____

_____

My opinion:_____

_____

Some evidence I could use:_____

_____

_____

6. Learning is an active process, not a passive one. Students learn best when they are actively engaged in their own learning, making decisions about what they learn and how they learn it.

Assignment: What is your view of the idea that students should be actively engaged in their own learning? Plan and write an essay that develops your point of view on the issue. Support your opinion with reasoning and examples from your reading, your class work, your personal experiences, or your observations.

Issue:_____

_____

My opinion:_____

_____

Some evidence I could use:_____

_____

_____

7. Technological progress will force all of society to confront tough new problems, only some of which we can foresee. But we should be prepared for change.
—William Gates, *The Road Ahead*

Assignment: What is your view of the idea that technology causes changes in society? Plan and write an essay that develops your point of view on the issue. Support your opinion with reasoning and examples from your reading, your class work, your personal experiences, or your observations.

Issue:_____

_____

My opinion:_____

_____

Some evidence I could use:_____

_____

_____

8. We make a living by what we get. We make a life by what we give.
—Winston Churchill

Assignment: What is your view of the idea that living a full and complete life includes helping others? Plan and write an essay that develops your point of view on the issue. Support your opinion with reasoning and examples from your reading, your class work, your personal experiences, or your observations.

Issue:_____

_____

My opinion:_____

_____

Some evidence I could use:_____

_____

_____

9. There are a few things that *everyone* is interested in. Virtually everyone is interested in *saving time, saving money,* and *reducing headaches,* that is, making life less complicated.
   —Adapted from *Guerrilla Selling,* Jay Conrad Levinson, Bill Gallagher, and Orvel Ray Wilson

Assignment: What is your view of the idea that saving time, saving money, and living a less stressful life are priorities for many, if not most, people? Plan and write an essay that develops your point of view on the issue. Support your opinion with reasoning and examples from your reading, your class work, your personal experiences, or your observations.

Issue:_____

_____

My opinion:_____

_____

Some evidence I could use:_____

_____

_____

10. The oppressor neither hates nor fears the weaknesses and failures of the oppressed. Rather, it is their strengths and successes that enrage and terrify him beyond reason.
    —James Jerry Clark, *Journal of a Champion,* Champions of Caring Program

Assignment: What is your opinion of the idea that oppressors actually fear their victims? Plan and write an essay that develops your point of view on the issue. Support your opinion with reasoning and examples from your reading, your class work, your personal experiences, or your observations.

Issue:_____

_____

My opinion:_____

_____

Some evidence I could use:_____

_____

_____

PRACTICAL ADVICE

As you begin to practice for the essay, keep the following strategies in mind:

- Read the excerpt carefully.

- Read the assignment carefully.

- Underline key words and phrases in the excerpt for possible use in your essay.

CHECK OFF

Before you go on to the next chapter,

- Can you dissect a writing prompt accurately to find out what you are supposed to write about?

- Is it becoming easier to think of at least three examples to support your essays?

ANSWERS AND EXPLANATIONS

CHECK YOUR WRITING SKILLS: DETERMINING WHAT'S BEING ASKED, PAGE 16

1. The issue is stated in the question: "Considerations of morality have no place in advertising."

2. What you are to write about is stated in the questions also: "your opinion of the idea that considerations of morality have no place in advertising."

3. Your sentence should state whether you agree or disagree with the issue as stated in the question.

4. Analyze your three examples. Do they offer strong support for your opinion? Is there any one that is weak that you could change? Why is the substitute better than your original piece of evidence?

5. Do you have a variety of kinds of evidence to support your opinion? You should try to find different sources; if they are all from cable TV shows, they may not impress the readers.

CHECK YOUR WRITING SKILLS: PRACTICING WITH WRITING PROMPTS, PAGE 18

1. *Issue:* It is better to be daring than to be cautious in living one's life.

   My opinion: You have to decide if you agree or disagree with the issue as stated. Remember that your opinion is less important to the reader than the way you will develop it.

   Some evidence: One way of approaching your answer is to consider some causes and effects, or outcomes, of being daring versus being cautious. For example, if the Wright Brothers had not been daring, they would never have tried to fly. Or, if Jackie Robinson had never dared to confront racism in Major League Baseball, he would never have become Rookie of the Year or the National League's Most Valuable Player.

2. *Issue:* It is acceptable to be radical when pursuing something that is just and right but conservative when in error.

   My opinion: Did you agree or disagree with the issue?

   Some evidence: One piece of evidence you could use that relates directly back to Dr. King is his use of nonviolence in the civil rights movement. While nonviolent, the civil rights marchers broke existing laws. In that sense, they were radical.

3. *Issue:* Knowledge is its own reward.

   My opinion: Do you agree that learning for learning's sake is enough? Or do you believe that what you learn has to be put to some use—from being a better basketball player by learning better ball control to earning a higher salary by getting a college degree?

   Some evidence: Real-world rather than historical examples would probably be the strongest support for this essay. However, the evidence you choose for your argument must be strong and convincing.

4. *Issue:* Good ideas generate more ideas, whereas bad ideas limit your creative thinking.

   My opinion: This is one of those times when you may have to think about your own experiences and observations of other's actions before you can decide how you feel about the issue. That's ok. But don't decide your opinion as you write. If you decided as you wrote, you would be writing without a plan. That's not a good way to get a good score.

   Some evidence: While you might have an historical anecdote you could use as an example, most probably the evidence to support your opinion would come from personal experiences or the experiences of friends, family, school situations, or employers.

5. *Issue:* In allowing ourselves the freedom to be and do our best, we aid others in being and doing their best.

   My opinion: It seems as though you should agree with the issue, or you would be a Scrooge—who would make a good example.

   Some evidence: Other examples could be Nelson Mandela himself and Mother Theresa. You may know someone in your own life who works to help others—a teacher, a coach, a physical therapist, or someone in the community who runs a foundation, a clinic, or an educational program.

6. *Issue:* Students should be actively engaged in their own learning.

   My opinion: You probably had no trouble in deciding how you feel about this issue.

   Some evidence: Using your own experience is probably the best source of examples. When a writer knows the subject very well, she can write so quickly that she forgets that the reader doesn't know any of the people or situations involved. Be careful in using personal experiences to explain as clearly and completely as space and time allow who the characters are and what happened.

7. *Issue:* Technology causes changes in society.

   My opinion: Be careful with this prompt. The excerpt doesn't claim that technology or technological change is good or bad. Nor does the question ask you if you think that technology or change caused by technology is good or bad. It just asks you if technology causes changes in society. That's why it's a good idea to read the excerpt and the actual question carefully and to highlight key words and phrases.

   Some evidence: There are any number of examples of technological change that you could use, such as how computers have created new jobs like computer programmers and eliminated or reduced the number of other jobs like secretaries; how cell phones mean that a person is never away from a phone call; how the Internet has increased the amount of information quickly available to people, as well as given people the ability to shop online at home instead of going to the mall.

8. *Issue:* Living a full and complete life includes helping others.

   My opinion: This is another issue where it might be difficult to disagree.

Some evidence: While you could use people you know as examples to support your argument, you could also use Winston Churchill himself and his steadfast service to Great Britain during World War II. When using the idea of helping others in humanitarian terms, Mother Theresa or Eleanor Roosevelt would be other good examples.

9. *Issue:* Saving time, saving money, and living a less stressful life are priorities for many, if not most, people.

   My opinion: You may agree with some parts of the issue, but not with others. If that is your opinion, you need to be clear in developing why you agree with some, but not all parts of the issue.

   Some evidence: Choosing examples to support your opinion will help you clarify your thoughts about the issue. If you agree and disagree with the issue, be sure that you use a similar number of examples and that they are strong examples to support your two-pronged opinion.

10. *Issue:* Oppressors actually fear their victims.

    My opinion: This prompt requires some consideration. Think in terms of cause and effect.

    Some evidence: Examples from history and current events would provide strong support for this issue. However, you might also think of an example of a local bully's tactics, which could support your opinion.

Chapter 3

ABOUT WRITING THE ESSAY

Your goals for this chapter are to
- Review the elements of an essay
- Review the writing process
- Identify the factors that make an essay "excellent"
- Identify the elements of a persuasive essay

You may be thinking that the College Board is asking for the impossible—an on-demand essay in a short period of time. Writing an essay in 20 or 25 or even 40 minutes is not an easy task. However, your experience writing essays on social studies, science, and literature tests has helped prepare you to write the SAT I essay. There is one difference though. Most of the essays that you have written for class are academic—that is, you are required to study, interpret, and present factual material. To answer the essay assignment, you do not need any specialized knowledge. Instead, you must present your own ideas clearly and effectively. Through your own life experience, reading, observation, and studies you already know everything that you need to answer the SAT I writing prompt.

THE ESSAY: A REVIEW

An essay is a group of paragraphs that work together to present a main point or thesis. An essay contains

- An introduction: the beginning, or introductory paragraph, that establishes the thesis

- A body: the middle paragraphs that develop support for the thesis

- A conclusion: the ending paragraph that ties together the points of the paragraph and reinforces the thesis

The following diagram is a graphic representation of a five-paragraph essay, a goal for your SAT I essay. While you may write as many paragraphs as you wish for your essay, your time is limited. Writing about five paragraphs will help ensure that you develop sufficient support to show the readers an accurate picture of your writing skills.

INTRODUCTION

Interesting Material and Background Information on Topic

Thesis Statement

*The introduction should catch the reader's attention,
establish the purpose and tone, and
present the thesis statement,
or the main idea.*

Body Paragraph 1

Supporting Information

*Each paragraph within the body of the essay should develop a subtopic
of the main point by providing strong supporting information.*

Body Paragraph 2

Supporting Information

*Each paragraph within the body of the essay should develop a subtopic
of the main point by providing strong supporting information.*

Body Paragraph 3

Supporting Information

*Each paragraph within the body of the essay should develop a subtopic
of the main point by providing strong supporting information.*

CONCLUSION

Reminder of Thesis Statement

Summary or Final Remarks

*The conclusion of an essay should bring the essay
to a satisfactory close and remind the reader of the main point.*

An essay is a sustained piece of communication and, therefore, requires more complex planning than a single paragraph does. To write the best essay you can for the SAT I Writing test—or any assignment—you need to

- Narrow your topic

- Formulate a thesis statement

- Develop support for the thesis

- Organize that support

- Draft your essay

- Polish your essay

This chapter will help you review the elements of an essay and provide practical advice for planning and writing your SAT I essay. Chapter 4 offers five sample essays for practice along with a timing guide to help you pace yourself.

THE WRITING PROCESS

You may have to plan and write your essay in 20 minutes, but the characteristics of the SAT I essay are no different from those of any good writing: unity, coherence, and adequate development. You already have the skill to put thoughts on paper because you have been writing essays for years. However, having some skill is not the same as excelling. To excel at writing, you must practice until certain techniques become second nature. In working your way through this chapter, you will have that opportunity to practice. You will review and practice the three steps that every serious writer uses to create a finished work: prewriting, writing, and revising.

AUDIENCE AND PURPOSE

Before we begin talking about prewriting, let's stop for a minute and consider audience and purpose. Any time you write something, you must decide how you will develop your topic. That decision is based on the audience for whom you are writing and your purpose—what you want to accomplish with your writing. Ask yourself: who is my audience for this essay and what is my purpose?

For the SAT I essay, you have an audience of two (or, in rare cases, three, if the first two readers are more than two points apart in their evaluation)—the College Board-trained readers who teach high school or college English and who will be reading hundreds of similar papers. The readers are experts in the conventions of English and will have a scoring guide, or rubric, to evaluate your paper. (We have discussed this scoring guide in Chapter 1.) The readers will score your essay holistically; that is, there is no single score for things like grammar and punctuation. The readers will consider every aspect of your writing for its impact on the overall impression of your essay. (The rubric in this workbook singles out the various descriptors, so you can pinpoint your weaknesses to work on and increase your overall score.)

Your purpose is very limited—to get the best score you can. To do that, you need to write a unified, coherent, and consistent essay that responds to the prompt. A well-written essay that misses the point of the question will not get you any credit.

PREWRITING

Several of the most important steps in writing an essay are the first ones—the initial planning stages involved in prewriting. At this point, you make decisions about content and format. Prewriting requires you to

- Explore ideas

- Narrow the topic

- Identify your audience and purpose

- Decide on your main idea, or thesis

- Determine your method for developing it

Although the SAT I gives you a prompt, or question, to be answered, you will need to generate the ideas to be developed in your essay. SAT I essays will always require that you express your own opinion or discuss your experiences. This should not be too difficult to do, but you need to consider your own opinions, ideas, interests, and experiences in relation to the question or prompt. If you are having trouble coming up with ideas, then psych yourself up by using one of the techniques described below.

Generating a Suitable Topic and Support

An initial part of the prewriting phase involves narrowing your topic. You must choose a position or response that you can cover well in the short amount of time you have to write. The SAT I wants you to show depth, not breadth.

If, after reading the prompt, no manageable topic leaps into your mind, try clustering. Write the broad topic in the center of a page. Think of all the words you can associate with it. Write these around the central word. One or more of these words may suggest a narrower topic for you.

After you have narrowed your topic, you must determine what pieces of information you will need to help you develop and support this topic. Try the following steps:

- Generate specific ideas and pieces of information

- Examine your personal feelings and thoughts about the topic

- Review your knowledge of the topic for more examples, details, facts, and reasons to use to support the point you want to make

You should generate as much information and as many ideas as time allows so that later you will be able to select only the strongest information to support your thesis.

We use the somewhat generic term *brainstorming* in this chapter, but there are several techniques that may be useful to you.

- Brainstorming—Think of anything and everything that is associated with the topic and jot your thoughts down. Do not make a judgment about the usefulness of your ideas. After you have exhausted all the ideas, cross off the unusable ones from your list.

- Self-interview—Ask yourself questions such as: "What experiences have I had that relate to the prompt?"; "What knowledge do I have about the topic?"; "What do I feel strongly about?"

- Free Writing—Assign yourself a certain number of minutes and begin writing. Do not stop until the required amount of time has passed. Don't worry about expressing yourself well or even making sense. Just keep writing. Since you have such a short period to complete your essay, allow only 1 or 2 minutes.

- Cueing—This technique involves giving yourself signals to respond to. Two cueing devices to stimulate your thinking are:

  –The 5 Ws. Answer the questions *Who? What? Where? When?* and *Why?*

  –The 5 senses. List details that relate to touch, smell, sound, taste, and sight.

Don't spend more than 2 minutes on this part, because you still have to develop your thesis statement and organize your ideas. That means stating your main idea and deciding how you are going to support it. This statement of the main idea is for you, not necessarily for your audience, because it may not be the final thesis statement. The main idea focuses on what you want to write about. The statement gives you a central point around which to organize information. While the actual statement may not appear in your essay, it is the thought that you want to leave with the readers.

Organization of Support

After you have chosen your specific topic and identified your audience and purpose, you must begin the job of pulling together the supporting information. First, organize the material that you created when you generated ideas into logical subtopics or natural subdivisions of the main idea. To order your supporting information, select one of the following methods of organization:

- Chronological order

- Spatial order

- Order of importance

- Comparison and contrast

- Developmental order

For more on organizational methods, see page 36.

If you had more time, you would create an outline at this point. However, you would lose too much time if you tried to outline your essay for the SAT I. Because of the time limit, you would do better to number your support in the order that makes the most sense to develop your main idea, or thesis statement, most effectively. This is also the time to eliminate quickly any irrelevant information and perhaps to replace it with stronger, more useful ideas if they come to you.

WRITING

Your next task is to turn your main point into a thesis statement, one that is a complete sentence. Weave it into an introductory paragraph that is both intriguing and informative. Usually, the writing stage begins with a first draft, the rough, unfinished version of what a piece of writing will become. You will not have time to polish your SAT I essay to perfection. As a result, when writing your draft, concentrate on paragraph development and overall organization. Give your readers a firm sense of the order of ideas within paragraphs and from paragraph to paragraph. Development and support count heavily in the evaluation of your SAT I essay. It is depth that matters.

The following are some ways to strengthen overall development and make your essay more interesting:

- Use transitional words and phrases to connect ideas. See page 37 for examples of transitions.

- Include repetitions of main words, synonyms, and parallelism to emphasize ideas.

- Use precise, vivid words and interesting sentence structure to express your thoughts.

Some ways to vary your sentence structure are by

- Beginning with a prepositional phrase

- Using adverbs and adverbial phrases

- Starting with dependent clauses

- Using various conjunctions, such as *not only, either, yet,* and *so*

- Including infinitives and participles

- Beginning with adjectives and adjective phrases

If new thoughts that sharpen your thesis and advance your purpose occur to you as you write, by all means add them to your essay. Do not be distracted by grammar, spelling, or punctuation as you write. However, be as correct as you can because there will be little time to proofread your essay.

REVISING

If you pace yourself, you will have time to revise your essay. Read through your work carefully. Concentrate on the flow of your thoughts to make sure that everything you have included helps you achieve your purpose. Check that your support is clearly stated and logically connected. Improve your clarity and coherence, if necessary. Ask yourself as you read:

- Does my introduction lead to the thesis statement? Does the paragraph capture the reader's interest?

- Have I clearly stated my main idea? Does my thesis present one main point?

- Do the body paragraphs develop significant subtopics of the thesis statement? Do those paragraphs have topic sentences?

- Have I included enough support?

- Have I organized my ideas logically?

- Do my ideas connect as clearly as possible? Have I used transitions?

- Does my conclusion remind the reader of my main point?

If you have time remaining, focus on your word choice and sentence variety. Check the sentences in order of importance—first, the thesis statement, then, the topic sentences of the body paragraphs, and last of all, the remaining lines. Check that every word and phrase says exactly what you mean. Make sure that your sentences are varied in structure. When editing for word choice and sentence variety, ask yourself:

- Does each word mean exactly what I have in mind?

- Is the language appropriate for the audience, the readers?

- Is every sentence clear?

- Have I varied the sentence length and structure?

- Are there any errors in grammar, mechanics, or spelling?

WRITING AN "EXCELLENT" ESSAY

You understand the established steps that professional writers follow, and you know the value of following those steps. However, you want more than that. You want to excel. You want your essay to stand out. To communicate clearly and precisely, which is what you must do to create an excellent SAT I essay, you need the proper tone and style, unity, coherence, and adequate development.

TONE AND STYLE

Your *tone* is the reflection of your attitude toward the subject of the essay. The words you choose express that attitude. Your words also reflect the audience for whom you are writing and provide clues to your purpose. A writer's tone, for example, may be lighthearted, brusque, or serious. In your SAT I essay, strive for a consistent tone. A superior essay maintains a consistent level of language and develops a consistent attitude toward the topic and the reader.

Decide if you are going to be serious, amusing, friendly and informal, or businesslike and formal. Then, choose words that fit that tone. The safest tone to adopt for this essay is formal and subjective, since you are being asked your opinion. You do not want to be stuffy and pretentious by using phrases such as "one understands" or "we can surmise." On the other hand, do not be too casual either, by writing things like "you know what I mean." Most students, however, err on the side of "faux" erudition, using big words and convoluted constructions. When in doubt, write what you mean simply and directly.

How do you develop the proper tone? Through *style*. Your style should be your own natural style that you use for school essays. That means

- Using proper grammar and punctuation

- Choosing words that convey your meaning in an interesting rather than a pedestrian or vague way: "Aunt Molly's illness set events in motion" versus "The reason it happened is because my aunt was ill"

- Avoiding the use of several words when one will do: "The extent of my feelings for the feline species is not a secret" versus "My love of cats is well-known"

- Avoiding hackneyed phrases and clichés such as "I was on cloud nine" versus "I was so happy that I hugged my little brother"

Your style adds interest to the essay. Vivid words and phrasing and a unique point of view about a subject can make your essay interesting to read.

UNITY

Unity is another word for clarity. All of your essay's ideas and information must belong together and be essential to the development of the thesis. The parts of the essay—the introduction, the body, and the conclusion—should all focus on the main idea. Each paragraph must relate to every other, and every paragraph must support the overall thesis. In addition, each paragraph within the essay must be unified. Each paragraph must have a topic sentence, and every sentence in the paragraph must relate to every other and add to the development of the topic sentence. In other words, a unified essay is one that is clearly developed. The introduction and the conclusion work together to create unity. The introduction establishes the main point. Then, the conclusion echoes the ideas or key words of the introduction.

Perhaps the most important element creating unity in an essay is the clarity of the thesis statement. Remember that your thesis statement contains the central idea that you have developed from brainstorming ideas in response to the essay prompt. As the *Harbrace College Handbook,* that venerable college English manual, states: "[Your thesis statement] is basically a claim statement, that is, it indicates what you claim to be true, interesting, or valuable about your subject."

If the thesis statement is focused and clear, it outlines the scope of the essay and the boundaries separating the relevant from the irrelevant. In the same way, the subtopics must logically grow out of the thesis. When the subtopics represent significant aspects of the main point and relate to each other, in all probability you will write a unified essay.

Although you can place your thesis statement anywhere in your essay, it is probably safest to put it in the introduction, even as the first sentence, so you can refer to it as you write to be sure that everything you are writing develops and supports it. Putting the thesis first also gets you started writing.

COHERENCE

In a coherent essay, a reader can move smoothly and logically from one thought to another. A *coherent* essay is one in which the ideas within each paragraph and within the essay as a whole are in logical order and their connections flow. Coherence depends on clear, relevant ordering of ideas and the introduction of transitional words and phrases. Many methods exist for organizing ideas logically. The chart below offers five methods for organizing your work.

Organization of Supporting Information

Chronological order	Information arranged in time sequence
Spatial order	Information arranged according to spatial relationships
Order of importance	Information arranged from most important to least important, or vice versa
Compare and contrast	Information arranged according to similarities and differences between two or more subjects
Developmental order	Information arranged so that one point leads logically to another

Transitions

Besides being logically organized, a coherent essay moves smoothly from one thought to the next because its ideas are connected by transitions, repetition of key words, synonyms, and pronouns. *Transitions* indicate how one idea relates to another, while *repetition* of words ties ideas together. The following are some transitions that can help you establish logical order in your writing.

Time Relationship		
after	finally	later
before	first	meanwhile
during	second	next
earlier	third	then
Spatial Relationship		
above	beneath	near
ahead	beyond	outside
before	here	over there
behind	inside	
Comparison or Contrast		
conversely	in like manner	similarly
however	instead	whereas
in contrast	likewise	yet
indeed	nonetheless	
Cause and Effect		
accordingly	inevitably	then
as a result	on account of	therefore
because of	since	thus
consequently		
Addition		
also	furthermore	not only
as well	in addition	too
besides	moreover	
Emphasis		
indeed	most of all	
in fact	most significantly	
in other words		
Examples		
also	for example	specifically
as an illustration	in particular	that is
for instance	namely	

ADEQUATE DEVELOPMENT

What is *adequate development*? In addition to the thesis statement, your essay must contain enough specific information to explain your main idea. Support consists of examples, details, facts, reasons, and/or events. The following chart presents five types of supporting information that you can use to develop your thesis.

KINDS OF SUPPORT		
Type of Support	**Definition**	**Example**
Examples	Particular instances of a general idea or principle	An essay about the best movies of the year might include a discussion of three or four films.
Details	Small items or pieces of information that make up something larger	An essay about a personal hero might describe details about appearance.
Facts	Specific pieces of information that can be verified	An essay about the New York Yankees might include names, backgrounds, and statistics of each player.
Reasons	Explanations, justifications, or causes, often answering the question *why?* about the main idea	An essay advocating gun control might include an explanation of ineffective current laws.
Events	Incidents or happenings	An essay on baby-sitting might include an amusing tale about a first-time baby-sitter.

A well-developed essay must contain enough support to meet the expectations established by the introduction and the thesis statement. In addition, the supporting information must make the essay seem complete.

THE SAT I ESSAY

According to the College Board, "students will be asked to write a short essay that requires them to take a position on an issue and use examples to support their position." This is a persuasive essay. Persuasive writing is often subjective. However, your essay must contain logical reasoning and factual information in order to defend your opinion effectively. A persuasive composition differs from other kinds of essays because it must present a forceful argument and be compelling in purpose and tone.

Your persuasive essay should use the three-part essay format just like other essays. The introduction presents the thesis, or point, that you are defending. It should be reasonable in tone. However, unlike a thesis for other types of essays, a persuasive thesis may be a controversial statement.

In a persuasive essay, supporting material provides convincing evidence to defend the thesis statement. Support may consist of logical reasons in examples, facts, and details. Your supporting information should never be based on unsubstantiated opinions. Your evidence should be solid, authoritative, rational, and believable, appealing to even those readers who disagree with you. You want to show your readers that you are well-informed and have thought about opposing arguments.

Your tone should be persuasive but reasonable, forceful but respectful of opposing viewpoints. In writing a persuasive essay for class, you would adjust your tone to your audience and take into consideration whether your audience might be sympathetic, apathetic, or strongly opposed to your position. You might choose a humorous, lighthearted approach or a serious, intellectual one. Do the same in writing your essay for the SAT I, and be sure to maintain whatever tone you choose throughout the essay.

GUIDELINES FOR PERSUASION

1. Use your knowledge and beliefs to choose an opinion/topic that you can support.
2. Decide how persuasive you must be to make your points—the intensity of your purpose and tone.
3. Brainstorm for specific examples, facts, details, reasons, and events that support your thesis statement.
4. State your opinion in a thesis statement that is direct, significant, and supportable.
5. Use concrete, precise words. Be sure your language is reasonable and compelling. Do not be emotional.
6. Employ smooth, logical transitions that emphasize your organization and your position on the issue.
7. Revise your essay by examining your word choices to ensure a balanced, forceful but rational, and consistent tone.

Order of importance is often a good method of organization for persuasive essays. Use transitions to create a road map for your argument—words such as *first, second, third,* or *then, next.* As you write your essay, focus on winning your audience's support. In the conclusion, rephrase your main point and summarize your support.

USING THE RUBRIC TO IMPROVE YOUR WRITING

In Chapter 1, you analyzed a scoring rubric similar to the one that the readers for the SAT I essays use. Take another look at it now, pages 6–9, and consider the characteristics in terms of persuasive essays.

The first area is **overall impression**. What factors specific to persuasive essays will create an excellent overall impression for your essay?

- Your ability to use language—words, phrases, sentences, and paragraphs—to state your position and to build support for your position on the issue
- Your ability to be clear and to the point in defending your position
- Adherence to the conventions of standard written English

The second area is **thesis and purpose**. What factors specific to persuasive essays will make the thesis and the purpose of your essay "excellent"?

- Your ability to develop and state your position on the issue thoughtfully and clearly
- Exhibiting an original, interesting, or unique approach to the position you take on the issue or to the way you develop the support for your position
- Using relevant and specific references, facts, and/or examples in support of your position

The third area is **organization and development**. What factors specific to persuasive essays will make the organization and development of your essay "excellent"?

- Selection of a method of organization that best develops your ideas
- Thorough development of all the ideas you introduce to support your position
- Coherence of thought in the development of ideas so that ideas flow logically from one to the other
- Unity of development so that all supporting ideas are essential to the overall development of your position on the issue

The fourth area is **use of sentences**. How would writing a persuasive essay affect your choice of sentence structure?
- The use of a device such as a rhetorical question to gain the reader's attention
- The use of a variety of sentence structures in explaining supporting ideas
- The correct use of different types of sentence structures

The fifth area is **word choice,** or **diction.** How would writing a persuasive essay affect your choice of words?
- The use of transitions to further or facilitate your organization
- The use of language that is specific to the issue and to your position on the issue
- The omission of highly emotional language to support your position

The sixth area is **grammar and usage**. Regardless of the type of writing you do, you should attempt to make your writing as error-free as possible.

Be sure to review this list after you score each essay in Chapter 4. Analyze each essay for areas of weakness. Focus on one area to work on as you write your next essay.

PRACTICAL ADVICE

The following are some suggestions to help you write clear, well-organized, coherent, and interesting essays in the time allotted. If you keep these suggestions in mind as you write your practice essays, these steps will come naturally to you on the day of the SAT I. You will see these steps again in Chapter 4.

Step 1   Read the question carefully.

Step 2   Restate to yourself what the question is asking. Underline the key words.

Step 3   Make a list by brainstorming all the ideas that come to mind. Write down your ideas.

Step 4   Create a thesis from the ideas you have brainstormed.

Step 5   Turn your brainstorm into an informal working plan by numbering the items that you want to include in your essay in the order in which you want to include them. Cross out ideas that no longer fit now that you have a thesis statement.

Step 6   Begin writing your introduction by stating your thesis clearly.

Step 7 Read your first paragraph to be sure that your ideas follow each other logically and support your thesis.

Step 8 Check your quick list of ideas. Choose the next idea and write a transition into your second paragraph. Keep writing until you use all the RELEVANT ideas on your quick list.

Step 9 Write a solid conclusion using one of the following techniques: (a) rephrasing your thesis, (b) summarizing your main points, or (c) referring in some way back to your introductory paragraph.

Step 10 Proofread and revise.

CHECK OFF

Before you practice writing essays in the next chapter, can you

- Identify the elements of an essay?

- Explain the steps in the writing process?

- Identify the factors that make an essay "excellent"?

- Explain the factors that make an effective persuasive essay?

Chapter 4
WRITING PRACTICE ESSAYS

Your goals for this chapter are to
- Write and revise five practice essays
- Identify areas for improvement in your essays
- Work to improve those specific areas

The writing prompt on the SAT I will ask you to take a position on an issue and defend it. You will be given answer sheets that will allow you to write about 200 to 250 words on the assigned question. The instructions will tell you to "plan and write" your essay. Up to this point, this book has discussed the writing prompt format, given you some practice in dissecting writing prompts similar to those on the test, and reviewed the elements of essays and how to write them. This chapter offers you five opportunities to write practice essays and then to revise them based on a rubric similar to the one used by the SAT readers.

PACING GUIDE FOR WRITING THE ESSAY

One of your worries is probably how to write an effective essay in what seems so little time. To help you learn to pace yourself, the answer sheets for the practice essays list a predetermined timing guide after the essay prompt. Use it as you write your essays. It will help you learn to pace yourself.

The pacing guide worksheets direct you through the step-by-step process for reading, planning, organizing, and writing your essay. If you practice the ten steps while you get ready for the real essay, you will learn them as you go. The idea behind the practice is to become so familiar with the steps that you will internalize them. On the day of the test, you will use the steps—read the question, plan, organize, and write your essay—without consciously thinking about the steps. They will just come naturally to you.

USING THE PRACTICE ESSAYS

1. Plan and write each essay and then evaluate it against the following rubric and score yourself. You can also make use of the SAT EssayEdge, if you wish.

2. According to the rubric, where could you do better? Turn back to the table on pages 41–42, to see how you might improve your persuasive essay.

3. Focus on one area in which you could improve. Revise your essay with the goal of enhancing your performance in the one area you chose to work on. Use a separate sheet of paper for your revision.

4. Reevaluate your revised essay against the rubric. How did you do this time? Can you see a difference? State to yourself how and why your revised essay is better than your first draft.

Repeat these four steps with each of the five practice essays in this chapter. See how well you can keep to the allotted time and still finish your essay.

PRACTICE ESSAY 1

Directions: Think carefully about the issue described in the excerpt below and about the assignment that follows it.

Behavioral scientists and psychologists have come to believe that success in the workplace is not so much determined by intellect, but by social intelligence—the ability to work with others, lead and motivate others, and inspire team spirit.

Assignment: What is your opinion of the idea that workplace success depends on the ability to work with others rather than on intellectual ability? Plan and write an essay that develops your point of view on the issue. Support your opinion with reasoning and examples from your reading, your classwork, your personal experiences, or your observations.

PRACTICE ESSAY 1

Follow these steps to writing your essay.

| TIP | Set aside 5 minutes for Steps 1 through 5. |

Step 1   Read the question carefully.

Step 2   Restate to yourself what the question is asking. Underline the key words.

_____

_____

_____

Step 3   Make a list by brainstorming all the ideas that come to mind. Write your ideas in the space below.

_____

_____

_____

_____

_____

_____

_____

_____

_____

_____

_____

_____

_____

_____

Step 4   Create a thesis from the ideas you brainstormed.

_____

_____

_____

Step 5   Turn your brainstorm into an informal working plan by numbering the items that you want
to include in your essay in the order in which you want to include them. Cross out ideas
that no longer fit now that you have a thesis statement.

TIP	**Take 3 minutes to write your introductory paragraph. You want to be sure that you are writing a clearly stated and interesting introduction.**

Step 6   Begin writing your introduction by stating your thesis clearly.

_____

_____

_____

_____

_____

_____

_____

_____

_____

_____

_____

Step 7   Read your first paragraph to be sure that the ideas you used follow each other logically and
support your thesis.

> **TIP**
>
> **By now you should be about 8 minutes into the 20 minutes you have to write your essay. Have you finished the first paragraph? You want to leave 2 minutes at the end for proofreading and revising.**

Step 8   Check your quick list of ideas. Choose the next idea and write a transition into your second paragraph. Keep writing until you use all the RELEVANT ideas on your quick list.

TIP
Don't forget to use transitions between your paragraphs.

TIP
If a new idea comes from the flow of your writing, use it IF IT FITS THE CONTEXT.

TIP	**You should have about 6 minutes of your writing time left. How much time do you have?**

Step 9 Allow about 4 minutes to write a solid conclusion using one of the following methods:

- Rephrase your thesis.
- Summarize your main points.
- Refer in some way back to your introductory paragraph.

_____

_____

_____

_____

_____

_____

_____

_____

_____

_____

_____

_____

_____

_____

_____

_____

TIP	**You should have paced yourself so that you have 2 minutes for your final review.**

Step 10 Proofread and revise neatly.

- Cross out any irrelevant ideas or words.
- Make any additions, especially transitions.
- Smooth out any awkward sentences.
- Check your grammar and mechanics.

SELF-EVALUATION RUBRIC

	6	5	4	3	2	1
Overall Impression	Demonstrates excellent command of the conventions of English; outstanding writing competence; thorough and effective; incisive	Demonstrates good command of the conventions of English; good writing competence; less thorough and incisive than the highest essays	Demonstrates adequate command of the conventions of English; competent writing	Demonstrates fair command of the conventions of English; some writing competency	Demonstrates little command of the conventions of English; poor writing skills; unacceptably brief; fails to respond to the question	Lacking skill and competence
Thesis and Purpose	Exhibits excellent perception and clarity; original, interesting, or unique approach; includes apt and specific references, facts, and/or examples	Exhibits good perception and clarity; engaging approach; includes specific references, facts, and/or examples	Clear and perceptive; somewhat interesting; includes references, facts, and/or examples	Somewhat clear but exhibits incomplete or confused thinking; dull, mechanical, overgeneralized	Very little clarity; confusing; flawed logic	Very confusing or completely off the topic
Organization and Development	Meticulously organized and thoroughly developed; coherent and unified	Well organized and developed; coherent and unified	Reasonably organized and developed; generally coherent and unified	Moderately organized and developed; some incoherence and lack of unity	Little or no organization and development; incoherent and void of unity	No apparent organization or development; incoherent
Use of Sentences	Effectively varied and engaging; virtually error free	Varied and interesting; a few errors	Adequately varied; some errors	Moderately varied and marginally interesting; one or more major errors	Little or no variation; dull and uninteresting; some major errors	Numerous major errors
Word Choice	Interesting and effective; virtually error free	Generally interesting and effective; a few errors	Occasionally interesting and effective; several errors	Moderately dull and ordinary; some errors in diction	Mostly dull and conventional; numerous errors	Numerous major errors; extremely immature
Grammar and Usage	Virtually error free	Occasional minor errors	Some minor errors	Some major errors	Severely flawed; frequent major errors	Extremely flawed

Instructions: Rate yourself in each of the categories on the rubric. Circle the description in each category that most accurately reflects your performance. Enter the numbers on the lines below. Then calculate the average of the six numbers to determine your final score. On the SAT I, at least two readers will rate your essay on a scale of 1 to 6, with 6 being the highest. Because it is difficult to score yourself objectively, you may wish to ask a respected friend or teacher to assess your writing to reflect more accurately its effectiveness.

SELF-EVALUATION

Each category is rated 6 (high) to 1 (low)
Overall Impression   _____
Thesis and Purpose   _____
Organization and Development _____
Use of Sentences   _____
Word Choice   _____
Grammar and Usage   _____

TOTAL   _____
　　Divide by 6 for final score   _____

OBJECTIVE EVALUATION

Each category is rated 6 (high) to 1 (low)
Overall Impression   _____
Thesis and Purpose   _____
Organization and Development _____
Use of Sentences   _____
Word Choice   _____
Grammar and Usage   _____

TOTAL   _____
　　Divide by 6 for final score   _____

www.petersons.com

PRACTICE ESSAY 2

Directions: Think carefully about the issue described in the excerpt below and about the assignment that follows it.

With the increasing importance of science and technology in the workplace, a liberal arts education is of little value for tomorrow's college graduates.

Assignment: What is your opinion of the idea that a liberal arts education will be of little value to college graduates in the future? Plan and write an essay that develops your point of view on the issue. Support your opinion with reasoning and examples from your reading, your classwork, your personal experiences, or your observations.

PRACTICE ESSAY 2

Follow these steps to writing your essay.

TIP	Set aside 5 minutes for Steps 1 through 5.

Step 1   Read the question carefully.

Step 2   Restate to yourself what the question is asking. Underline the key words.

_____

_____

_____

Step 3   Make a list by brainstorming all the ideas that come to mind. Write your ideas in the space below.

_____

_____

_____

_____

_____

_____

_____

_____

_____

_____

_____

_____

Step 4   Create a thesis from the ideas you brainstormed.

_____

_____

_____

Step 5   Turn your brainstorm into an informal working plan by numbering the items that you want to include in your essay in the order in which you want to include them. Cross out ideas that no longer fit now that you have a thesis statement.

| TIP | **Take 3 minutes to write your introductory paragraph. You want to be sure that you are writing a clearly stated and interesting introduction.** |

Step 6   Begin writing your introduction by stating your thesis clearly.

_____

_____

_____

_____

_____

_____

_____

_____

_____

_____

_____

_____

_____

Step 7   Read your first paragraph to be sure that the ideas you used follow each other logically and support your thesis.

TIP	By now you should be about 8 minutes into the 20 minutes you have to write your essay. Have you finished the first paragraph? You want to leave 2 minutes at the end for proofreading and revising.

Step 8 Check your quick list of ideas. Choose the next idea and write a transition into your second paragraph. Keep writing until you use all the RELEVANT ideas on your quick list.

_____

_____

_____

_____

TIP

Don't forget to use transitions between your paragraphs.

_____

_____

_____

_____

_____

_____

TIP

If a new idea comes from the flow of your writing, use it IF IT FITS THE CONTEXT.

_____

_____

_____

_____

_____

_____

_____

TIP	**You should have about 6 minutes of your writing time left. How much time do you have?**

Step 9 Allow about 4 minutes to write a solid conclusion using one of the following methods:

- Rephrase your thesis.
- Summarize your main points.
- Refer in some way back to your introductory paragraph.

_____

_____

_____

_____

_____

_____

_____

_____

_____

_____

_____

_____

_____

_____

_____

_____

TIP	**You should have paced yourself so that you have 2 minutes for your final review.**

Step 10 Proofread and revise neatly.

- Cross out any irrelevant ideas or words.
- Make any additions, especially transitions.
- Smooth out any awkward sentences.
- Check your grammar and mechanics.

SELF-EVALUATION RUBRIC

	6	5	4	3	2	1
Overall Impression	Demonstrates excellent command of the conventions of English; outstanding writing competence; thorough and effective; incisive	Demonstrates good command of the conventions of English; good writing competence; less thorough and incisive than the highest essays	Demonstrates adequate command of the conventions of English; competent writing	Demonstrates fair command of the conventions of English; some writing competency	Demonstrates little command of the conventions of English; poor writing skills; unacceptably brief; fails to respond to the question	Lacking skill and competence
Thesis and Purpose	Exhibits excellent perception and clarity; original, interesting, or unique approach; includes apt and specific references, facts, and/or examples	Exhibits good perception and clarity; engaging approach; includes specific references, facts, and/or examples	Clear and perceptive; somewhat interesting; includes references, facts, and/or examples	Somewhat clear but exhibits incomplete or confused thinking; dull, mechanical, overgeneralized	Very little clarity; confusing; flawed logic	Very confusing or completely off the topic
Organization and Development	Meticulously organized and thoroughly developed; coherent and unified	Well organized and developed; coherent and unified	Reasonably organized and developed; generally coherent and unified	Moderately organized and developed; some incoherence and lack of unity	Little or no organization and development; incoherent and void of unity	No apparent organization or development; incoherent
Use of Sentences	Effectively varied and engaging; virtually error free	Varied and interesting; a few errors	Adequately varied; some errors	Moderately varied and marginally interesting; one or more major errors	Little or no variation; dull and uninteresting; some major errors	Numerous major errors
Word Choice	Interesting and effective; virtually error free	Generally interesting and effective; a few errors	Occasionally interesting and effective; several errors	Moderately dull and ordinary; some errors in diction	Mostly dull and conventional; numerous errors	Numerous major errors; extremely immature
Grammar and Usage	Virtually error free	Occasional minor errors	Some minor errors	Some major errors	Severely flawed; frequent major errors	Extremely flawed

57

Instructions: Rate yourself in each of the categories on the rubric. Circle the description in each category that most accurately reflects your performance. Enter the numbers on the lines below. Then calculate the average of the six numbers to determine your final score. On the SAT I, at least two readers will rate your essay on a scale of 1 to 6, with 6 being the highest. Because it is difficult to score yourself objectively, you may wish to ask a respected friend or teacher to assess your writing to reflect more accurately its effectiveness.

SELF-EVALUATION

Each category is rated 6 (high) to 1 (low)

Overall Impression   _____

Thesis and Purpose   _____

Organization and Development   _____

Use of Sentences   _____

Word Choice   _____

Grammar and Usage   _____

TOTAL   _____

 Divide by 6 for final score   _____

OBJECTIVE EVALUATION

Each category is rated 6 (high) to 1 (low)

Overall Impression   _____

Thesis and Purpose   _____

Organization and Development   _____

Use of Sentences   _____

Word Choice   _____

Grammar and Usage   _____

TOTAL   _____

 Divide by 6 for final score   _____

PRACTICE ESSAY 3

Directions: Think carefully about the issue described in the excerpt below and about the assignment that follows it.

In the last few years, a number of athletes have gone directly from high school to professional sports teams instead of going to college. Some people in sports and education think that these players are too young to deal with the pressures and problems of professional sports.

Assignment: What is your opinion of the idea that high school athletes are too young to handle the celebrity and competitive pressures of professional sports? Plan and write an essay that develops your point of view on the issue. Support your opinion with reasoning and examples from your reading, your classwork, your personal experiences, or your observations.

PRACTICE ESSAY 3

Follow these steps to writing your essay.

TIP	Set aside 5 minutes for Steps 1 through 5.

Step 1 Read the question carefully.

Step 2 Restate to yourself what the question is asking. Underline the key words.

_____

_____

_____

Step 3 Make a list by brainstorming all the ideas that come to mind. Write your ideas in the space below.

_____

_____

_____

_____

_____

_____

_____

_____

_____

_____

_____

_____

_____

Step 4   Create a thesis from the ideas you brainstormed.

_____

_____

_____

Step 5   Turn your brainstorm into an informal working plan by numbering the items that you want
to include in your essay in the order in which you want to include them. Cross out ideas
that no longer fit now that you have a thesis statement.

TIP	**Take 3 minutes to write your introductory paragraph. You want to be sure that you are writing a clearly stated and interesting introduction.**

Step 6   Begin writing your introduction by stating your thesis clearly.

_____

_____

_____

_____

_____

_____

_____

_____

_____

_____

Step 7   Read your first paragraph to be sure that the ideas you used follow each other logically and
support your thesis.

TIP	By now you should be about 8 minutes into the 20 minutes you have to write your essay. Have you finished the first paragraph? You want to leave 2 minutes at the end for proofreading and revising.

Step 8 Check your quick list of ideas. Choose the next idea and write a transition into your second paragraph. Keep writing until you use all the RELEVANT ideas on your quick list.

_____

_____

_____

TIP

Don't forget to use transitions between your paragraphs.

_____

_____

_____

_____

_____

TIP

If a new idea comes from the flow of your writing, use it IF IT FITS THE CONTEXT.

_____

_____

_____

_____

_____

TIP	**You should have about 6 minutes of your writing time left. How much time do you have?**

Step 9   Allow about 4 minutes to write a solid conclusion using one of the following methods:

- Rephrase your thesis.
- Summarize your main points.
- Refer in some way back to your introductory paragraph.

_____

_____

_____

_____

_____

_____

_____

_____

_____

_____

_____

_____

_____

_____

_____

_____

TIP	**You should have paced yourself so that you have 2 minutes for your final review.**

Step 10   Proofread and revise neatly.

- Cross out any irrelevant ideas or words.
- Make any additions, especially transitions.
- Smooth out any awkward sentences.
- Check your grammar and mechanics.

SELF-EVALUATION RUBRIC

	6	5	4	3	2	1
Overall Impression	Demonstrates excellent command of the conventions of English; outstanding writing competence; thorough and effective; incisive	Demonstrates good command of the conventions of English; good writing competence; less thorough and incisive than the highest essays	Demonstrates adequate command of the conventions of English; competent writing	Demonstrates fair command of the conventions of English; some writing competency	Demonstrates little command of the conventions of English; poor writing skills; unacceptably brief; fails to respond to the question	Lacking skill and competence
Thesis and Purpose	Exhibits excellent perception and clarity; original, interesting, or unique approach; includes apt and specific references, facts, and/or examples	Exhibits good perception and clarity; engaging approach; includes specific references, facts, and/or examples	Clear and perceptive; somewhat interesting; includes references, facts, and/or examples	Somewhat clear but exhibits incomplete or confused thinking; dull, mechanical, overgeneralized	Very little clarity; confusing; flawed logic	Very confusing or completely off the topic
Organization and Development	Meticulously organized and thoroughly developed; coherent and unified	Well organized and developed; coherent and unified	Reasonably organized and developed; generally coherent and unified	Moderately organized and developed; some incoherence and lack of unity	Little or no organization and development; incoherent and void of unity	No apparent organization or development; incoherent
Use of Sentences	Effectively varied and engaging; virtually error free	Varied and interesting; a few errors	Adequately varied; some errors	Moderately varied and marginally interesting; one or more major errors	Little or no variation; dull and uninteresting; some major errors	Numerous major errors
Word Choice	Interesting and effective; virtually error free	Generally interesting and effective; a few errors	Occasionally interesting and effective; several errors	Moderately dull and ordinary; some errors in diction	Mostly dull and conventional; numerous errors	Numerous major errors; extremely immature
Grammar and Usage	Virtually error free	Occasional minor errors	Some minor errors	Some major errors	Severely flawed; frequent major errors	Extremely flawed

Instructions: Rate yourself in each of the categories on the rubric. Circle the description in each category that most accurately reflects your performance. Enter the numbers on the lines below. Then calculate the average of the six numbers to determine your final score. On the SAT I, at least two readers will rate your essay on a scale of 1 to 6, with 6 being the highest. Because it is difficult to score yourself objectively, you may wish to ask a respected friend or teacher to assess your writing to reflect more accurately its effectiveness.

SELF-EVALUATION

Each category is rated 6 (high) to 1 (low)
Overall Impression _____
Thesis and Purpose _____
Organization and Development _____
Use of Sentences _____
Word Choice _____
Grammar and Usage _____

TOTAL _____
Divide by 6 for final score _____

OBJECTIVE EVALUATION

Each category is rated 6 (high) to 1 (low)
Overall Impression _____
Thesis and Purpose _____
Organization and Development _____
Use of Sentences _____
Word Choice _____
Grammar and Usage _____

TOTAL _____
Divide by 6 for final score _____

PRACTICE ESSAY 4

Directions: Think carefully about the issue described in the excerpt below and about the assignment that follows it.

Odd as it may sound, personality is a skill. You can choose and develop aspects of it that will draw people to you and make them want to help you learn and improve.
—Twyla Tharp, *The Creative Habit: Learn It and Use It for Life*

Assignment: What is your opinion of the idea that a person can choose and develop personality traits that will attract others or turn them away? Plan and write an essay that develops your point of view on the issue. Support your opinion with reasoning and examples from your reading, your classwork, your personal experiences, or your observations.

PRACTICE ESSAY 4

Follow these steps to writing your essay.

TIP	Set aside 5 minutes for Steps 1 through 5.

Step 1   Read the question carefully.

Step 2   Restate to yourself what the question is asking. Underline the key words.

_____

_____

_____

Step 3   Make a list by brainstorming all the ideas that come to mind. Write your ideas in the space below.

_____

_____

_____

_____

_____

_____

_____

_____

_____

_____

_____

_____

_____

Step 4   Create a thesis from the ideas you brainstormed.

_____

_____

_____

Step 5   Turn your brainstorm into an informal working plan by numbering the items that you want to include in your essay in the order in which you want to include them. Cross out ideas that no longer fit now that you have a thesis statement.

TIP	Take 3 minutes to write your introductory paragraph. You want to be sure that you are writing a clearly stated and interesting introduction.

Step 6   Begin writing your introduction by stating your thesis clearly.

_____

_____

_____

_____

_____

_____

_____

_____

_____

_____

_____

Step 7   Read your first paragraph to be sure that the ideas you used follow each other logically and support your thesis.

TIP	By now you should be about 8 minutes into the 20 minutes you have to write your essay. Have you finished the first paragraph? You want to leave 2 minutes at the end for proofreading and revising.

Step 8 Check your quick list of ideas. Choose the next idea and write a transition into your second paragraph. Keep writing until you use all the RELEVANT ideas on your quick list.

_____

_____

_____

_____

TIP
Don't forget to use transitions between your paragraphs.

_____

_____

_____

_____

_____

_____

TIP
If a new idea comes from the flow of your writing, use it IF IT FITS THE CONTEXT.

_____

_____

_____

_____

_____

_____

TIP	**You should have about 6 minutes of your writing time left. How much time do you have?**

Step 9   Allow about 4 minutes to write a solid conclusion using one of the following methods:

- Rephrase your thesis.
- Summarize your main points.
- Refer in some way back to your introductory paragraph.

_____

_____

_____

_____

_____

_____

_____

_____

_____

_____

_____

_____

_____

_____

_____

_____

_____

TIP	**You should have paced yourself so that you have 2 minutes for your final review.**

Step 10   Proofread and revise neatly.

- Cross out any irrelevant ideas or words.
- Make any additions, especially transitions.
- Smooth out any awkward sentences.
- Check your grammar and mechanics.

SELF-EVALUATION RUBRIC

	6	5	4	3	2	1
Overall Impression	Demonstrates excellent command of the conventions of English; outstanding writing competence; thorough and effective; incisive	Demonstrates good command of the conventions of English; good writing competence; less thorough and incisive than the highest essays	Demonstrates adequate command of the conventions of English; competent writing	Demonstrates fair command of the conventions of English; some writing competency	Demonstrates little command of the conventions of English; poor writing skills; unacceptably brief; fails to respond to the question	Lacking skill and competence
Thesis and Purpose	Exhibits excellent perception and clarity; original, interesting, or unique approach; includes apt and specific references, facts, and/or examples	Exhibits good perception and clarity; engaging approach; includes specific references, facts, and/or examples	Clear and perceptive; somewhat interesting; includes references, facts, and/or examples	Somewhat clear but exhibits incomplete or confused thinking; dull, mechanical, overgeneralized	Very little clarity; confusing; flawed logic	Very confusing or completely off the topic
Organization and Development	Meticulously organized and thoroughly developed; coherent and unified	Well organized and developed; coherent and unified	Reasonably organized and developed; generally coherent and unified	Moderately organized and developed; some incoherence and lack of unity	Little or no organization and development; incoherent and void of unity	No apparent organization or development; incoherent
Use of Sentences	Effectively varied and engaging; virtually error free	Varied and interesting; a few errors	Adequately varied; some errors	Moderately varied and marginally interesting; one or more major errors	Little or no variation; dull and uninteresting; some major errors	Numerous major errors
Word Choice	Interesting and effective; virtually error free	Generally interesting and effective; a few errors	Occasionally interesting and effective; several errors	Moderately dull and ordinary; some errors in diction	Mostly dull and conventional; numerous errors	Numerous major errors; extremely immature
Grammar and Usage	Virtually error free	Occasional minor errors	Some minor errors	Some major errors	Severely flawed; frequent major errors	Extremely flawed

Instructions: Rate yourself in each of the categories on the rubric. Circle the description in each category that most accurately reflects your performance. Enter the numbers on the lines below. Then calculate the average of the six numbers to determine your final score. On the SAT I, at least two readers will rate your essay on a scale of 1 to 6, with 6 being the highest. Because it is difficult to score yourself objectively, you may wish to ask a respected friend or teacher to assess your writing to reflect more accurately its effectiveness.

SELF-EVALUATION

Each category is rated 6 (high) to 1 (low)
Overall Impression _____
Thesis and Purpose _____
Organization and Development _____
Use of Sentences _____
Word Choice _____
Grammar and Usage _____

TOTAL _____
Divide by 6 for final score _____

OBJECTIVE EVALUATION

Each category is rated 6 (high) to 1 (low)
Overall Impression _____
Thesis and Purpose _____
Organization and Development _____
Use of Sentences _____
Word Choice _____
Grammar and Usage _____

TOTAL _____
Divide by 6 for final score _____

PRACTICE ESSAY 5

Directions: Think carefully about the issue described in the excerpt below and about the assignment that follows it.

Webster's dictionary defines perfectionism "as an extreme or obsessive striving for perfection." Some people believe that perfectionism inhibits a person's ability to work productively and well. Some colleges and universities have been sending their students the message to take things less seriously and to enjoy their college years more.

Assignment: What is your view of the message to college students to relax a little? Plan and write an essay that develops your point of view on the issue. Support your opinion with reasoning and examples from your reading, your classwork, your personal experiences, or your observations.

PRACTICE ESSAY 5

Follow these steps to writing your essay.

TIP	Set aside 5 minutes for Steps 1 through 5.

Step 1   Read the question carefully.

Step 2   Restate to yourself what the question is asking. Underline the key words.

_____

_____

_____

Step 3   Make a list by brainstorming all the ideas that come to mind. Write your ideas in the space below.

_____

_____

_____

_____

_____

_____

_____

_____

_____

_____

_____

Step 4   Create a thesis from the ideas you brainstormed.

_____

_____

_____

Step 5   Turn your brainstorm into an informal working plan by numbering the items that you want
to include in your essay in the order in which you want to include them. Cross out ideas
that no longer fit now that you have a thesis statement.

> **TIP**   **Take 3 minutes to write your introductory paragraph. You want to be sure
that you are writing a clearly stated and interesting introduction.**

Step 6   Begin writing your introduction by stating your thesis clearly.

_____

_____

_____

_____

_____

_____

_____

_____

_____

_____

_____

_____

_____

Step 7   Read your first paragraph to be sure that the ideas you used follow each other logically and
support your thesis.

TIP	By now you should be about 8 minutes into the 20 minutes you have to write your essay. Have you finished the first paragraph? You want to leave 2 minutes at the end for proofreading and revising.

Step 8   Check your quick list of ideas. Choose the next idea and write a transition into your second paragraph. Keep writing until you use all the RELEVANT ideas on your quick list.

_____

_____

_____

_____

TIP
Don't forget to use transitions between your paragraphs.

_____

_____

_____

_____

_____

TIP
If a new idea comes from the flow of your writing, use it IF IT FITS THE CONTEXT.

_____

_____

_____

_____

_____

_____

TIP	**You should have about 6 minutes of your writing time left. How much time do you have?**

Step 9 Allow about 4 minutes to write a solid conclusion using one of the following methods:

- Rephrase your thesis.
- Summarize your main points.
- Refer in some way back to your introductory paragraph.

_____

_____

_____

_____

_____

_____

_____

_____

_____

_____

_____

_____

_____

_____

_____

_____

_____

_____

TIP	**You should have paced yourself so that you have 2 minutes for your final review.**

Step 10 Proofread and revise neatly.

- Cross out any irrelevant ideas or words.
- Make any additions, especially transitions.
- Smooth out any awkward sentences.
- Check your grammar and mechanics.

SELF-EVALUATION RUBRIC

	6	5	4	3	2	1
Overall Impression	Demonstrates excellent command of the conventions of English; outstanding writing competence; thorough and effective; incisive	Demonstrates good command of the conventions of English; good writing competence; less thorough and incisive than the highest essays	Demonstrates adequate command of the conventions of English; competent writing	Demonstrates fair command of the conventions of English; some writing competency	Demonstrates little command of the conventions of English; poor writing skills; unacceptably brief; fails to respond to the question	Lacking skill and competence
Thesis and Purpose	Exhibits excellent perception and clarity; original, interesting, or unique approach; includes apt and specific references, facts, and/or examples	Exhibits good perception and clarity; engaging approach; includes specific references, facts, and/or examples	Clear and perceptive; somewhat interesting; includes references, facts, and/or examples	Somewhat clear but exhibits incomplete or confused thinking; dull, mechanical, overgeneralized	Very little clarity; confusing; flawed logic	Very confusing or completely off the topic
Organization and Development	Meticulously organized and thoroughly developed; coherent and unified	Well organized and developed; coherent and unified	Reasonably organized and developed; generally coherent and unified	Moderately organized and developed; some incoherence and lack of unity	Little or no organization and development; incoherent and void of unity	No apparent organization or development; incoherent
Use of Sentences	Effectively varied and engaging; virtually error free	Varied and interesting; a few errors	Adequately varied; some errors	Moderately varied and marginally interesting; one or more major errors	Little or no variation; dull and uninteresting; some major errors	Numerous major errors
Word Choice	Interesting and effective; virtually error free	Generally interesting and effective; a few errors	Occasionally interesting and effective; several errors	Moderately dull and ordinary; some errors in diction	Mostly dull and conventional; numerous errors	Numerous major errors; extremely immature
Grammar and Usage	Virtually error free	Occasional minor errors	Some minor errors	Some major errors	Severely flawed; frequent major errors	Extremely flawed

Instructions: Rate yourself in each of the categories on the rubric. Circle the description in each category that most accurately reflects your performance. Enter the numbers on the lines below. Then calculate the average of the six numbers to determine your final score. On the SAT I, at least two readers will rate your essay on a scale of 1 to 6, with 6 being the highest. Because it is difficult to score yourself objectively, you may wish to ask a respected friend or teacher to assess your writing to reflect more accurately its effectiveness.

SELF-EVALUATION

Each category is rated 6 (high) to 1 (low)

Overall Impression _____

Thesis and Purpose _____

Organization and Development _____

Use of Sentences _____

Word Choice _____

Grammar and Usage _____

TOTAL _____

Divide by 6 for final score _____

OBJECTIVE EVALUATION

Each category is rated 6 (high) to 1 (low)

Overall Impression _____

Thesis and Purpose _____

Organization and Development _____

Use of Sentences _____

Word Choice _____

Grammar and Usage _____

TOTAL _____

Divide by 6 for final score _____

Chapter 5
THE TOP 10 RULES OF EFFECTIVE WRITING

Your goals for this chapter are to
• Learn 10 important rules for making your writing effective
• Practice these 10 rules to become confident in your writing

---

What is *effective writing?* Effective writing is writing that gets your point across clearly and concisely. It accomplishes the purpose you have established for your piece—to explain, to entertain, or, in the case of the SAT I essay, to persuade.

When you write, you have to make choices about the content, organization, structure, and word usage that will be appropriate for the assignment. You must decide on the right words, the right sentence structure, the right organizational style, and the right tone for your purpose. As you gain knowledge about and experience in good writing, your decisions become easier—and your writing becomes more confident.

Before you reach the point where your choices come effortlessly to you, you need to learn what makes a piece of writing effective. You also need to think about how to create effective writing. This chapter offers 10 rules that will help you make informed decisions for effective writing. You will analyze and then practice

• Using action verbs and active voice

• Using precise words

• Saying exactly what you mean

• Maintaining consistent tone throughout a piece of writing

• Avoiding words that may not be understood

• Being concise in your development of ideas

• Improving sentences by combining or shortening sentences

• Developing sentence variety

• Using the conventions of standard written English for capitalization and punctuation

These same rules apply when you have to answer the SAT's multiple-choice questions about improving sentences and paragraphs. The practice you complete in this chapter will help you when you start to work on Part II of this book.

USING THE PRACTICE ITEMS

After each rule, there is a set of practice items called *Check Your Writing Skills*. The practice sentences for rules 9 and 10 about capitalization and punctuation are combined at the end of rule 10. Review the recommendations for creating effective writing that apply for each rule and then read and complete each practice set. If you do not understand what to do to fix or rewrite a particular sentence, you may read the answer immediately.

On pages 113–124, there is a single set of 50 items. Before reading and completing them, review the 10 rules for effective writing. Then, complete the entire set of 50 items. Try not to check the suggested responses until you have finished a group of sentences.

On page 128, you will find some additional suggestions for practice. By practicing writing effectively now, you can gain confidence for writing your SAT I essay.

RULE 1: USE ACTION VERBS AND THE ACTIVE VOICE

Your job as a writer is to communicate effectively with your reader. To do this, you need to make your writing interesting. Using action verbs and active voice adds life to writing.

ACTION VERBS

Action verbs in the active voice make your sentences vivid and easy to understand. While parts of the verb *to be,* such as *is* or *was,* are necessary for expressing some ideas, too many of them make your writing dull. Wherever possible, replace the parts of the verb *to be* with *action verbs* by

- Changing an important noun in a sentence into an action verb
  Verb *to be:* The use of leaf blowers before 8 a.m. *is* a violation of local noise abatement laws.
  Action Verb: The use of leaf blowers before 8 a.m. *violates* local noise abatement laws.

- Substituting a verb that has a meaning similar to that of one of the important nouns or adjectives in the sentence
  Verb *to be:* The quarterback's wretched performance *was a disgrace* to his team.

Action Verb: The quarterback's wretched performance *humiliated* his team.

- Rephrasing your sentence if you can think of no related verbs
  Verb *to be:* Jamie *was* happy to be part of the all-star soccer team.
  Action Verb: Being a part of the all-star soccer team *thrilled* Jamie.

In the examples above, notice how the substitutions create more interesting sentences. Replacing weak verbs with strong, precise action verbs adds vitality to your writing.

CHOOSE THE ACTIVE VOICE

In addition to using action verbs, you can make your essay more direct and more interesting by writing in the active voice. A verb is in the *active voice* when its subject performs the action. Verbs in the passive voice usually force your reader to wait until the end of the sentence to find the doer, or the subject, of the action. Notice how much more effective the sentences in active voice are in the following examples.

Passive Voice: The main idea for my essay was stated as the first sentence in the first paragraph.
Active Voice: I stated the main idea of my essay in the first sentence in the first paragraph.

Passive Voice: Money for the new recreation building was raised quickly.
Active Voice: The recreation committee quickly raised money for the new building.

CHECK YOUR WRITING SKILLS

Rewrite each sentence, using an action verb in the active voice.

1. The completion of the homework assignment was immensely pleasing to Tori.

_____

_____

2. Laughing and joking was heard from the sailors as they scrubbed the decks of the ship.

_____

_____

3. A study of the life cycles of various South American monkeys was made by the zoologists.

_____

_____

4. Since Liz was pursuing her goal to be a physician, all her spare time was spent studying.

_____

_____

5. The sounds that were made by the ghosts in the haunted house were frightening to me.

_____

_____

RULE 2: USE PRECISE WORDS

When you write, use the most precise words you can to make your ideas stand out. In addition to using action verbs in the active voice, you make your writing clearer by using the most specific words you can.

REPLACE OVERLY GENERAL WORDS WITH SPECIFIC IMAGES

Words with specific meanings will give your readers a mental picture that allows them to see what you see and understand what you are thinking. General words such as *said* or *animal* are useful but sometimes fall short of expressing an idea clearly and may leave readers uninformed. To communicate effectively, use specific nouns, verbs, and modifiers. Notice how the following examples become more interesting when specific verbs replace overly general ones.

General: Tom got into his car and drove off.
Specific: Tom leaped into his SUV and roared off.

General: The writer wrote a three-page critique of the painting in which he said he did not like it.
Specific: In his three-page critique, the art critic squeezed every drop of meaning—and enjoyment—out of the 3-inch by 3-inch pastel.

Overly general words about people, places, and things can leave your readers wondering about details. Substitute specific nouns to clarify your thoughts.

General: An old dog came up the street.
Specific: An ancient, gray-muzzled golden retriever wandered up Bluebird Canyon Road.

General: My coach illustrates the point about playing fairly.
Specific: My basketball coach, Ms. Berry, illustrates the essayist's point about playing fairly.

You can further sharpen the meaning of your sentences by using well-chosen, vivid adjectives and adverbs.

General: The *Star Wars* saga is an interesting group of movies.
Specific: The *Star Wars* saga is a memorable series of films, filled with amazing aliens and noble heroes.

General: At the end of the day, the workmen walked up the snow-covered road.
Specific: At the end of the day, the tired workmen trudged wearily up the snow-covered road.

Vague modifiers, such as *interesting* and *good,* may show your feelings and opinions, but more colorful modifiers add details that help focus your writing, as well as show your opinions and feelings.

General: I thought the essay was well written and interesting.
Specific: I thought the writer effectively organized her essay to move from the specific to the general.

CHOOSE THE RIGHT CONNOTATION

The *denotation* of a word is its literal meaning, whereas the *connotation* is a broader area of meanings that a word suggests. Often, when you are searching for a word, two or more possibilities occur to you. Most probably, the words are synonyms. While the words have definitions that are close in meaning, they neither share the same precise meaning nor do they call the same ideas to mind. One synonym probably has a different connotation, a different shade of meaning, from the other. Choose the right word with the best connotation for your essay. By choosing the right shade of meaning, you can present your ideas more precisely. Consider the following examples:

- Claire was *crafty,* and she would distract her mother so that her dog could sneak snacks off the dinner table.
  (*Crafty* has the negative connotation of deception.)

- Claire was *shrewd,* and she would distract her mother so that her dog could sneak snacks off the dinner table.
  (*Shrewd* can also have a negative connotation, but it can also mean skill in practical matters.)

- Claire was *clever,* and she would distract her mother so that her dog could sneak snacks off the dinner table.
  (*Clever* has a more positive connotation than the other words. It suggests Claire's actions are harmless and playful instead of secretive and deceptive.)

Choose the word with the most appropriate connotation, depending on the ideas you want to communicate. The best way to learn word connotations and denotations is to read widely. Use a thesaurus and a dictionary to look up the meanings of words to help you see the subtle difference between meanings of similar words.

CHECK YOUR WRITING SKILLS

For sentences 6 through 8, rewrite the sentences, using more specific verbs, nouns, and modifiers.

6. The soccer players worked hard for a goal.

_____

_____

7. I enjoyed my United States history class because Ms. Lim made it interesting.

_____

_____

8. Tom brought the huge fish over the side of the boat.

_____

_____

For sentences 9 and 10, rewrite the sentences, substituting a synonym with a different connotation for the italicized word.

9. Eva seems *cold* to people who do not know her.

   _____

   _____

10. The politician *preached* against the dangers of unlimited wetlands development.

   _____

   _____

RULE 3: SAY WHAT YOU MEAN

Be careful to avoid *clichés, trite expressions,* and *euphemisms* in your writing. Including overused clichés and trite expressions in your writing makes you appear lazy because you haven't taken the time and effort to express your exact meaning. In addition, trite expressions don't give your audience a clear idea of what you mean. Using details will do that. Euphemisms can lead to wordiness and make your writing stilted.

To help you avoid clichés and trite expressions, start a Word Bank of words and phrases that you could use in writing the kinds of essays that the College Board asks for on the SAT I Writing test.

REPLACE CLICHÉS WITH FRESHER IMAGES AND WORDS

A *cliché* is any stale, worn-out phrase that has been used so often it has become virtually meaningless. Clichés make your writing seem commonplace and secondhand. Some clichés and trite expressions include the following:

Ugly as sin	Like finding a needle in a haystack
Pretty as a picture	Like a bump on a log
Happy as a lark	Like a hot potato
Hard as a rock	Sky high
Fresh as a daisy	Sparkling clean
Skinny as a rail	Filthy rich
Sly as a fox	Dirt cheap
Stiff as a board	Costing an arm and a leg
Old as the hills	Heart of gold
Mad as a hornet	One in a million
Soft as silk	Between a rock and a hard place
Warm as toast	Out of the frying pan and into the fire
Dumb as a doorknob	When push comes to shove
Smart as a whip	Working fingers to the bone
Crazy as a loon	Come out smelling like a rose
Honest as the day is long	Tooting my/your/one's own horn
As much fun as a barrel of monkeys	In a New York minute
Quiet as a mouse	Variety is the spice of life.
Loose as a goose	Stand up and be counted
Phony as a three-dollar bill	Raining cats and dogs
Pure as the driven snow	The sixty-four dollar question
Crystal clear	Day in and day out
True blue	Have a nice day
Like pulling teeth	Like a fish out of water

Replace clichés and trite expressions with livelier, more concrete language. For example:

Cliché: I was *shaking in my boots* before the interview, but I was *happy as a lark* when the personnel manager offered me the job.

Improved: I was *terrified* before the interview, but I was *ecstatic* when the personnel manager offered me the job.

www.petersons.com

Cliché: Whether the author really believed what he wrote was the sixty-four dollar question.

Improved: Whether the author really believed what he wrote was difficult to determine from the answers he gave the interviewer.

AVOID EUPHEMISMS

A *euphemism* is a word or phrase that is less direct but that may be considered less offensive than another word or phrase with the same meaning; for example, saying someone is *no longer with us* instead of *dead*. Euphemisms can lead to wordiness, as in the above example, because you may need several words to say what one direct word could convey. Euphemisms also lessen the impact of a thought or idea, and they can mislead your readers. Occasionally, you may choose to use a euphemism to protect someone's feelings—yours, the subject of your writing's, or your audience's—but eliminate euphemisms whenever possible, so your writing does not seem insincere.

Euphemism: Amit could not attend the meeting Thursday because he was *indisposed.*

Improved: Amit could not attend the meeting Thursday because he was *sick.*

Euphemism: Because she was constantly late for work, Leslie was *let go.*

Improved: Because she was constantly late for work, Leslie was *fired.*

CHECK YOUR WRITING SKILLS

For sentences 11 through 13, rewrite the sentences, replacing the italicized clichés with more interesting language.

11. I tried to start my car, but the battery was *dead as a doornail.*

_____

_____

12. Ms. Lim is a *one-in-a-million* teacher.

_____

_____

13. Every time I have to make a presentation in class, my stomach gets *tied up in knots.*

_____

_____

For sentences 14 and 15, rewrite the sentences, replacing the italicized euphemisms with more precise words.

14. Marli's room was in a *state of severe disorder.*

_____

_____

15. One of Armando's weekly chores was to *eliminate the refuse.*

_____

_____

RULE 4: MAINTAIN YOUR TONE

The words you choose express your attitude—feelings and opinions—about the subject of your essay. This attitude is called *tone.* Good writers maintain a consistent tone about their subject. As you begin to write a paper, choose a tone that is appropriate for your topic, audience, and purpose and then pick words to fit that tone. Maintain the same tone throughout whatever you are writing, whether it is the SAT I essay, your college application essay, or a research report. The right tone for your SAT I essay is the same tone you use in writing an essay for class. Just as clichés and euphemisms reduce the effectiveness of your writing, so, too, can inappropriate word choice by confusing the tone.

AVOID SELF-IMPORTANT LANGUAGE

If a writer tries to impress readers with unnecessarily obscure words and lengthy, complicated sentences, that author has used self-important language. The result can destroy the tone and confuse the message. When you write, avoid that type of language. Eliminate vague, general nouns and long verbs that end in *-ate* or *-ize.*

Self-important: To facilitate input by the maximum number of potential purchasers, questionnaires were designed and posted well in advance of the launch of the promotional marketing campaign.

Improved: Before we began advertising, we designed and mailed a marketing survey to find out what customers were looking for.

AVOID FLOWERY LANGUAGE AND EMOTIONALLY LOADED WORDS

Good writing should include vivid modifiers and interesting phrases. However, your writing should never become overloaded with unnecessary adjectives and adverbs that serve only as decoration. Usually, a simpler way of expressing yourself is more effective.

Flowery: The glimmering, golden rays of the brilliant orb of the sun shimmered above the white-hot sands of the vast desert, sere and lifeless.

Improved: The rays of the sun shimmered above the hot, dry desert.

Similarly, overly emotional language can produce a harsh tone and make your readers reject your point of view. Avoid emotional language and substitute more rational diction.

Emotional: The idiot who wrote that essay should have his head examined.

Improved: The writer who developed that argument based it on a faulty assumption.

CHECK YOUR WRITING SKILLS

For sentences 16 through 18, rewrite the sentences, replacing self-important language with precise, direct language.

16. To develop an appropriate level of competency, users of the paintbrush practice their art endlessly.

_____

_____

17. Luis tried to ameliorate his grade by fawning over his teacher.

_____

_____

18. In my opinion, the author penned a brilliant and incandescent essay illuminating and extolling the multiplicity of benefits to be derived from a post-prandial nap.

For sentences 19 and 20, rewrite the sentences, eliminating overly emotional words and flowery language.

19. The ponderous vehicle rumbled through the newly fallen crystal white snow.

20. The stupidity of people can be seen in the idiotic reasons that they give for not voting.

RULE 5: USE DIRECT LANGUAGE

Whether you are writing the SAT I essay or an essay for a U.S. history class, you should use only vocabulary and expressions that your readers will understand. In general, regardless of the type of writing, avoid *slang* words and expressions because you cannot be sure that your audience is familiar with them. Slang becomes quickly outdated and has no place in a formal piece of writing. Your essay for the SAT I Writing test is a formal essay, even if it's only a draft.

> **Slang:** Brian's mother reprimanded him for bombing his physics test.
> **Improved:** Brian's mother reprimanded him for failing his physics test.

Similarly, jargon can confuse readers and destroy the tone you are trying to create. *Jargon* is language aimed at specialists. You would use it only if you were writing a highly technical report that requires specialized terms. This is not the case with your SAT I essay. Choose concrete, understandable words and phrases to develop your ideas.

> **Jargon:** Close-support, transport, and reconnaissance assistance is provided by the S-3X helicopter, which is the most cost effective in a crane configuration.
> **Improved:** The S-3X helicopter provides support, transportation, and reconnaissance. However, the helicopter is most cost effective when it works as a crane.

CHECK YOUR WRITING SKILLS

Rewrite the following sentences, removing slang or jargon. Use precise, direct language.

21. Ian raced ahead of the curl and carved a bottom turn that would do credit to a butcher.

_____

_____

22. The police collared the man and woman as they ran from the store that they had ripped off.

_____

_____

23. Sergio thought that Pearl was awesome because of the way that she protected the goal.

_____

_____

RULE 6: USE CONCISE LANGUAGE

As you write your essay, strive to be *concise*. Deadwood, redundancy, and wordiness can bore your readers. Eliminating unnecessary words and phrases will make the important words and ideas stand out.

ELIMINATE "DEADWOOD"

Check your essay for words that contribute nothing to your ideas. Discard these empty words that pad your sentences and create roundabout constructions. You will find some of the most common "empty words" in this box.

Commonly Used Empty Words and Phrases		
a great deal of	due to	which is to say
is the one who is	it is a fact that	the area of
there is	the thing that	what I mean is
there are	of the opinion that	for the reason that
by way of	to the extent that	in a manner that

"Deadwood": It is a fact that sunburn can cause skin cancer.
Improved: Sunburn can cause skin cancer.

"HEDGING" WORDS AND PHRASES

Other "deadwood" you should eliminate are "hedging" words and phrases, or qualifiers. Writers use qualifiers to be noncommittal, but using them results in a vague and indefinite essay. However, don't eliminate all hedging words in your writing. For example, "Everyone in the stadium cheered the touchdown" needs to be qualified unless you know that the opposing team had no supporters in the stands. The following list contains words and phrases that unnecessarily qualify what you want to say.

Commonly Used "Hedging" Words and Phrases		
almost	rather	it seems
tends to	in a way	sort of
somewhat	kind of	that may or may not

Hedging: A major earthquake that may or may not occur in this region can cause a great deal of damage.

Improved: If a major earthquake occurs in this region, it will cause a great deal of damage.

AVOID REDUNDANCY

Redundancy occurs when you repeat an idea unnecessarily. It prevents writing from being concise. Saying the same thing repeatedly not only sounds awkward but adds "deadwood" to your essay. To eliminate redundancy in your writing, look for words or phrases that repeat the meaning of another word.

Redundant: Tamiko prefers the written letter to the telephone.
Improved: Tamiko prefers letters to the telephone.

Redundant: The consensus of opinion in our community is that commercial building should be restricted.
Improved: The consensus in our community is that commercial building should be restricted.

BE SUCCINCT

Less obvious than "deadwood" and redundant language are wordy phrases and clauses that can weaken the impact of your writing. Shorten wordy phrases and clauses if you can without changing the meaning of your sentence. Sentences can be rewritten by shortening into appositives, prepositional phrases, adjectives, adverbs, or possessive nouns. Sometimes, you can replace a phrase with a single word.

Wordy: Denee sang every Christmas carol in a loud voice.
Improved: Denee sang every Christmas carol loudly.

Wordy: Tourists from Germany and Canada love to vacation in the Caribbean.
Improved: Many German and Canadian tourists love to vacation in the Caribbean.

If your essay has a great many adjective clauses, you can simplify sentences by dropping the clause's subject, verb, and other unnecessary words. Also, substitute appositives, participial phrases, and compounds for wordy clauses.

Wordy: The painting, which hangs on the museum's third floor, accurately portrays the signing of the Declaration of Independence.
Improved: The painting on the museum's third floor accurately portrays the signing of the Declaration of Independence.

CHECK YOUR WRITING SKILLS

For sentences 24 through 28, rewrite sentences, removing "dead-wood" and redundancy. Use precise, direct language.

24. The goal of the firefighters is to save lives to the extent that they don't jeopardize their or other people's lives.

_____

_____

25. Most people are of the opinion that work should be completed before play begins.

_____

_____

26. Outside the house the snow was like a blanket in appearance covering the front yard.

_____

_____

27. Anna, who loves painting, enjoys drawing pictures of seascapes, trees, and people.

_____

_____

28. Akeem argued with Marcus about a disagreement they had over who should clean up the kitchen.

_____

_____

For sentences 29 and 30, rewrite the sentences, making them more succinct.

29. Hope should never be found to be the only possible basis that you rely on for your future.

_____

_____

30. The challenge that was confronted by Ira was to convince his boss that he could take a week off to go skiing.

_____

_____

RULE 7: IMPROVE SENTENCES

SENTENCE COMBINING TECHNIQUES

A good mixture of long and short sentences adds interest to your essay. Aim for a varied pattern of sentence lengths and structures.

If you find your writing is choppy and disconnected, try combining short sentences. One way is to create a *compound subject* or *verb*. You might try rewriting an idea as a *modifying phrase*, or an *appositive*. There are many methods of combining short sentences.

Sentence-Combining Techniques	
Choppy Sentences	**Improved Sentences**
The glee club held a fundraiser. The basketball team also held a fundraiser.	The glee club and the basketball team held fundraisers. (Compound subject)
Kareem opened the door. He invited all of us in.	Kareem opened the door and invited all of us in. (Compound verb)
The most valuable player on the basketball team will give the graduation speech. She is the star of this year's musical.	The most valuable player on the basketball team, who is also the star of this year's musical, will give the graduation speech. (Appositive)
The wide receiver ran down the field. He caught the winning touchdown pass.	Running down the field, the wide receiver caught the winning pass. (Modifying phrase)
The writer wanted to finish his reading. He did not want to be interrupted with questions.	The writer did not want to be interrupted with questions before he finished his reading. (Complex sentence)
Kim, Julio, and Billy ate the casserole. Billy became ill.	Kim, Julio, and Billy ate the casserole, but only Billy became ill. (Compound sentence)
Alan decided to go to law school. He applied to five universities. All accepted him.	When Alan decided to go to law school, he applied to five universities and all five accepted him. (Compound-complex sentence)

SHORTEN LONG SENTENCES

Not only can you damage the flow of your essay with short, choppy sentences, but you can also hamper your writing by putting too many ideas in long sentences. If you have overused compound, complex, and compound-complex sentences, you can make your thoughts more accessible by shortening the sentences. Break up your long sentences into shorter, simpler ones, but remember that you want to achieve variety. Not all long sentences need to be divided.

Too Long: After Rick flipped the starter switch on his motorcycle, it made a clicking sound, but the engine did not start because the battery was dead and needed a jump.

Improved: After Rick flipped the starter switch on his motorcycle, it made a clicking sound, but the engine did not start. The battery was dead and needed a jump.

CHECK YOUR WRITING SKILLS

Rewrite passages 31 and 32 by combining sentences. Make sure to use precise, concise language, and do not alter the author's meaning.

31. The most interesting person I know is Sean O'Neill. He started his own business forty years ago. He now owns a fleet of 100 long-distance trucks. He never forgot how hard it was to get his first loan to start his business. He started a program to help enterprising college graduates who want to start their own business.

_____

_____

_____

_____

_____

32. The hills went from the valley to the sea. Where the hills met the ocean, they formed a small lagoon. The lagoon is home to shellfish, small fish, and water birds. The lagoon is shallow and fairly clear. It has interesting ecology to study.

_____

_____

_____

_____

For sentences 33 and 34, rewrite the sentences, making them shorter without changing their meaning. Keep in mind that there is no one correct answer.

33. Stevedores removed countless items from the cargo ship, while sailors lounged around the deck, and small boats cruised by on the other side of the ship.

_____

_____

34. The NCAA has many rules regarding the recruiting of athletes, and these guidelines have been developed over time to protect the athletes and to make sure that all colleges and universities are following the same policies.

_____

_____

RULE 8: DEVELOP SENTENCE VARIETY

Remember to use sentence combining and sentence restructuring when you edit your writing. Also, focus on the beginnings of your sentences as you write and edit. Using a variety of sentence structures will come naturally to you the more you practice. It is, after all, the way you speak.

USE A VARIETY OF SENTENCE OPENERS

Using too many similar openers for your sentences makes your writing monotonous. Vary sentence openers by using some of the techniques listed in the following chart:

Options for Sentence Beginnings	
Subject-Verb	The crowd could see the band very clearly.
Adjective	Wet and cold, we decided to leave the lake.
Adverb	Suddenly, the puppy jumped at the ball.
Prepositional Phrase	In an instant, the magician made the tiger disappear from the cage.
Participial Phrase	Diving into the waves, Suzanne raced out to the buoy.
Infinitive Phrase	To learn the dance routine, Hua practiced with the cheerleaders two hours a day.
Adverbial Clause	Because the roads were iced over, the sheriffs allowed no one to drive to Lake Tahoe.
One-Word Transition	However, Jasper prefers to eat his hamburger with salsa.
Transitional Phrase	On the other hand, many people enjoy a vacation in the country.
Inverted Order	Out of the evening sky shot a magnificent meteor shower.

100

VARY SENTENCE STRUCTURES

As you write, include some compound, some complex, and some compound-complex sentences. Structural variety highlights your ideas and engages your reader. An occasional short sentence, for example, could be used to emphasize your major idea, while supporting details are expressed in longer sentences.

Types of Sentence Structure	
Simple Sentence	California has a milder climate than Connecticut.
Compound Sentence	Southern California has a Mediterranean climate, and Connecticut has a humid continental climate.
Complex Sentence	Because of its latitude and proximity to the ocean, Southern California has a Mediterranean climate.
Compound-Complex Sentence	Because of its latitude and proximity to the ocean, Southern California has a warm, sunny climate, and the region often experiences drought.

CHECK YOUR WRITING SKILLS

Rewrite sentence 35 using each of the openers identified by the letters (A), (B), and (C). You may substitute words, but do not change the author's meaning. Keep in mind that there is no one correct answer.

NOTE: Not all of these new beginnings are ones that you are likely to use in an SAT I essay, because they may not be concise or clear to the reader. However, learning which ones work in particular situations and which don't will help you with your revision process.

35. Francesca was not the type of person who would run from her responsibilities to her friends and family, so she paid for her brother's education.

(A) Transitional phrase:

_____

_____

_____

(B) Participial phrase:

_____

_____

_____

(C) Adverbial clause:

_____

_____

_____

Rewrite passage 36 using each of the sentence structures identified by the letters (A), (B), (C), and (D). Although it may not be possible to keep all of the author's original thoughts in each sentence structure, try to keep as many as possible.

36. Lida and Sarah teamed together to write a biography on Alex Haley. In the process, they not only learned a great deal about the life of the noted author, but they also learned a lot of United States history.

(A) Simple sentence:

_____

_____

_____

_____

(B) Compound sentence:

_____

_____

_____

_____

(C) Complex sentence:

_____

_____

_____

_____

(D) Compound-complex sentence:

_____

_____

_____

RULE 9: USE STANDARD RULES OF ENGLISH FOR CAPITALIZATION

The SAT I Writing test evaluators may not expect you to write a flawless essay, but you do want to make sure that your mechanics are as correct as possible. Everything you do well adds to the favorable impression necessary for a high score.

CAPITALIZATION

You have studied capitalization throughout your school years. The following list recaps the rules for capitalization you have learned.

Nouns

- Capitalize the first word in interjections and incomplete questions.

- Capitalize the first word in a quotation if the quotation is a complete sentence.

- Capitalize the first word after a colon if the word begins a complete sentence.

- Capitalize geographical and place names.

103

- Capitalize names of specific events and periods of time.

- Capitalize the names of organizations, government bodies, political parties, races, nationalities, languages, and religions.

Adjectives

- Capitalize most proper adjectives; for example *African* in *African American*.

- Do not capitalize certain frequently used proper adjectives; for example, *french fries, venetian blinds*.

- Capitalize a brand name used as an adjective, but not the common noun it modifies; for example, *Jello pudding*.

- Do not capitalize a common noun used with two proper adjectives; for example, *Iron Age tools*.

- Do not capitalize prefixes attached to proper adjectives unless the prefix refers to a nationality; for example, *pre-Columbian art* but *Franco-American music*.

Capitals in Titles

- Capitalize titles of people when used with a person's name or when used in direct address.

- Capitalize titles showing family relationships when they refer to a specific person, unless they are preceded by a possessive noun or pronoun.

- Capitalize the first word and all other key words in the titles of books, periodicals, plays, poems, stories, paintings, and other works of art. Do not capitalize prepositions or articles unless they begin or end the title.

RULE 10: USE STANDARD RULES OF ENGLISH FOR PUNCTUATION

Just as you should use proper capitalization in your essay, use standard English punctuation to make a good impression on the scorers. Remember, you want to eliminate errors that interfere with clarity. The following rules will help you review punctuation rules that are important in writing.

End Marks

- Use a period to end a declarative sentence, a mild imperative, and an indirect question.

- Use a question mark to end an interrogative sentence, an incomplete question, or a statement intended as a question.

- Use an exclamation mark to end an exclamatory sentence, a forceful imperative sentence, or an interjection of strong emotion.

Commas

Many writers overuse commas. Make certain that you know why you are adding a comma to a sentence.

- Use a comma before a conjunction that separates two independent clauses in a compound sentence.

- Use commas to separate three or more words, phrases, or clauses in a series.

- Use commas to separate adjectives of equal rank.

- Do not use commas to separate adjectives that must stay in a specific order.

- Use a comma after an introductory word, phrase, or clause.

- Use commas to set off parenthetical expressions.

- Use commas to set off nonessential expressions.

- Use commas to set off a direct quotation from the rest of the sentence.

- Use a comma to prevent a sentence from being misunderstood.

Semicolons and Colons

- Use a semicolon to join independent clauses not already joined by a coordinating conjunction *(and, or, but, so, yet)*.

- Use a semicolon to join independent clauses separated by either a conjunctive adverb or a transitional expression.

- Use a colon before a list of items following an independent clause.

- Use a colon to introduce a formal or lengthy quotation or one that is missing an introductory expression.

- Use a colon to introduce a sentence that summarizes or explains the sentence before it.

Quotation Marks and Underlining

If a word, a title, or a name would be italicized in printed material, then you need to underline it when you write it by hand. If you were writing your essay on a computer, you would use the italics function. Do not use quotation marks around an indirect quotation (a restatement of someone's words).

- Use quotation marks to enclose a person's exact words.

- Place a comma or a period inside the final quotation mark.

- Place a semicolon or a colon outside the final quotation mark.

- Place a question mark or exclamation mark inside the final quotation if the end mark is part of the quotation.

- Place a question mark or exclamation mark outside the final quotation if the end mark is not part of the quotation.

- Use three ellipsis marks in a quotation to indicate that words have been omitted.

- Use single quotation marks for a quotation within a quotation.

- Use quotation marks around titles of short written works, shows, films, and other works of art.

- Underline or italicize titles of long written works, shows, films, and other works of art.

- Underline or italicize the names of individual air, sea, space, and land craft.

- Underline or italicize words and phrases from a foreign language when not used commonly in English.

- Underline or italicize numbers, symbols, letters, and words used as names for themselves.

Dashes, Parentheses, and Brackets

- Use dashes to indicate an abrupt change of thought, a dramatic interrupting idea, or a summary statement.

- Use dashes to set off a nonessential appositive, modifier, or parenthetical expression when it is long, already punctuated, or especially dramatic.

- Use parentheses to set off asides and explanations only when the material is not essential or when it consists of one or more sentences.

- Place all punctuation after the parentheses in a sentence with a set-off phrase.

- Use brackets to enclose words you insert into a quotation when you are quoting someone else.

Hyphens

- Use a hyphen when writing out the numbers twenty-one through ninety-nine.

- Use a hyphen with fractions used as adjectives.

- Don't use a hyphen with a fraction when the fraction is a noun; for example, Two thirds of the legislators were needed to pass the bill.

- Use a hyphen in words with the prefixes *all-*, *ex-*, and *self-* and words with the suffix *-elect*.

- Use a hyphen to connect a compound modifier before a noun unless it includes a word ending in *-ly*, or is a compound proper adjective; for example, beautifully dressed, Native American jewelry.

- If a word must be divided at the end of a line, place a hyphen between syllables.

- Use a hyphen between two words that are used together to modify another word; for example, twentieth-century writers.

Apostrophes

- Add an apostrophe and an *s* to show the possessive case of most singular nouns; for example, *the cat's dish, the tomato's flavor.*

- Add an apostrophe to show the possessive case of plural nouns ending in *-s* or *-es*; for example, *the boys' club, the teachers' lounge.*

- Use an apostrophe and an *s* to show possession with plural nouns that do not end in *-s*; for example, *women's clothing, the mice's nests.*

- Add an apostrophe and an *s* or just an apostrophe (if the word is plural and ends in *-s*) to the last word of a compound noun to form the possessive; for example, *the Joint Committee's decision, the mutual funds' investors.*

- To show joint ownership, make the final noun possessive. To show individual ownership, make each noun possessive; for example, *Marie and Leslie's apartment, but Mike's and Tom's cars.*

- Use an apostrophe and an *s* with indefinite pronouns to show possession; for example, *one's jacket, somebody's chair.*

- Use an apostrophe and an *s* to write the plurals of numbers, symbols, and letters; for example, *8's, &'s, p's.*

- Do not use an apostrophe with the possessive forms of personal pronouns; for example, *hers.*

CHECK YOUR WRITING SKILLS

Sentences 37 to 50 may have an error in capitalization or punctuation. Circle the error and then rewrite the sentence correctly on the blank line.

37. I think that Kellogg's Cereals are the best.

_____

38. Planning for the future is important, but living in today is important too I think.

_____

39. *Things Fall Apart* is a strong moving novel.

_____

40. The movie contained some exciting moments; but it had a very predictable ending.

_____

41. Lenny yelled, "Get out of my way"!

_____

42. Ali commented that she hated the song <u>Blue Moon</u>.

_____

43. Clarissa said that she was going to study a novel concept to her parents for her final exam.

_____

44. Lucy said that the invitation must be her's because Marion knew that it didn't belong to her.

_____

45. A two thirds majority was needed to pass the bill.

_____

46. Thankfully the political candidate's speech finally ended.

_____

47. The city seemed alive with activity as the New Year approached, it was a time of great expectation for many people.

_____

48. The city council called for the expulsion of Council member Davis for theft, this is a point under considerable dispute, before the members went on to new business.

_____

49. The recipe called for the following ingredients, milk, eggs, flour, sugar, orange flavoring, and baking powder.

_____

50. On Valentine's Day, Sharif called his girlfriend "mon amour."

_____

ANSWERS AND EXPLANATIONS

Study Strategy: Read these sample sentences next to the original sentences. See how much more the rewritten sentences tell you and how they help to give you a picture of the event or person. Strive for this in your own writing.

CHECK YOUR WRITING SKILLS: USING ACTION VERBS AND ACTIVE VOICE, PAGE 82

1. Tori completed the homework assignment, to her immense pleasure.

2. The sailors laughed and joked as they scrubbed the decks of the ship.

3. The zoologists studied the life cycles of various South American monkeys.

4. Liz pursued her goal to be a physician by spending all her spare time studying.

5. The sounds of the ghosts in the haunted house frightened me.

CHECK YOUR WRITING SKILLS: USING PRECISE WORDS, PAGE 85

6. The soccer team fought hard to score the deciding goal.

7. I enjoyed my U.S. history class because Ms. Lim made history come alive for me.

8. With a mighty effort, Tom hauled the huge silvery sailfish over the side of the heaving boat.

9. Eva seems arrogant to people who do not know her.

10. The politician spoke forcefully against the dangers of unlimited wetlands development.

CHECK YOUR WRITING SKILLS: SAYING WHAT YOU MEAN, PAGE 88

11. I tried to start my car, but the battery was not charged.

12. Ms. Lim always seems genuinely interested in what her students have to say.

13. Every time I have to make a presentation in class, my hands get clammy, my stomach hurts, and my voice comes out as a squeak.

14. Marli's room was a mess.

15. One of Armando's weekly chores was to throw out the trash.

CHECK YOUR WRITING SKILLS: MAINTAINING YOUR TONE, PAGE 90

16. Good painters spend a great deal of time practicing.

17. Luis tried to improve his grade by flattering his teacher.

18. In my opinion, the author wrote a witty essay about the benefits of an after-lunch nap.

19. The huge truck plowed through the snow.

20. People use poor reasons to justify not voting.

CHECK YOUR WRITING SKILLS: USING DIRECT LANGUAGE, PAGE 92

21. Ian rode down the wave and made an excellent turn.

22. The police apprehended the man and woman as they ran from the store that they had robbed.

23. Sergio thought that Pearl was a great goalkeeper because of the many saves she made.

CHECK YOUR WRITING SKILLS: USING CONCISE LANGUAGE, PAGE 95

24. The goal of firefighters is to save lives but not at the risk of jeopardizing their own or other people's lives.

25. Most people believe that work should be completed before play begins.

26. Outside the house, the snow covered the front yard like a blanket.

27. Anna enjoys drawing pictures of seascapes, trees, and people.

28. Akeem argued with Marcus about who would clean up the kitchen.

29. Your future should not be based solely on hope.

30. Ira needed to convince his boss to let him take a week off to go skiing.

CHECK YOUR WRITING SKILLS: IMPROVING SENTENCES, PAGE 98

31. The most interesting person that I know is Sean O'Neill. He started his own business forty years ago and now owns 100 long-distance trucks. Mr. O'Neill has never forgotten how hard it was to get his first loan. As a result, he started a program to help enterprising college graduates who want to start their own business.

32. A small lagoon was formed by the hills that went from the valley to the ocean. The lagoon is home to shellfish, small fish, and water birds. The ecology of the shallow, fairly clear lagoon is an interesting one to study.

33. As boats cruised by and sailors lounged on the deck, stevedores removed countless items from the cargo ship.

34. The NCAA has developed recruiting rules to protect athletes and to ensure that no college or university has an unfair advantage.

CHECK YOUR WRITING SKILLS: DEVELOPING SENTENCE VARIETY, PAGE 101

35. (A) **Transitional phrase**
    On the contrary, Francesca was not the type of person who would run from her responsibilities to her friends and family, so she paid for her brother's education.
    (B) **Participial phrase**
    Being the type of person who would not run from responsibilities to friends and family, Francesca paid for her brother's education.
    (C) **Adverbial clause**
    Because Francesca did not run from her responsibilities to her family and friends, she paid for her brother's education.

36. (A) **Simple sentence**
    Lida and Sarah learned a lot about Alex Haley and United States history.
    (B) **Compound sentence**
    Lida and Sarah wrote a biography about Alex Haley, and they also learned a lot about United States history.

(C) Complex sentence
Because they wrote a biography of Alex Haley, Lida and Sarah learned a lot about United States history.

(D) Compound-complex sentence
Because they wrote a biography of Alex Haley, Lida and Sarah learned a great deal about the author's life, and they learned a lot about United States history, too.

Check Your Writing Skills: Capitalization and Punctuation, page 107

37. I think that Kellogg's cereals are the best.
Rule: Capitalize a brand name used as an adjective, but not the common noun it modifies.

38. Planning for the future is important, but living in today is important, too, I think.
Rule: Use commas to set off parenthetical expressions (too and I think).

39. *Things Fall Apart* is a strong, moving novel.
Rule: Use commas to separate adjectives of equal rank.

40. The movie contained some exciting moments, but the ending was very predictable.
Rule: Use a comma before a conjunction separating two independent clauses in a compound sentence.

41. Lenny yelled, "Get out of my way!"
Rule: Place a question mark or exclamation point inside the final quotation if the end mark is part of the quotation.

42. Ali commented that she hated the song "Blue Moon."
Rule: Use quotation marks around titles of short written works, episodes in a series, songs, parts of musical compositions, or collections.

43. Clarissa said that she was going to study for her final exam—a novel concept to her parents.
Rule: Use dashes to indicate an abrupt change of thought, a dramatic interrupting idea, or a summary statement.

44. Lucy said that the invitation must be hers because Marion knew that it didn't belong to her.
Rule: Do not use an apostrophe with the possessive forms of personal pronouns.

45. A two-thirds majority was needed to pass the bill.
Rule: Use a hyphen with fractions used as an adjectives.

46. Thankfully, the political candidate's speech finally ended.
Rule: Use a comma after an introductory word, phrase, or clause.

47. The city seemed alive with activity as the New Year approached; it was a time of great expectation for many people.
Rule: Use a semicolon to join two independent clauses not already joined by a coordinating conjunction.

48. The city council called for the expulsion of Council member Davis for theft (this is a point under considerable dispute) before the members went on to new business.
Rule: Use parentheses to set off asides and explanations only when the material is not essential or when it consists of one or more sentences.

49. The recipe called for the following ingredients: milk, eggs, flour, sugar, orange flavoring, and baking powder.
Rule: Use a colon before a list of items following an independent clause.

50. On Valentine's Day, Sharif called his girlfriend <u>mon amour</u>.
Rule: Underline words and phrases from a foreign language.

CHECK YOUR WRITING SKILLS

Review the 10 rules of effective writing, and then try to complete the following 50 items without looking at the answers. There is no time limit for this practice, so really concentrate on what the directions are asking you to do and then on doing it. The more practice in analyzing and creating effective sentences you have now, the more confident you can be that your own writing will be clear and to the point.

> Rewrite the following sentences, using more specific verbs, nouns, and modifiers.

1. The streetlights were brighter and then were dimmer as the electricity was interrupted by the storm.

_____

_____

2. The moviegoers were angry with the people talking.

_____

_____

Rewrite each sentence, using an action verb in the active voice.

---

3. Only two questions were missed by John on his history examination.

_____

_____

4. The opposing team's large half-time lead was overcome, and the game was easily won by our team.

_____

_____

5. Her fear of an avalanche was Kathy's reason to ski as fast as she could.

_____

_____

6. The first cold morning of autumn is invigorating to me.

_____

_____

7. Jamie and Ali were focused on their game.

_____

_____

> Rewrite the following sentences, substituting for the italicized word a synonym with a different connotation.

8. Surveys often use *guesses* to calculate certain statistics.

_____

_____

9. The poet's image of a *golden* day seemed to establish the overall mood of the poem very well.

_____

_____

10. The robin's egg *was concealed* in its home of twigs.

_____

_____

> Rewrite the following sentences, replacing clichés with fresher language.

11. A light went off in Carla's head and she figured out the solution to her problem.

_____

_____

12. When the supervisor told me that I was getting a raise, it was music to my ears.

_____

_____

> Rewrite the following sentences, replacing euphemisms with precise words.

13. The political candidates had a frank exchange of views.

   _____

   _____

14. Dave enjoyed going out to eat with his friends, but his table manners were lacking in polish.

   _____

   _____

15. As children, the boys relied on the pugilistic arts to solve their disagreements.

   _____

   _____

> Rewrite the following sentences, replacing self-important language with precise, direct language.

16. The nimble dashing flow of water changed from a bluish hue to moving snow as it cascaded over the granite pillows below.

   _____

   _____

17. The book society sought celebrated wordsmiths to elevate its literary audience.

   _____

   _____

> Rewrite the following passages, eliminating overly emotional words and flowery language.

18. Reggie's decision not to have a DJ for the party shows how stubborn and inept he is at planning social engagements.

_____

_____

19. The generous and giving nature of Tan was manifested by his gift to the university.

_____

_____

20. The sustaining values that parents convey to their progeny is created through the multitudinous experiences one has in a lifetime.

_____

_____

> Rewrite the following sentences, removing slang or jargon. Use precise, direct language.

21. The stockbroker told his client that the company's earnings and P/E multiple indicated that the equity would increase in value.

_____

_____

22. The interaction of the pressure gradients was indicative of a coming rainstorm.

_____

_____

Rewrite the following sentences, removing "deadwood" and redundancies. Use precise, direct language.

---

23. It is a fact that Sun is the fastest runner in the school.

_____

_____

24. Kristalle did not get the job that she wanted due to the fact that she did not turn in her application on time.

_____

_____

25. A great deal of time and money is spent on scientific projects that have uncertain benefits.

_____

_____

26. I find that to understand an assignment I often have to read it a couple of times and take notes.

_____

_____

27. The golden retriever ran around the side of the corner of the building to get the stray ball that was thrown by the girl.

_____

_____

Rewrite the following passages, making them more succinct.

---

28. The tasks that are placed before American politicians change from time to time due to new priorities.

_____

_____

29. Mary worked hard to complete her reading, and then she worked on her term paper.

_____

_____

30. The sailors watched from the deck as the golden orb of the setting sun made its final appearance as it set behind the clouds.

_____

_____

Rewrite the following passages by combining sentences. Make sure to use precise, concise language and do not alter the author's meaning.

---

31. In the past, it was common to find social functions for the young centered on the family. Today, most social functions are associated with school in some fashion.

_____

_____

32. Wonda, Carla, and Jaresa were in an argument. They were upset because each of them wanted to be the lead singer.

_____

_____

> Rewrite the following sentences, making them shorter without changing their meaning. Keep in mind that there is no one correct answer.

33. Since the United States was first created, political parties were developed so that people with essentially the same viewpoint had a means of expressing their thoughts as to how the government should be run.

_____

_____

_____

_____

34. A lunar eclipse occurs when a shadow caused by the earth blocking the light from the sun falls across the visible portion of the moon, but not all observers see the same thing because of their unique view of the moon.

_____

_____

_____

_____

Rewrite the following sentence by using each of the openers identified by the letters (A), (B), and (C). You may substitute words, but do not change the author's meaning. Keep in mind that there is no one correct answer.

Note: Not all of these new beginnings are ones that you are likely to use in an SAT I essay because they may not be as concise or clear to the reader. But learning which ones work and which ones don't in particular situations helps you with your revision process.

35. Moreover, the rights of the many must be limited in order to prevent individuals from a loss of their rights and freedoms.

    (A) Prepositional phrase:

    _____

    _____

    _____

    (B) Infinitive phrase:

    _____

    _____

    _____

    (C) Inverted order:

    _____

    _____

    _____

Rewrite the following passage by using each of the sentence structures identified by the letters (A), (B), (C), and (D). Although it may not be possible to maintain all of the author's original thoughts in each sentence structure, try to keep as much as possible.

36. The urban environment is one of the most complex on Earth. People too often focus only on the human elements, but many animals and plants thrive in the city.

   (A) Simple sentence:

   _____

   _____

   _____

   _____

   (B) Compound sentence:

   _____

   _____

   _____

   _____

   (C) Complex sentence:

   _____

   _____

   _____

   _____

(D) Compound-complex sentence:

_____

_____

_____

_____

The following sentences may have an error in capitalization, abbreviation, or punctuation. Identify the error and the means to correct the mistake.

---

37. The instructions for the test include the following: mark the correct answer in the proper oval and make sure to darken the entire oval.

_____

38. 11 players can form a football team.

_____

39. The colors of the American flag are red, white and blue.

_____

40. Mark yelled at his brother, "Dad said, Don't play in the junk-yard!"

_____

41. There were eighty three volunteers who went to paint the building.

_____

42. Juanita was talking to Rosa (a beautiful dancer) about the ballet auditions.

_____

43. The team was devastated by its loss, however, the players recovered quickly.

_____

44. The author was quoted as saying, "I believe that writers can sway public opinion—these people can be hard to convince."

_____

45. The "Bible" is the most widely owned book in the United States.

_____

46. Many people mistakenly believe that San Francisco California is the state's capital.

_____

47. Hakeem said, "I feel that this is the best movie I've seen in a long time."

_____

48. The cars lights were being turned on as it grew dark.

_____

49. The earthquake hit at rush hour; commuters still remember the shaking motion.

_____

50. All of us sometimes forget to cross our *t*s.

_____

ANSWERS AND EXPLANATIONS

CHECK YOUR WRITING SKILLS, PAGES 113–124

Check your answers against these suggested responses. Remember that except for the capitalization and punctuation sentences, there is no one correct way to rework a sentence. If you are still unsure about some of the ways to revise your writing, review the 10 rules again. Complete the additional exercises presented on page 128.

1. The streetlights brightened and dimmed as the storm interrupted the electricity.

2. The moviegoers complained about the people talking.

3. John missed only two questions on his history examination.

4. Our team overcame the opposing team's large half-time lead and went on to win the game easily.

5. Kathy skied as fast as she could to avoid an avalanche.

6. The first frost of autumn energizes me.

7. Jamie and Ali concentrated on their game.

8. Surveys often use estimates to calculate certain statistics.

9. The poet's image of a sunny day seemed to establish the overall mood of the poem very well.

10. The robin's egg was nestled in its home of twigs.

11. Carla suddenly understood and was able to solve her problem.

12. When the supervisor told me that I was getting a raise, I was happy.

13. The political candidates disagreed.

14. Dave enjoyed going out to eat with his friends, but his table manners were poor.

15. As children, the boys solved their disagreements by fighting.

16. The river changed from blue to white as it cascaded over the rocks.

17. The literary society searched for well-known authors to interest its members.

18. Reggie's decision not to have a DJ for the party shows how little experience he has in planning parties.

19. Tan's generosity was evident in his gift to the university.

20. A lifetime of experiences creates lasting values that parents pass on to children.

21. The stockbroker told his client that based on past performance, the company's stock price would rise.

22. The forecast called for rain.

23. Sun is the fastest runner in the school.

24. Kristalle did not get the job that she wanted because she did not turn in her application on time.

25. Significant time and money is spent on scientific projects that have uncertain benefits.

26. To understand an assignment, I often have to read it several times and take notes.

27. The golden retriever ran around the corner of the building to get the stray ball that the girl had thrown.

28. The tasks for American politicians periodically change due to new priorities.

29. Mary worked hard to complete her reading and then her term paper.

30. The sailors on the deck watched the setting sun disappear behind the clouds.

31. Social functions in the past were family-oriented, but today they are school-centered.

32. Wonda, Carla, and Jaresa argued passionately about who should be the lead singer.

33. Political parties were developed in the United States so that like-minded people could express their opinions about the government.

34. Observers in various areas of the earth see different views of a lunar eclipse, which is created by the earth's shadow on the moon blocking the sunlight.

35. **(A) Prepositional phrase**
    In addition, the rights of the many must be limited in order to prevent individuals from a loss of their rights and freedoms.
    (B) Infinitive phrase
    To clarify the point, the rights of the many must be limited in order to prevent individuals from a loss of their rights and freedoms.
    (C) Inverted order
    To prevent individuals from a loss of their rights and freedoms, the rights of the many must be limited.

36. **(A) Simple sentence**
The complex urban environment has a thriving population of plants and animals.
(B) Compound sentence
People focus on the human elements in the complex urban environment, but many plants and animals thrive there.
(C) Complex sentence
While many plants and animals thrive in the city, people focus on the human element.
(D) Compound-complex sentence
Because the urban environment is complex, people focus only on the human element, but many animals and plants thrive in the city.

37. The instructions for the test include the following: Mark the correct answer in the proper oval and make sure to darken the entire oval.
Rule: Capitalize the first letter after a colon if the word begins a complete sentence.

38. Eleven players can form a football team.
Rule: Spell out numbers that begin a sentence.

39. The colors in the American flag are red, white, and blue.
Rule: Use commas to separate three or more words, phrases, or clauses in a series.

40. Mark yelled at his brother, "Dad said, 'Don't play in the junk-yard!' "
Rule: Use single quotation marks for a quotation within a quotation.

41. There were eighty-three volunteers who went to paint the building.
Rule: Use a hyphen when writing out the words twenty-one through ninety-nine.

42. Juanita was talking to Rosa, a beautiful dancer, about the ballet auditions.
Rule: Use commas to set off nonessential elements.

43. The team was devastated by its loss; however, the players recovered quickly.
Rule: Use a semicolon to separate two independent clauses not already joined by a coordinating conjunction.

44. The author was quoted as saying, "I believe that writers can sway public opinion . . . these people can be hard to convince."
Rule: Use ellipsis marks in a quotation to indicate that words have been omitted.

45. The Bible is the most widely owned book in the United States.
     Rule: Do not underline or place in quotation marks the titles of holy books such as the Koran or the Bible, or their parts.

46. Many people mistakenly believe that San Francisco, California, is the state's capital.
     Rule: Use a comma to separate each part of a geographical name of two or more parts.

47. Hakeem said, "I feel that this is the best movie I've seen in a long time."
     Rule: Place a comma or period inside the final quotation mark.

48. The cars' lights were being turned on as it grew dark.
     Rule: Add an apostrophe to show the possessive case of plural nouns ending in s or es.

49. The earthquake hit at rush hour—commuters still remember the shaking motion.
     Rule: Use dashes to indicate an abrupt change of thought, a dramatic interrupting idea, or a summary statement.

50. All of us sometimes forget to cross our *t*'s.
     Rule: Use an apostrophe and an s to write the plurals of numbers, symbols, and letters.

MORE PRACTICE

For additional practice in revising your own writing to make it more effective, complete the following suggested activities:

1. Choose one of the practice essays that you wrote when working through Chapter 4. Review it for passive voice and the use of precise words. Circle any verbs, nouns, and adjectives that you could improve. Underline any passive voice.

    Choose one sentence to improve. Rework it here.

    _____

    _____

    _____

Choose another sentence and revise it here.

_____

_____

Compare your revised sentences to your original sentences. Do they tell you more about your topic? Are they more interesting? Remember to use active voice and precise words in whatever you write.

2. Choose any two of your practice essays. Review them for trite expressions, clichés, slang, and jargon. Circle any instances that you find. Use the blank lines below to rephrase the sentences to make them clearer and more precise.

Essay 1

_____

_____

_____

Essay 2

_____

_____

_____

_____

Didn't find any examples of tired, overused expressions or slang? Great! That's one area that you won't have to worry about for the SAT I essay. Be sure to keep up the good work.

Found a couple of worn-out expressions, some slang, or jargon? Recognize that this is one area that you will have to be careful about in your writing. From now on, avoid using them in all your writing.

3. Choose two other of your practice essays. Check them for redundancies and "deadwood." On separate sheets of paper, revise each essay once to eliminate redundancies and "deadwood."

As you write essays and papers for your classes, watch out for this habit of repeating what you have to say. It is a major weakness of writers and means they haven't organized their ideas before they begin to write.

4. On a separate sheet of paper, revise one of your practice essays by combining and breaking apart sentences to see how much sentence variety you can introduce—and still keep the sense of what you have to say.

Practice this skill of varying sentence structures as you write essays and papers for class. It makes your writing much more interesting than a paragraph of simple sentences all beginning with a subject followed by a verb.

5. Revise the following sentence three different ways to remove the dash.
The earthquake hit at rush hour—commuters still remember the shaking motion.

Semicolon:

_____

_____

Comma:

_____

_____

Period:

_____

_____

CHECK OFF

Before you continue on to Part II,

- Can you summarize what you learned about writing effective prose?

- Do you know which rules apply to areas of your own writing?

- Do you know how you are going to work on those areas in your writing?

Make a plan to practice writing and revising your own work every day between now and SAT I test day. Even if all you write is the answers to textbook review questions, practice using a variety of sentence structures, active voice, and precise words.

Part II
Practicing Standard English for Writing

In Chapters 6 through 9, you will learn

- Basic information about the multiple-choice section on the SAT I

- General test-taking strategies for the multiple-choice questions

- The differences between the Identifying Sentence Errors, Improving Sentences, and Improving Paragraphs sections on the Writing test

- Strategies for answering each type of test item

- How to recognize 100 of the most common usage errors in standard written English

You will also practice

- Answering simulated test items for each type of multiple-choice question on the SAT I Writing test

Chapter 6

ABOUT THE MULTIPLE-CHOICE SECTION

Your goals for this chapter are to
- Learn basic information about the multiple-choice section on the SAT I Writing test
- Analyze the question types for sentence errors, improving sentences, and improving paragraphs
- Answer simulated test items to become familiar with the different types of multiple-choice question formats used on the SAT I Writing test

The Writing test on the SAT I includes multiple-choice questions that assess your knowledge of standard written English. This chapter provides basic information for the multiple-choice section on the Writing test, as well as suggestions for developing a strategy for attacking the questions. Chapters 7, 8, and 9 will help you review the conventions of standard English while mastering techniques for answering the specific types of multiple-choice questions.

In addition to helping you identify sentence errors, improve sentences, and improve paragraphs in the multiple-choice section, the reviews in Chapters 7, 8, and 9 can also help you with your own writing. The grammar, usage, mechanics, and word choice decisions you need to make to answer the multiple-choice questions correctly can sensitize you to look for and correct similar problems in your own writing.

The idea is to become so familiar with good writing that it becomes second nature to you. You will have sharpened your writing skills so much that your first drafts will need fewer and fewer revisions.

BASIC INFORMATION ABOUT THE MULTIPLE-CHOICE SECTION

1. The multiple-choice section contains three types of questions:
   - **Identifying Sentence Errors**
     You must recognize errors in grammar and standard English usage.
   - **Improving Sentences**
     You must choose the most effective and correct version of a sentence. This section tests your knowledge of grammar and standard English usage as well as sentence structure.
   - **Improving Paragraphs**
     You must improve the logic, coherence, or organization of a paragraph, again using the most effective and correct choice given.

2. Each set of Sentence Error and Sentence Improvement questions has items arranged in order of difficulty.

3. Improving Paragraph questions are not arranged in order of difficulty. They follow the order of the essay.

4. The SAT I Writing test allots 25 minutes for the multiple-choice section.

5. You receive one point for each correct answer. You receive no points for questions you leave blank. If you answer incorrectly, a quarter point is subtracted. This is the guessing penalty.

GENERAL TEST-TAKING STRATEGIES FOR THE MULTIPLE-CHOICE QUESTIONS

Besides the obvious importance of understanding the material, you have probably discovered that there are three significant considerations to remember when taking standardized multiple-choice tests:

- Accurate reading and analysis of test material and instructions

- Time management

- Educated guessing

The consequences of failing to do any of the above can lower your score:

- If you fail to read the directions and the questions carefully, you may make errors that are unnecessary.

- If you neglect the time, you may miss opportunities to show what you know.

- If you do not make educated guesses to answer questions you are not sure of, you are missing out on a higher score.

How do you prevent these missteps from happening and ensure your highest score? You need to develop a plan to

1. Read effectively
2. Manage your time well
3. Use all of your knowledge to the best possible effect

When you take the SAT I Writing test, you will want to have every advantage possible. The ideal is to know the correct answer as soon as you read the answer choices, but that does not always happen. However, knowing what to do ahead of time will give you an edge—a little extra time. You can use that additional minute to answer another question or check a response that you are unsure of. Here are some methods to help you score well.

- Answer the easy questions first.
  NOTE: Be sure to skip the answer ovals for the questions you skip.

- Look for errors according to difficulty:
  1. Capitalization and punctuation errors
  2. Grammar and syntax errors
  3. Usage, sequence of tenses, parallel structure, redundancy, and then other errors

- Read a sentence or passage twice before making any decision about answers.

- Identify the subject and the predicate of each sentence to help you find errors in usage, redundancy, and relevance.

- Be sure to use educated guessing—
  1. If you know something about the content of the question
     AND
  2. If you can eliminate one or more answer choices

EDUCATED GUESSING

One technique that is especially helpful is "educated guessing." Use this strategy when you do not know the correct answer immediately, but you do know something about the content of the question and can eliminate at least one answer choice. Some of these tips work better with some types of multiple-choice questions on the SAT I Writing test than others.

- First, ignore answers that are absolutely wrong.
- Eliminate choices in which part of the answer is incorrect.

- Check the key words in the question again.

- Reread remaining answers to discover which seems most correct.

- Choose the answer that feels right. Trust yourself. Your subconscious usually will guide you to the correct choice. Do not argue with yourself.

You are probably thinking about the quarter-point deduction for an incorrect answer, and you are wondering if taking a chance is worth the possible point loss. Recognize that if you use this strategy, your chances of scoring higher are excellent. You are not guessing but making an "educated guess." You will have to answer four questions wrong to lose a single point. If you have an idea about which choice is correct, act on it. Even the College Board suggests that you guess as long as you can eliminate some answer choices as wrong.

PLANNING YOUR TIME

It is important to remember that you may not be able to answer all the questions even by using the educated-guess technique. You must pace yourself so you can read all the questions, answer the easier ones, and leave the more difficult ones until the end. By planning your time, you can be confident that you will be able to correctly answer as many questions as you possibly can.

Because the questions at the beginning of each section (except for the Paragraph Improvement set) tend to be easier, you might plan to spend more time on those questions and less time on the final questions.

Instead of allotting yourself about 35 seconds to read and answer each question, consider dividing your multiple-choice time into 5-to-10 minute segments. Then, divide the questions so that you tackle more in the first segment when you are fresh than in the last segment when you are tired and the questions are more difficult. If you are a slow starter, rearrange the time segments so you answer the most questions during the middle period. One of the benefits of taking the Practice Exercise Sets in this book is that you can devise a strategy that fits your work pattern.

- Don't spend too much time on a difficult question.

- If you read a question and the content and none of the answer choices seem correct, skip the question. Put a check mark (√) next to it in the test booklet and be sure you skip the answer oval.

- If you read a question and don't know the answer immediately but at least one of the answer choices seems wrong, try the steps for making an educated guess. If you can't immediately eliminate any other answer choices, don't spend any more time. Put an *X* next to it and move on, skipping the answer oval for the question.

When you have read through the entire test and answered what you can immediately or with a few seconds' thought, go back first to the questions marked with an *X* and try those again. If you still have time, try the questions marked with a check.

One word of advice: Don't worry if a question at the beginning of a section seems difficult to you. Remember that all things are relative. What may be an easy question for one student because agreement problems were her teacher's pet peeve, may be a blank to another student because his class spent more time working on creating imagery in their writing.

USING THE PRACTICE ITEMS

In this chapter, you will learn about each multiple-choice question type on the SAT I Writing test. After the discussion of each question type, there is a set of exercises called Check Your Writing Skills. Complete each exercise to familiarize yourself with the question formats. Apply the techniques described in this chapter as you answer each question. If you do not understand what to do to fix a particular sentence, you may read the answer immediately. The Answers and Explanations for each question will help you to pinpoint your weaknesses and improve your language skills. It is a good idea to read the answer explanations to all the questions, whether you answered the question correctly or not. You may find ideas or tips that will help you better analyze the answer choices to the questions on the real test.

On pages 156–159, there is a single set of 20 items. Try not to check the suggested responses until you have finished the entire set. Again, be sure to read all the explanations.

After you have finished answering the questions and reading all the answer explanations for the Check Your Writing Skills exercises, review the test-taking strategies in this chapter. Before you begin to answer questions in the following chapters and in the Practice Exercise Sets, be sure to review these strategies again. Your goals should be to:

- Apply the test-taking system carefully

- Work the system to get a greater number of correct responses

- Be careful with your time and strive to answer more questions in the allotted time period

ANALYZING THE QUESTION TYPES

Multiple-choice questions on the SAT I Writing test measure what you have learned about standard English. If you have studied grammar and usage, you should be very comfortable taking the examination. If you have not, use this book to study. Knowing what each question type tests and understanding the directions will also help you to score your highest.

FOCUSING ON IDENTIFYING SENTENCE ERRORS

The first type of multiple-choice question asks you to identify errors in grammar and standard English usage. Each question is independent and unrelated to other questions on the test. The following strategy may help you to better discover the answers to Sentence Error questions.

- Read the sentence to yourself, taking care to hear what it sounds like.

- Concentrate on any jarring words or phrases.

- If any part sounds awkward, you may have found the mistake.

- Use your expertise in English usage and grammar to explain to yourself the possible error you discovered.

- Always examine the verbs carefully. Many errors result from faulty verb usage. Check for tense errors, subject-verb agreement mistakes, and nonstandard irregular forms. (See Chapter 7 for a review of verbs.)

- If the sentence seems fine, choose choice (E), *No error*. If you have more than six *No error* responses, double-check them. You could be missing some mistakes.

Identifying Sentence Error Instructions

It is a good idea to familiarize yourself with the instructions for the parts of the test beforehand. Then, you will not have to struggle with them on test day. Take a look now at the instructions for the section on sentence errors.

Instructions: The sentences in this section test your knowledge of grammar, usage, diction (choice of words), and idiom.

Some sentences are correct.

No sentence contains more than one error.

The underlined and lettered parts of each sentence below may contain an error in grammar, usage, word choice, or expression. Read each sentence carefully, and identify the item that contains the error according to standard written English.

Indicate your choice by filling in the corresponding oval on your answer sheet. Only the underlined parts contain errors. Assume that the balance of the sentence is correct. No sentence contains more than one error.

Some sentences may contain no error. In those cases, the correct answer will always be No error (E).

SAMPLE QUESTION   SAMPLE ANSWER

The meteor showers <u>attracted</u>   (A) (B) (C) ● (E)
                    A

astronomers from all over the world, <u>for</u>
                                       B

there <u>had never been</u> such a brilliant <u>one</u>
       C   D

in recent times. <u>No error</u>
                   E

Notice that you only have to recognize the mistake; you do not need to correct or name it. Once you have found the error, if there is one, you simply fill in the proper oval.

Analyzing Some Sample Questions

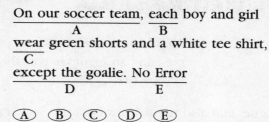

On our soccer team, each boy and girl
        A   B
wear green shorts and a white tee shirt,
    C
except the goalie. No Error
     D   E

Ⓐ Ⓑ Ⓒ Ⓓ Ⓔ

Did you choose choice (C)? The mistake in this sentence occurs in the verb; the sentence has an error in subject-verb agreement. Ordinarily when a compound subject is joined by *and,* the verb is plural. However, when the word *each* or *every* is used before a compound subject, the sentence requires a singular verb. The subject of this sentence, *boy and girl,* is preceded by *each,* so the verb must be singular, *wears.*

Trust yourself. Even if you did not remember the exact rule, your ear probably told you something was wrong with the *each/wear* construction.

Try another sample question.

Venice is a very picturesque city to visit because
     A   B
of its canals and their great museums. No Error
   C   D   E

Ⓐ Ⓑ Ⓒ Ⓓ Ⓔ

If you picked choice (D), you are correct. This sentence has an error in pronoun and antecedent agreement. A personal pronoun must agree with its antecedent in number. *Museums* refers back to *Venice,* which is singular, so the pronoun should be singular, *its.* As the sentence reads now, it appears that the canals have the museums.

CHECK YOUR WRITING SKILLS

Circle the underlined part of the following sentences that you think contains an error. If you think the sentence seems fine, circle choice (E).

1. The achievements and also the failures of the British monarchy has been important
A
issues in the discussion
B
regarding the continuation of that institu-
C   D
tion. No error
E

2. From the drivers' point of view, the new
A
speed limits enacted by the state were
B
more stricter than the old laws. No error
C   D   E

3. Every evening of his adult life, the old
A
man put on a pair of glasses, shuffled over
B   C
to his easy chair, he turned on the light,
D
and opened the newspaper. No error
E

4. Abandoning reason and defying fear, the
A   B
refugees dashed toward the border and
C
freedom. No error
D   E

5. Outside of Jean, there was no one
A   B
interested in going skiing at Mammoth
C
over the weekend. No error
D   E

6. More than once, José thought of stepping
A
on the ugly monster, but the thought of
B
touching such a dangerous hard-shelled
C

creature with his bare foot was too
D
revolting. No error
E

7. I walked along a narrow path through
dark pines; beside a brook swollen with
A   B
melting snow I found the old man I came
C
to see, sitting silent and alone before his
D
deteriorating cottage. No error
E

8. I exercised regularly for a month,
A
running, lifting weights, and skipping rope,
B
and for the first time I made the varsity
C   D
boxing team. No error
E

9. When it comes to unpleasant things to do,
A   B
I hate weeding and raking as much as
C
having to eat brussels sprouts upsets me.
D
No error
E

10. If the operator of the caterpillar
would have checked the control levers
A
before beginning the heavy roadwork, the
B
machine might never have rolled and the
C
driver would not be lying in the
D
hospital. No error
E

FOCUSING ON IMPROVING SENTENCES

The second set of questions, Improving Sentences, asks you to choose the best, most effective revision of a sentence from five alternatives. These errors may be in

- Usage

- Expression

- Style

Some of the sentences may have no errors. In this case, you would pick choice (A), which simply repeats the sentence presented in the question. Rarely are more than 10 percent of the sentences correct. So, although each test is different, if you find many sentences where you select choice (A), you may not be reading carefully. The following suggestions will help you to attack the Improving Sentences questions.

- Carefully read the entire sentence, NOT just the underlined phrases. The underlined words may seem correct unless you read the whole statement.

- Always substitute into the sentence the choices for the part that you think is incorrect.

- Do not spend the time to substitute for choice (A), because it repeats the original sentence.

- Find the best answer, not one that is simply correct. More than one choice may be correct, but only one best fits the context.

- If the sentence sounds correct to your ear, the correct choice is (A).

The common errors in this section of the writing test often involve

- Verbs

- Incorrect comparisons

- Pronoun reference

- Standard English usage

These are some of the same errors you may find in the Identifying Sentence Errors section of the test. You will also find errors in sentence structure, such as

- Sentence fragments

- Run-on sentences

- Confusing sentences

Chapter 8 will help you review sentence structure.

Improving Sentences Instructions

Familiarize yourself with the directions for this section. The instructions below are very similar to those you will find on the actual test.

Instructions: The underlined sections of the sentences below may contain errors in standard written English, including awkward or ambiguous expressions, poor word choice, incorrect sentence structure, or faulty grammar, usage, and punctuation. In some items, the entire sentence may be underlined.

Read each sentence carefully. Identify which of the five alternative choices is most effective in correctly conveying the meaning of the original statement. Choice (A) always repeats the original. Select (A) if none of the other choices improves the original sentence.

Indicate your choice by filling in the corresponding oval on the answer sheet. Your choice should make the most effective sentence—clear and precise, with no ambiguity or awkwardness.

SAMPLE QUESTION

Ansel Adams photographed landscapes <u>and they communicate</u> the essence of Yosemite and other mountainous regions.

(A) and they communicate

(B) landscapes, they communicate

(C) landscapes, and communicating

(D) which communicate

(E) that communicate

SAMPLE ANSWER

Ⓐ Ⓑ Ⓒ Ⓓ ●

Analyzing Sample Questions

<u>The principal presented the trophy to the debate team captain that was engraved with the championship year.</u>

(A) The principal presented the trophy to the debate team captain that was engraved with the championship year.

(B) Trophy was presented to the debate team captain by the principal that was engraved with the championship year.

(C) Engraved with the championship year, the principal presented the trophy to the debate team captain.

(D) The trophy engraved with the championship year and presented to the debate team captain by the principal.

(E) The principal presented the trophy, engraved with the championship year, to the captain of the debate team.

 Ⓐ Ⓑ Ⓒ Ⓓ Ⓔ

Choice (A) is incorrect because it contains a misplaced modifier; the clause *that was engraved with the championship year* modifies *captain* instead of *trophy*. Choice (B) not only has the same clause now incorrectly modifying *principal*, but also is in the less desirable passive voice. Choice (C) is incorrect because the clause modifies *principal*. Choice (D) is an incomplete sentence. Choice (E) is correct and the best answer.

Here is another example.

> Ana is a new member of the choir, and she comes from Venezuela.

(A)   Ana is a new member of the choir, and she comes from Venezuela.

(B)   Ana, a new member of the choir and from Venezuela.

(C)   Being from Venezuela, Ana is a new member of the choir.

(D)   Ana, a new member of the choir, comes from Venezuela.

(E)   Ana is a new member from Venezuela in the choir.

Ⓐ   Ⓑ   Ⓒ   Ⓓ   Ⓔ

The sentence is grammatically correct, but it could be more effective if it used a subordinate clause rather than a coordinate. Choice (B) is an incomplete sentence. Choice (C) does have subordination, but it suggests that being from Venezuela is a reason why Ana is in the choir. Choice (E) changes the meaning of the sentence. Choice (D) is grammatically correct and properly subordinates one clause and embeds it into the other, the main clause. It is the best choice.

CHECK YOUR WRITING SKILLS

Read each sentence carefully. Circle the answer choice you think is the most effective. Choice (A) always repeats the original.

1. As long as lamb was not served, <u>anything that the caterers suggested for the al fresco buffet was alright with the host and hostess.</u>

   (A) anything that the caterers suggested for the al fresco buffet was alright with the host and hostess.

   (B) anything the caterers suggested for the al fresco buffet was alright with the host and hostess.

   (C) anything that the caterers suggested for the *al fresco buffet* was alright with the host and hostess.

   (D) anything that the caterers suggested for the al fresco buffet was cool with the host and hostess.

   (E) anything that the caterers suggested for the al fresco buffet was all right with the host and hostess.

2. <u>Although the troupe was not professional, the entire audience was mesmerized by them pantomiming and dancing.</u>

   (A) Although the troupe was not professional, the entire audience was mesmerized by them pantomiming and dancing.

   (B) Although the troupe was not professional, the entire audience was mesmerized by their pantomiming and dancing.

   (C) The entire audience was mesmerized by them pantomiming and dancing although the troupe was not professional.

   (D) The entire audience was mesmerized by their pantomiming and dancing although the troupe was not professional.

   (E) Although the troupe was not professional, the entire audience was mesmerized by their pantomiming and the way they danced.

3. <u>The witness stated that, on the evening in question, he heard shooting while watching the 6 o'clock news on television.</u>

   (A) The witness stated that, on the evening in question, he heard shooting while watching the 6 o'clock news on television.

   (B) While watching the 6 o'clock news on television, the witness stated that, on the evening in question, he heard the shots.

   (C) The witness stated that, on the evening in question, while watching the 6 o'clock news on television, he heard shooting.

   (D) The witness stated that on the evening in question, he heard shooting, he was watching the 6 o'clock news on television.

   (E) The witness stated that, on the evening in question, he heard shooting, watching the 6 o'clock news on television.

4. <u>Learning to parallel park was frightening to Margaret, and she mastered the technique on her second try.</u>

   (A) Learning to parallel park was frightening to Margaret, and she mastered the technique on her second try.

   (B) Although learning to parallel park was frightening to Margaret, she mastered the technique on her second try.

   (C) Learning to parallel park was frightening to Margaret; and she mastered the technique on her second try.

   (D) Because learning to parallel park was frightening to Margaret, she mastered the technique on her second try.

   (E) Mastering the technique on her second try, learning to parallel park was frightening to Margaret.

5. Stephanie, <u>who loves to dance, enjoys tap dancing, ballet, and jazz.</u>

   (A) who loves to dance, enjoys tap dancing, ballet, and jazz.
   (B) who loves dancing, enjoys tap dancing, ballet, and jazz.
   (C) who loves to dance—enjoys tap dancing, ballet, and jazz.
   (D) enjoys tap dancing, ballet, and jazz.
   (E) who enjoys dancing and loves tap dancing, ballet, and jazz.

6. After reading Patrick O'Brian's novel, <u>with its in-depth look at the British Royal Navy, science, and medical practices in the nineteenth century, in style so much like that of the period about which O'Brian wrote.</u>

   (A) with its in-depth look at the British Royal Navy, science, and medical practices in the nineteenth century, in style so much like that of the period about which O'Brian wrote.
   (B) with its in-depth look at the British Royal Navy, science, and medical practices in the nineteenth century, in style so much like that of the period that O'Brian wrote about.
   (C) with its in-depth look at the British Royal Navy, science, and medical practices in the nineteenth century. Its style recreates that of the period about which O'Brian wrote.
   (D) with its in-depth look at the British Royal Navy, science, and medical practices in the nineteenth century and written in the style of the period, I recommended the book to my friends.
   (E) with its in-depth look at the British Royal Navy, nineteenth century science, and medical practices styled so much like that of the period about which O'Brian wrote.

7. The radio, <u>blaring as I attempted to study the research material, made concentration impossible.</u>

   (A) The radio, blaring as I attempted to study the research material, made concentration impossible.
   (B) The radio blared as I attempted to study the research material; made concentration impossible.
   (C) The radio blared while attempting to study the research material and made concentration impossible.
   (D) The radio, blaring as I attempted to study the research material, making concentration impossible.
   (E) The radio, blaring, I attempted to study the research material, thus it made concentration impossible.

147

FOCUSING ON IMPROVING PARAGRAPHS

Two techniques exist for answering the questions in the Improving Paragraphs section—reading the essay first and reading the questions first. Try both and choose the one that works better for you.

Essay First

If you prefer to read the essay first, you can choose from three techniques.

Strategies for Reading the Essay First		
Option 1	**Option 2**	**Option 3**
• Read the essay carefully. • Do not look for errors immediately. • Do not worry about details. • Ask yourself: What is the thesis of this essay? • Use the main point to answer organization, function, and Sentence Combining questions.	• Skim the essay for general meaning. • Reread it more slowly. • Answer the questions.	• Skim the essay for general meaning. • Begin to answer the questions. • Reread the essay or parts of the essay as needed.

Questions First

You might also try reading the questions before you read the essay. This technique gives you an overview of what you must do. You will discover the number of questions that you will need to answer and which paragraphs generate the most questions and, therefore, which paragraphs require your strongest focus. You may even find some questions that you can answer without even reading the essay. After you read the questions, read the essay, keeping in mind what you must answer.

No matter which technique you decide to use on the actual test, you will need to understand the directions. Here are the instructions for the Improving Paragraphs section.

Improving Paragraphs Instructions

Familiarize yourself with the directions for this section. The instructions below are very similar to what you will find on the test.

Instructions: The selections below are unedited drafts of students' essays. Carefully read each essay. Sections of each essay need to be rewritten to make the meaning clearer and more precise.

Each essay is followed by a series of questions about changes that might improve all or part of its organization, development, sentence structure, language usage (diction), audience focus, or use of the conventions of standard written English.

Choose the answer that most clearly and effectively expresses the writer's intended meaning. Indicate your choice by filling in the appropriate oval on the answer sheet.

Analyzing a Sample Paragraph

The questions below are based on the following essay about environmental pollutants.

(1) *What causes a normal human cell to mutate and become a menace to its body?* (2) *Scientists found a connection over two hundred years ago.* (3) *A major culprit, they discovered, is environmental agents—chemicals in the air you breathe, the food they eat, and the water we drink.* (4) *Today, the World Health Organization estimates that 60 to 90 percent of all cancers are associated with environmental pollutants.*

(5) *Carcinogens are those cancer-producing agents.* (6) *They are predominantly hydrocarbons.* (7) *Such cancer-producing agents are found in cigarettes.* (8) *Scientific data disclosed by the Surgeon General of the United States support a strong link between smoking and lung cancer.* (9) *Of all lung-cancer patients, 90 percent are smokers.*

(10) *Another environmental carcinogen is radiation.* (11) *The ultra-violet rays of the sun can cause genetic mutations in the cells of the skin.* (12) *Such mutations can lead to cancer.* (13) *In fact, extensive exposure to the sun*

makes skin cancer a common type of malignancy for light-skinned people.

(14) Emissions, from radioactive materials, can trigger wild growth of cancerous cells. (15) The tragic cases of deadly cancers after the Chernobyl reactor accident illustrate this danger. (16) Certainly survivors of Hiroshima and Nagasaki have extremely elevated cancer rates.

(17) Environmental factors contribute to cancer. (18) While people cannot avoid all of them, they certainly can take precautions. (19) Eliminating use of tobacco products, apply sun screens, and if you avoid dangerous situations, individuals will help to curtail their risk of contracting cancer.

1. Which sentence contains the thesis statement of this essay?

   (A) Sentence 1
   (B) Sentence 2
   (C) Sentence 3
   (D) Sentence 4
   (E) Sentence 17

   Ⓐ Ⓑ Ⓒ Ⓓ Ⓔ

This question is asking you to identify where the author states the point of the essay. Choice (A), a question, is an opening sentence intended to hook the audience. Sentence 2, choice (B), adds interest. Choice (D) adds a fact in support of the thesis. Choice (E) restates the thesis in the conclusion. The correct answer is choice (C), the statement that environmental factors can cause cancer.

Try another sample question.

2. What is the best revision of sentence 3 for clarity and style?

    (A)   A major culprit, they discovered, is environmental agents—chemicals in the air we breathe, the food we eat, and the water we drink.

    (B)   They discovered a major culprit, environmental agents; for example, chemicals in the air you breathe, the food they eat, and the water we drink.

    (C)   A major culprit, they discovered, are environmental agents—chemicals in the air you breathe, the food you eat, and the water you drink.

    (D)   They discovered environmental agents are a major culprit; chemicals in the air you breathe, the food they eat, and the water we drink.

    (E)   Environmental agents are a major culprit, scientists discovered. Chemicals in the air you breathe are one. The food that you eat is one. The water you drink is another.

    Ⓐ Ⓑ Ⓒ Ⓓ Ⓔ

Did you find the problem with parallel structure and pronoun shift in sentence 3? Notice that three pronouns—*you, they, we*—are used. To correct that error and create parallel structure, one pronoun should be used. Choices (B) and (D) do not correct the mistake. Choice (C) has a subject-verb agreement error. Choice (E) corrects the grammatical errors, but the result is choppy. Choice (A) is the best choice.

CHECK YOUR WRITING SKILLS

Reread the sample essay on pages 149–150 about carcinogens. Then, answer these additional questions. Mark the answer you think is correct.

1. What is the best way to revise and combine sentences 5, 6, and 7?

   (A) Carcinogens are those cancer-producing agents, are predominantly hydrocarbons, and such cancer producing agents are found in cigarettes.
   (B) Carcinogens, cancer-producing agents, are predominantly hydrocarbons, such as those found in cigarettes.
   (C) Carcinogens, cancer-producing agents, are predominantly hydrocarbons; they are cancer-producing agents and are found in cigarettes.
   (D) Carcinogens, those cancer-producing agents that are predominantly hydrocarbons found in cigarettes.
   (E) Carcinogens, those cancer-producing agents, are predominantly hydrocarbons, such cancer-producing agents are found in cigarettes.

2. Which revision of sentence 13 is the best for increasing coherence?

   (A) Emissions from radioactive materials can trigger wild growth of cancerous cells.
   (B) A third environmental factor, emissions from radioactive materials, can trigger wild growth of cancerous cells.
   (C) Also, emissions, from radioactive materials, can trigger wild growth of cancerous cells.
   (D) Emissions, chemicals from radioactive materials, can trigger wild growth of cancerous cells.
   (E) Emissions from radioactive materials, triggering wild growth of cancerous cells, another factor of environmental pollution.

3. What organizational method does this essay employ?

   (A) Order of importance
   (B) Spatial order
   (C) Chronological
   (D) Compare and contrast
   (E) Descriptive order

ANSWERS AND EXPLANATIONS

CHECK YOUR WRITING SKILL: IDENTIFYING SENTENCE ERRORS, PAGE 142

1. **The correct answer is (A).** The error is subject-verb agreement. Use *have* instead of *has*.

2. **The correct answer is (C).** The error is a double comparative. Eliminate *more*.

3. **The correct answer is (D).** Faulty parallelism is the error. Eliminate *he*.

4. **The correct answer is (E).** The participles correctly modify the subject *refugees*.

5. **The correct answer is (A).** The error is in usage. Use *Except for* or *Besides*.

6. **The correct answer is (E).** The use of a comma to separate two independent clauses joined by a coordinating conjunction, the use of a hyphen to combine two adjectives modifying a noun (*hard-shelled*), and the use of singular verb form *was* are correct.

7. **The correct answer is (E).** The use of a semicolon to separate two independent clauses not joined by a conjunction, the use of the participle *swollen* to modify the noun *brook*, and the use of the preposition *before* are all correct.

8. **The correct answer is (C).** The sentence's faulty coordination can be corrected by eliminating *and* and making the first clause subordinate beginning with *Because*.

9. **The correct answer is (D).** The faulty parallelism can be corrected by revising the underlined section to read *eating brussels sprouts*.

10. **The correct answer is (A).** The form of the verb is incorrect. When a clause begins with *if*, the verb should be past perfect: *had checked*.

CHECK YOUR WRITING SKILLS: IMPROVING SENTENCES, PAGE 145

1. **The correct answer is (E).** *All right* replaces the nonstandard *alright*.

    Choice (A)   This response includes the nonstandard word *alright*.

    Choice (B)   This response has the nonstandard word *alright*.

    Choice (C)   This choice includes the nonstandard word and erroneously italicizes *al fresco buffet*. The words *al fresco* and *buffet* are used commonly in English, so italics are not required.

    Choice (D)   The slang word *cool* is substituted for *alright*.

2. **The correct answer is (B).** This choice properly uses a possessive pronoun before the gerunds.

    Choice (A)   This response uses the objective form of the pronoun instead of the possessive before the gerunds.

    Choice (C)   It does not correct the erroneous pronoun and adds a misplaced modifying clause.

Choice (D)   The pronoun is correct, but the sentence now contains a misplaced clause.

Choice (E)   This response contains faulty parallel construction.

3. **The correct answer is (C).** The clause *while watching the 6 o'clock news on television* is placed properly to modify *heard*.

Choice (A)   This response has a misplaced modifying clause.

Choice (B)   This response has a misplaced modifying clause. In this sentence, it modifies *stated*.

Choice (D)   This response is a run-on sentence with an incorrect comma.

Choice (E)   This response contains a misplaced clause modifying *shooting*.

4. **The correct answer is (B).** This choice corrects the faulty coordination.

Choice (A)   This response uses a coordinating conjunction, which creates a faulty relation between the clauses.

Choice (C)   This sentence has faulty coordination and is not logical.

Choice (D)   This response corrects the coordination problem but creates illogical subordination.

Choice (E)   The modifiers are misplaced.

5. **The correct answer is (D).** This choice eliminates the redundancy.

Choice (A)   This response contains a redundant clause, *who loves to dance,* since the rest of the sentence conveys the love of dance.

Choice (B)   This choice contains the same error as (A).

Choice (C)   This response is redundant and has an error in the use of the dash.

Choice (E)   This is another example of redundancy and also has a faulty parallelism.

6. **The correct answer is (D).** This choice creates a complete sentence.

Choice (A)   This response is an incomplete sentence.

Choice (B)   This response is an incomplete sentence.

Choice (C)   This response continues the long sentence fragment even though a complete sentence has been created from the last clause.

Choice (E)   This response contains a misplaced modifier that modifies *practices* instead of the intended meaning, the author's style.

7.   **The correct answer is (A).** The sentence is correct.

    Choice (B)   This response is a run-on sentence with a comma splice.

    Choice (C)   The modifying clause *while attempting to study the research materials* is misplaced.

    Choice (D)   This response is an incomplete sentence.

    Choice (E)   This choice is not only a run-on sentence but also has incorrect comma placement.

CHECK YOUR WRITING SKILLS: IMPROVING PARAGRAPHS, PAGE 152

1.   **The correct answer is (B).** This is the most straightforward, understandable choice.

    Choice (A)   There is no parallel structure.

    Choice (C)   This choice contains redundancies.

    Choice (D)   This response is a lengthy sentence fragment.

    Choice (E)   This response is a run-on sentence.

2.   **The correct answer is (B).** The words *a third environmental factor* create an effective transition.

    Choice (A)   There is no transition in this choice.

    Choice (C)   The prepositional phrase does not need to be surrounded by commas.

    Choice (D)   This response contains no transition.

    Choice (E)   This choice is an incomplete sentence.

3.   **The correct answer is (A).** The paragraphs are arranged from the weakest to the strongest point.

    Choice (B)   No direction or area is involved.

    Choice (C)   Time is not involved.

    Choice (D)   There is no comparison.

    Choice (E)   There is no description.

MORE PRACTICE

Review the strategies in this chapter for each type of multiple-choice question on the SAT I Writing test. Then, try to complete the following 20 items without looking at the answers until you have finished the exercise. Reread the directions for each section before answering the questions. There is no time limit for this practice, so really concentrate on what the directions are asking you to do and then on doing it.

IDENTIFYING SENTENCE ERRORS

1. In last Thursday night's performance,
    _____
    A
    Allison was the strongest of the singers
    _____
    B
    who entertain for the children's ward of
    _____   _____
    C   D
    the hospital. No error
    _____
    E

2. The article in the local newspaper that
    _____
    A
    circulated last Sunday accuses corruption
    _____ _____
    B   C
    by the mayor. No error
    _____   _____
    D   E

3. The tourists thought Yosemite was
    _____ _____   ____
    A   B   C
    more beautiful than any national park they
    _____
    D
    visited. No error
    _____
    E

4. When Jorgé met the members of the club,
    _____   ____
    A   B
    he was aggravated by their rude manners.
    _____   _____
    C   D
    No error
    _____
    E

5. The Army of the Cumberland operated
    ____   _____
    A   B
    mainly in the states of Georgia, Tennessee,
    _____
    C
    and Kentucky during the Civil War.
    _____
    D

    No error
    _____
    E

6. According to psychologists and counse-
    _____
    A
    lors, a message conveyed by telephone is
    _____
    B
    less effective than in person. No error
    _____   _____   _____
    C   D   E

7. Mr. Hancock was torn because he both
    _____   _____   ____
    A   B
    wanted to keep his job in New York and
    _____
    C
    to move to a farming community. No error
    _____   _____
    D   E

8. Because she dreams of playing profes-
    _____   _____
    A   B
    sional basketball, Jana wishes that she was
    _____   ___
    C   D
    a few inches taller. No error
    _____
    E

9. As hurricane Olivia stormed along the
    _____
    A
    predicted path up the mid-Atlantic coast,
    _____
    B
    it left record-breaking destruction in her
    ____   ___
    C   D
    path. No error
    _____
    E

10. In Joan Aiken's novel *Go Saddle the Sea,*
    _____
    A
    the main character Felix just escapes

    death in a series of adventures after he

    runs away from his grandfather's estate in
    _____   _____
    B   C
    Spain in search of his father's relatives in
    _____
    D
    England. No error
    _____
    E

IMPROVING SENTENCE ERRORS

11. The summation of the student whose name alphabetically preceded Tom's own was listened to by Tom, standing in the wings of the auditorium.

   (A) The summation of the student whose name alphabetically preceded Tom's own was listened to by Tom, standing in the wings of the auditorium.
   (B) The summation of the student whose name alphabetically preceded Tom's own was listened to by him, standing in the wings of the auditorium.
   (C) Standing in the wings of the auditorium, Tom listened to the summation of the student whose name alphabetically preceded his own.
   (D) Standing in the wings of the auditorium, the summation of the student whose name alphabetically preceded his own was listened to by Tom.
   (E) Tom, standing in the wings of the auditorium, was listened to by the students whose name alphabetically preceded his own.

12. I am sunburned due to exposure at the beach because I fell asleep on my blanket.

   (A) I am sunburned due to exposure at the beach because I fell asleep on my blanket.
   (B) Due to exposure at the beach, I am sunburned because I fell asleep on my blanket.
   (C) My sunburn is due to exposure because I fell asleep on my blanket at the beach.
   (D) I am sunburned due to exposure because I fell asleep on my blanket at the beach.
   (E) Because I fell asleep on my blanket at the beach, I am sunburned due to exposure.

13. The standards are exacting and those criteria, therefore, prevent many manuscripts from being published.

   (A) The standards are exacting, and those criteria, therefore, prevent many manuscripts from being published.
   (B) The standards are exacting and therefore, that criteria prevent many manuscripts from being published.
   (C) The standards are exacting and therefore, those criteria prevents many manuscripts from being published.
   (D) The standards are exacting and therefore, that criteria prevents many manuscripts from being published.
   (E) The standards are exacting, therefore, those criteria prevent many manuscripts from being published.

14. Just as the peace treaty was being signed, the revolutionary council hung three officers of the loyalist army, and fighting broke out again.

   (A) Just as the peace treaty was being signed, the revolutionary council hung three officers of the loyalist army, and fighting broke out again.
   (B) Before the peace treaty was to be signed, the revolutionary council hung three officers of the loyalist army, and fighting broke out again.
   (C) Fighting broke out again just as the peace treaty was being signed because the revolutionary council hung three officers of the loyalist army.
   (D) Just as the peace treaty was being signed, the revolutionary council hung three officers of the loyalist army, as a result, fighting broke out again.
   (E) Just as the peace treaty was being signed, the revolutionary council hanged three officers of the loyalist army, and fighting broke out again.

PART II: PRACTICING STANDARD ENGLISH FOR WRITING

15. Beside swollen glands, high fever, and a painful rash, victims of the flu epidemic had severely inflamed joints.

(A) Beside swollen glands, high fever, and a painful rash, victims of the flu epidemic had severely inflamed joints.

(B) Victims of the flu epidemic had severely inflamed joints beside swollen glands, high fever, and a painful rash,

(C) Beside swollen glands, high fever, and a painful rash, joints of victims of the flue epidemic were severely inflamed.

(D) Besides swollen glands, high fever, and a painful rash, victims of the flu epidemic had severely inflamed joints.

(E) Beside swollen glands, high fever, and a painful rash, victims of the flu epidemic also had severely inflamed joints.

16. The Silk Road which carried the rich goods of ancient China was filled with caravans composed of many camels, donkeys, and merchants on foot.

(A) The Silk Road which carried the rich goods of ancient China was filled

(B) The Silk Road, which carried the rich goods of ancient China, was filled

(C) The Silk Road, that carried the rich goods of ancient China, was filled

(D) The Silk Road carrying the rich goods of ancient China was filled

(E) The Silk Road was the route which carried the rich goods of ancient China, and was filled

17. In *Les Miserables* the major character, Jean Valjean, was sent to prison because desperately needing food, he had stole a loaf of bread.

(A) In *Les Miserables* the major character, Jean Valjean, was sent to prison because desperately needing food, he had stole a loaf of bread.

(B) In *Les Miserables* the major character, Jean Valjean, was sent to prison because desperately needing food, he steals a loaf of bread.

(C) In *Les Miserables* the major character, Jean Valjean, was sent to prison because, desperately needing food, he had stolen a loaf of bread.

(D) In *Les Miserables* the major character, Jean Valjean, was sent to prison because desperately needing food he had stolen a loaf of bread.

(E) In *Les Miserables* Jean Valjean, the major character, was sent to prison because desperately needing food for which he had stole a loaf of bread.

www.petersons.com

158

IMPROVING PARAGRAPHS

Reread the sample essay on pages 149–150 about carcinogens. Then, answer these additional questions.

18. Which of the following is the best combination of the following sentences?

    The ultra-violet rays of the sun can cause genetic mutations in the cells of the skin. Such mutations can lead to cancer.

    (A) The ultra-violet rays of the sun can cause genetic mutations in the cells of the skin; such mutations can lead to cancer.

    (B) The ultra-violet rays of the sun can cause genetic mutations in the cells of the skin that can lead to cancer.

    (C) The sun's ultra-violet rays can cause genetic mutations in the cells of the skin. Such mutations can lead to cancer.

    (D) Mutating cells caused by the ultra-violet rays can cause genetic mutations in the cells of the skin, resulting in cancer.

    (E) The sun's ultra-violet rays that can cause genetic mutations in the cells of the skin and can lead to cancer.

19. What is the best revision of the following sentence?

    Eliminating use of tobacco products, apply sun screens, and if you avoid dangerous situations, individuals will help to curtail their risk of contracting cancer.

    (A) Eliminate use of tobacco products. Apply sun screens. If you avoid dangerous situations, individuals will help to curtail their risk of contracting cancer.

    (B) Eliminating use of tobacco products, applying sun screens, and if you avoid dangerous situations, you will help to curtail your risk of contracting cancer.

    (C) Eliminating use of tobacco products, applying sun screens, and avoiding dangerous situations will help individuals to curtail their risk of contracting cancer.

    (D) Eliminating use of tobacco products; applying sun screens, if you avoid dangerous situations, you will help to curtail your risk of contracting cancer.

    (E) If you eliminate use of tobacco products, apply sun screens, and if you avoid dangerous situations, people can curtail their risk of contracting cancer.

20. What is the purpose of sentences 18 and 19?

    (A) Conclude the essay
    (B) Offer solutions
    (C) Serve as a reminder of the thesis
    (D) Entertain and amuse the audience
    (E) Support the main idea of the essay

ANSWERS AND EXPLANATIONS

Quick-Score Answers									
1.	C	5.	E	9.	D	13.	A	17.	C
2.	B	6.	D	10.	E	14.	E	18.	B
3.	D	7.	B	11.	C	15.	D	19.	C
4.	C	8.	D	12.	C	16.	B	20.	B

IDENTIFYING SENTENCE ERRORS

1. **The correct answer is (C).** The verb is incorrect. The tense should be past, *entertained.*

2. **The correct answer is (B).** Substitute *alleges* for *accuses* to correct improper diction.

3. **The correct answer is (D).** When comparing one member of a group with the rest of the group, include the word *other, more beautiful than any other national park.*

4. **The correct answer is (C).** The sentence has a diction error. *Aggravated* means to make worse; use *annoyed.*

5. **The correct answer is (E).** *Army of the Cumberland* is the title, so capitalizing the initial "A" is correct. All other elements are correct.

6. **The correct answer is (D).** Sentences must compare only like items. Add the words *one delivered.*

7. **The correct answer is (B).** The faulty parallelism can be corrected by placing *both* after the verb.

8. **The correct answer is (D).** Since the sentence expresses an idea contrary to fact, use the subjunctive mood, *were.*

9. **The correct answer is (D).** The sentence contains an improper pronoun shift in gender. Replace *her* with *its.*

10. **The correct answer is (E).**

IMPROVING SENTENCE ERRORS

11. **The correct answer is (C).** The sentence is in the active voice.

    Choice (A)   This response is written in the awkward passive voice.

> Choice (B)　This response contains an ambiguous pronoun reference. Is it Tom or the student speaker who is standing in the wings?
>
> Choice (D)　As written, the summation is standing in the wings. This is an example of a misplaced modifier.
>
> Choice (E)　This response changes the meaning of the sentence completely.

12. **The correct answer is (C).** *Due to* means *caused by* and should be used only when the words *caused by* can logically be substituted.

> Choice (A)　*Due to* is used incorrectly.
>
> Choice (B)　This response does not correct the error and is awkward.
>
> Choice (D)　This response contains the same diction error.
>
> Choice (E)　This response contains the same diction error.

13. **The correct answer is (A).** There is no error.

> Choice (B)　*Criteria* is plural, so *that* should be *those.*
>
> Choice (C)　This response has an error in subject-verb agreement. The plural subject requires *prevent.*
>
> Choice (D)　This response contains the same errors as choices (B) and (C).
>
> Choice (E)　This sentence contains a comma splice.

14. **The correct answer is (E).** The choice corrects the error in diction.

> Choice (A)　*Hung,* meaning *suspended,* is used incorrectly for *hanged, executed.*
>
> Choice (B)　This response contains the same error as choice (A).
>
> Choice (C)　This response contains the same error as choice (A).
>
> Choice (D)　This sentence has a comma splice.

15. **The correct answer is (D).** This sentence corrects the misuse of *beside.*

> Choice (A)　This response incorrectly uses *beside,* which means "at the side of" or "close to" for *besides,* which means "in addition to."
>
> Choice (B)　This sentence contains the same error as choice (A).
>
> Choice (C)　This choice worsens the sentence by making it passive.
>
> Choice (E)　Adding *also* does not improve the sentence.

16. **The correct answer is (B).** The choice correctly surrounds the nonessential clause with commas.

   Choice (A)   This response does not set off the nonessential clause with commas.

   Choice (C)   This response erroneously sets off an essential clause.

   Choice (D)   A comma is needed to enclose the modifying clause.

   Choice (E)   This response changes the meaning of the sentence.

17. **The correct answer is (C).** The choice corrects the error in verb usage.

   Choice (A)   This response contains an incorrect past participle. Use *stolen.*

   Choice (B)   Since the stealing occurred before the prison sentence, the clause requires the past perfect.

   Choice (D)   This does not set off with a comma the introductory phrase in the dependent clause.

   Choice (E)   This response is so flawed that it does not make sense.

IMPROVING PARAGRAPHS

18. **The correct answer is (B).** The sentence is grammatically correct and succinct.

   Choice (A)   This choice does not really combine the sentences; rather, it simply joins them with a semicolon.

   Choice (C)   This response only changes the prepositional phrase, *of the sun,* to a possessive noun, *sun's.*

   Choice (D)   This response contains many redundancies.

   Choice (E)   This response is not a complete sentence.

19. **The correct answer is (C).** The sentence has proper parallel construction.

   Choice (A)   This response results in choppy sentences.

   Choice (B)   This response results in faulty parallelism.

   Choice (D)   This response results in faulty parallelism.

   Choice (E)   This response results in faulty parallelism.

20. **The correct answer is (B).** Offering solutions to situations makes for an effective conclusion.

   Choice (A)   The entire paragraph concludes the essay.

   Choice (C)   The first sentence of that paragraph serves as a reminder of the thesis.

   Choice (D)   The sentences are not amusing.

   Choice (E)   The body paragraphs support the main idea.

CHECK OFF

Before you move on to the next chapter, can you

- Explain what each type of multiple-choice question on the SAT I Writing test assesses?

- Describe your general strategy for answering the multiple-choice questions?

- Explain how to make educated guesses?

- Describe your plan for making the most efficient use of your time on the multiple-choice section?

If you still need help with general strategies, see page 135.

If you are unsure of how to make educated guesses, see page 136.

If you still need help with time management, see page 137.

Chapter 7

ABOUT IDENTIFYING SENTENCE ERRORS

> Your goals for this chapter are to
> • Learn how to recognize and correct common sentence errors
> • Practice identifying and correcting common sentence errors

WHAT IS STANDARD ENGLISH?

The majority of educated people speak and write what is called "standard English." It includes the most widely accepted uses of grammar, mechanics, and spelling. Standard English can be informal or formal. "Informal English" is everyday English, the English used in advertising, on television, in conversation, or in personal letters. While informal English may contain contractions and casual phrases, it usually does not contain slang or improper grammar.

Formal English is just that—formal. It is the English that people use to express themselves in serious writing and speaking. Using formal English well means being precise and effective in your expression. This is the kind of English that you must demonstrate on the SAT I Writing test.

Much of the multiple-choice portion of the writing test deals with problem sentences, and some of the questions in the Improving Paragraph section also ask about sentences. As a result, understanding the parts of a sentence and correct usage in sentences is crucial to earn a good score on the test. This chapter will discuss common sentence errors. Chapter 8 will examine improving sentences by correcting flaws in structure.

USING THE PRACTICE ITEMS

After the following explanations of each question type, there is a set of exercises called Check Your Writing Skills. If you do not understand what to do to fix a particular sentence, you may read the answer immediately. The Answers and Explanations for each question will help you to find any weaknesses you may have. Be sure to read the answer explanations to all the questions.

VERBS

When you write in formal English, the chances of making errors with verbs are great. Consider the many forms and uses of verbs, the multitude of words that can function as verbs, and the probability of there being more than one verb in a sentence. To avoid making mistakes, you must take special care to understand the various uses of verbs.

VERB TENSES

When you write, you often need to indicate time. You want to indicate that something is happening now, yesterday, or tomorrow. The tense of the verb shows time—in the past, in the present, or in the future. Verbs have six tenses to reveal the time of an action or condition. Verb tense may also have basic, progressive, and emphatic forms.

Tenses and Forms of Verbs		
	Basic Form	**Progressive Form**	**Emphatic Form**
Present	I talk a lot.	I am talking about it now.	I do talk more than most students.
Past	I talked with the group.	I was talking when you interrupted.	I did talk with you about that.
Future	I will talk to you Sunday.	I will be talking at the conference.	
Present Perfect	I have talked for almost an hour.	I have been talking too much.	
Past Perfect	I had talked to him a year ago.	I had been talking with you when he arrived.	
Future Perfect	I will have talked to the recruiter by the end of the week.	I will have been talking about this project for a month before I get approval.	

Irregular Verbs

Most verbs are regular; that is, the past and the past participle are formed by adding *-ed* or *-d* to the present form. Although most verbs are regular, many of our most common verbs are irregular. An irregular verb is one whose past and past participle are not formed by adding *-ed* or *-d.* It is important for you to master irregular verbs because they often cause usage errors. The following charts show some of the common irregular verbs.

Irregular Verbs with the Same Present, Past, and Past Participle			
Present	**Present Participle**	**Past**	**Past Participle**
bid	bidding	bid	(have) bid
burst	bursting	burst	(have) burst
cost	costing	cost	(have) cost
cut	cutting	cut	(have) cut
hit	hitting	hit	(have) hit
hurt	hurting	hurt	(have) hurt
let	letting	let	(have) let
put	putting	put	(have) put
set	setting	set	(have) set
shut	shutting	shut	(have) shut
split	splitting	split	(have) split
spread	spreading	spread	(have) spread
thrust	thrusting	thrust	(have) thrust

Irregular Verbs with the Same Past and Past Participle

Present	Present Participle	Past	Past Participle
bind	binding	bound	(have) bound
build	building	built	(have) built
catch	catching	caught	(have) caught
creep	creeping	crept	(have) crept
find	finding	found	(have) found
get	getting	got	(have) got or gotten
hang	hanging	hung	(have) hung
keep	keeping	kept	(have) kept
lead	leading	led	(have) led
lend	lending	lent	(have) lent
pay	paying	paid	(have) paid
shine	shining	shone or shined	(have) shone or shined
spin	spinning	spun	(have) spun
teach	teaching	taught	(have) taught
wring	wringing	wrung	(have) wrung

Irregular Verbs That Change in Other Ways

Present	Present Participle	Past	Past Participle
arise	arising	arose	(have) arisen
become	becoming	became	(have) become
break	breaking	broke	(have) broken
draw	drawing	drew	(have) drawn
eat	eating	ate	(have) eaten
freeze	freezing	froze	(have) frozen
go	going	went	(have) gone
know	knowing	knew	(have) known
rise	rising	rose	(have) risen
see	seeing	saw	(have) seen
shrink	shrinking	shrank	(have) shrunk
slay	slaying	slew	(have) slain
steal	stealing	stole	(have) stolen
take	taking	took	(have) taken
write	writing	wrote	(have) written

Sequence of Tenses

Sentences with more than one verb must be consistent in their time sequences. Sentences should not shift tenses unnecessarily when showing a sequence of events. In deciding on tense, ask yourself if the events in the sentence are *simultaneous*—happening at the same time—or *sequential*—happening one after the other. The tense of the main verb often determines the tense of the verb in the subordinate clause. The tense of the subordinate clause should follow logically from the tense of the main verb. Look for a logical relationship and choose the verb forms that convey the proper meaning. Here are some examples:

All Events Taking Place at the Same Time
Present I understand that *you talk a great deal.* I understand that *you are talking at graduation.*
Past I understood that *you talked to my brother.* I understood that *you were talking about auto repair yesterday.*
Future I will understand if *you speak slowly.* I will understand if *you are speaking French.*

Events Taking Place in Sequence
Present I understand that *you talked to the supervisor.* I understand that *you will be talking to the supervisor.*
Past I understood that *you had talked with the owners.* I understood that *you had been talking about the environment for years.*
Future I will understand *if you have talked to my friends.* I will understand *if you have been talking to a lawyer.*

When checking the sequence of tenses in sentences, rely on logic rather than on hard-and-fast rules. Decide if the events discussed are simultaneous or sequential. Then, use a tense for the subordinate verb that makes sense.

Mood

In standard English, there are three *moods*, or ways to express action or condition:

- *Indicative mood*—when you make factual statements or ask questions
- *Imperative mood*—when you give orders or directions
- *Subjunctive mood*—when you express an idea contrary to fact or when you express a request, a demand, or a proposal

The subjunctive mood has limited use. Because of that, it is often the source of errors. Verbs in this mood differ from other verbs in three ways:

- In the present tense, the third person singular verb does not have the usual *-s* or *-es* ending.

   For example: I insist that he come to the party.

- In the present tense, the subjunctive form of *be* is *be*.

   For example: I prefer that my employees be punctual.

- In the past tense, the subjunctive mood of *be* is *were*, regardless of the subject.

   For example: If I were you, I would not eat that wild mushroom.

Subject-Verb Agreement

Another area in which you may find sentence errors is subject-verb agreement. For a subject and its verb to agree, you must make sure that both are either singular or plural. You are virtually guaranteed that you will be tested on agreement of subject and verb in the Identify Sentence Errors section of the Writing test. The following list will help you recognize difficult agreement problems:

- A phrase or clause that interrupts a subject and its verb does not affect subject-verb agreement.

   For example: Birds of a feather flock together.

- The antecedent of a relative pronoun determines its agreement with a verb.

   For example: Richard is the only one of our players who performs well.

- Two or more singular subjects joined by *or* or *nor* must have a singular verb.

  For example: Neither the cat nor the dog has been outside today.

- Two or more plural subjects joined by *or* or *nor* must have a plural verb.

  For example: Tortilla chips or wheat crackers make tasty snacks.

- If one or more singular subjects are joined to one or more plural subjects by *or* or *nor*, the subject closest to the verb determines agreement.

  For example: The twins or Maria takes us to the movies every month.
  Maria or the twins take us to the movies every month.

- A compound subject joined by *and* is generally plural and must have a plural verb.

  For example: Black and orange are my favorite colors.

- When parts of a compound subject equal a single thing and when the word *each* or *every* is used before a compound subject, the sentence must have a singular verb.

  For example: Pork and beans is a camping staple.
  Each of the children was given an apple.

- If a subject comes after its verb, it must still agree with the verb.

  For example: Overhead sail the dark storm clouds.

- A linking verb must agree with its subject, regardless of the number of its predicate nominative.

  For example: Brilliantly colored leaves are a sign of autumn.
  A sign of autumn is brilliantly colored leaves.

- A collective noun takes a singular verb when the group it names acts as a single unit.

  For example: That family eats together every night.

- A collective noun takes a plural verb when the group it names act as individuals with different points of view.

  For example: That family are unable to agree on a restaurant.

- Nouns that are plural in form but singular in meaning take singular verbs.

  For example: The news about the airplane accident was not good.

- Singular indefinite pronouns take singular verbs.

  For example: Each of his brothers drives a sports car.

- Plural indefinite pronouns take plural verbs.

  For example: Both of my dogs require a great deal of exercise.

- The pronouns *all, any, more, most, none,* and *some* take a singular verb if the pronoun's antecedent is singular and a plural verb if it is plural.

  For example: Some of the meat is spoiled.
  Some of the bananas are still green.

- A noun expressing an amount or measurement is usually singular and takes a singular verb.

  For example: Three cups of chocolate chips is required for the cookies.

CHECK YOUR WRITING SKILLS

Find the error in each of the following sentences.

- Write the letter of the correct answer choice on the line marked "Answer."

- Correct the error on the lines marked "Correction."

- Explain the reason for your answer choice and correction on the lines marked "Reason."

You will not need to write out steps 2 and 3 on the real test, but you cannot pick the correct answer without recognizing the error. Having to write out all three steps here will help you become accustomed to recognizing the error.

1. During the summer vacation, Jamie's
   <u>   A   </u>
   grandmother <u>teached</u> <u>her</u> how to <u>crochet</u>.
           B   C   D
   <u>No error</u>
      E

   Answer _____

   Correction _____

   _____

   Reason _____

   _____

   _____

2. As <u>the prisoner of war</u> <u>will talk</u> about his
           A   B
   experiences, the reporters <u>discovered</u> the
                          C
   true horror of what he encountered.
   <u> D</u>
   <u>No error</u>
      E

   Answer _____

   Correction _____

   _____

   Reason _____

   _____

   _____

3. The judge <u>ordered</u> <u>that</u> the defendant
               A   B
<u>stands</u> trial tomorrow, in spite of the fact
 C
that his lawyer <u>is not prepared.</u> <u>No error</u>
                    D   E

Answer _____

Correction _____

_____

Reason _____

_____

_____

4. Although <u>she has started</u> at the high
             A
school <u>recently,</u> Alexandra <u>is</u> popular with
       B   C
those classmates who <u>enjoys</u> her vitality
                   D
and exuberance. <u>No error</u>
                 E

Answer _____

Correction _____

_____

Reason _____

_____

_____

5. *The Untouchables* <u>were</u> a <u>television series</u>
      A   B   C
and a movie <u>starring</u> Kevin Costner.
             D
<u>No error</u>
 E

Answer _____

Correction _____

_____

Reason _____

_____

_____

PRONOUNS

Pronoun usage is a common source of errors. Sentence-error identification questions regularly test pronoun usage.

PRONOUN-ANTECEDENT AGREEMENT

Antecedents are the nouns (or words that take the place of nouns; see bullets 5 and 6) for which pronouns stand. Pronouns must agree with their antecedents in number, person, and gender. Pronoun agreement can cause problems when antecedents are compound.

- Use a singular personal pronoun with two or more singular antecedents joined by *or* or *nor*.

    For example: Neither Julio nor Billy wants to spend his time painting the basketball court.

- Use a plural personal pronoun with two or more antecedents joined by *and*.

    For example: Cleo and Ali bought their jackets at the same store.

- If two individuals share ownership of an item, use a plural pronoun to show joint ownership.

    For example: Neither Ann nor Karina let me borrow her basketball. (Each girl owns a basketball.)
    Neither Ann nor Karina let me borrow their basketball. (Both girls own one basketball jointly.)

- Use a plural pronoun if any part of a compound antecedent joined by *or* or *nor* is plural.

    For example: If my brothers or Nguyen calls, tell them to call back later.

- Use a plural personal pronoun when the antecedent is a plural indefinite noun.

    For example: Many of the students were excited about their field trip.

- Use a singular personal pronoun when the antecedent is a singular indefinite pronoun.

    For example: Only one of the scouts forgot his uniform.

- A reflexive pronoun must agree with an antecedent that is clearly stated. Replace a reflexive pronoun if you can substitute a personal pronoun.

    For example: The people who have the best chance to be elected are you. (Not yourselves)

Other errors in agreement sometimes occur because of a person or gender shift. When dealing with pronoun-antecedent agreement, check that the pronouns agree in person and gender.

REFERENCE

In all areas of pronoun usage, one rule governing reference is paramount. A pronoun requires an antecedent that is either clearly stated or clearly understood. A common error, vague or ambiguous pronoun references can obscure the meaning of sentences.

- Pronouns such as *it, they, you, which, this, that,* and *these* should always have a clear antecedent. Correct errors by replacing the pronoun with a specific noun or by revising the sentence completely. In many idiomatic expressions, the personal pronoun *it* has no specific antecedent. When using an idiom such as *It is raining* or *It is late,* the use of *it* without a specific antecedent is acceptable.

  Flawed: The dog was carsick, and the heater was broken. These made the drive miserable.

  Improved: The dog was carsick, and the heater was broken. These disasters made the drive miserable.

  Improved: The dog's carsickness and the broken heater made the drive miserable.

- A pronoun should never refer to more than one antecedent.

  Flawed: Tom told Vladimir that he must stay and clean up.

  Improved: Tom told Vladimir that Vladimir must stay and clean up.

  Improved: Cleaning up was Vladimir's responsibility, according to Tom.

- A personal pronoun should always be tied to a single, obvious antecedent.

  Flawed: The Bothells serve smoked fish at their picnics, which not everybody likes.

  Improved: The Bothells serve smoked fish at their picnics, a food that not everybody likes.

- A personal pronoun should always be close enough to its antecedent to prevent confusion.

  Flawed: The hikers saw the Mayan pyramid, rising majestically out of the forest. It was a long climb to the top, but they felt the effort was necessary. They had, after all, walked miles just to reach it.

  Improved: The hikers saw the Mayan pyramid, rising majestically out of the forest. It was a long climb to the top, but they felt the effort was necessary. They had, after all, walked miles just to reach the pyramid.

CHECK YOUR WRITING SKILLS

Find the error in each of the following sentences.

- Write the letter of the correct answer choice on the line marked "Answer."

- Correct the error on the lines marked "Correction."

- Explain the reason for your answer choice and correction on the lines marked "Reason."

You will not need to write out steps 2 and 3 on the real test, but you cannot pick the correct answer without recognizing the error. Having to write out all three steps here will help you become accustomed to recognizing the error.

1. Although both are over thirty, neither Bob
        A B   C
   nor David has finished their education.
                D
   No error
     E

   Answer _____

   Correction _____

   _____

   Reason _____

   _____

   _____

2. Neither of the women brought their
            A   B   C
   husband to the school board meeting.
     D
   No error
     E

   Answer _____

   Correction _____

   _____

   Reason _____

   _____

   _____

3. Our parents always trust my sister and
            A   B C
   myself. No error
     D   E

   Answer _____

   Correction _____

   _____

   Reason _____

   _____

   _____

4. From where I live, you can see the ocean
           A   B   C
   as well as the canyon. No error
     D   E

   Answer _____

   Correction _____

   _____

   Reason _____

   _____

   _____

5. Kyra <u>was wearing</u> a skirt with
          A

<u>garish horizontal</u> stripes, a baseball cap,
          B

high-top tennis shoes, and an aviator

jacket. <u>It</u> made <u>her</u> look odd. <u>No error</u>
          C   D   E

Answer _____

Correction _____

_____

Reason _____

_____

_____

MODIFIERS AND COMPARISONS

Almost certainly, you will be presented with some questions about comparisons on the SAT I Writing test. One important use of modifiers—adjectives and adverbs—is to make comparisons. Most adjectives and adverbs have different forms to show the three degrees of comparison—*positive, comparative,* and *superlative.* Two rules govern the formation of regular modifiers.

- Use *more* and *most* to form the comparative and superlative degrees of all modifiers with three or more syllables.

- Use *-er* or *more* to form the comparative degree and *-est* or *most* to form the superlative degree of most one-syllable or two-syllable modifiers.

The comparative and superlative degrees of a few modifiers are not formed according to the rules governing standard English.

Irregular Modifiers		
Positive	**Comparative**	**Superlative**
bad	worse	worst
badly	worse	worst
far (distance)	farther	farthest
far (extent)	further	furthest
good	better	best
ill	worse	worst
late	later	last or latest
little (amount)	less	least
many	more	most
much	more	most
well	better	best

One basic rule determines the correct use of comparative and superlative forms. When comparing two persons, places, or things, use the comparative. When comparing more than two persons, places, or things, use the superlative.

Comparisons are involved in some common usage problems. The following are some examples:

- A double comparison is an error in usage caused by using both *-er* and *more* or both *-est* and *most.* A double comparison can also result from adding any one of these to an irregular modifier.

  Flawed: Your bowling ball is more lighter than mine.

  Improved: Your bowling ball is lighter than mine.

- Another usage error results from unbalanced comparisons. Be certain that a sentence compares two or more things of a similar kind.

  Flawed: The bill of a chicken is narrower and rounder than a duck.

  Improved: The bill of a chicken is narrower and rounder than the bill of a duck.

- Another illogical comparison results when something is inadvertently compared with itself. Make sure a sentence contains the other element to be compared or that it compares one of a group with the rest of the group.

  Flawed: Ling was faster than any runner in the mile race.

  Improved: Ling was faster than any other runner in the mile race.

CHECK YOUR WRITING SKILLS

Find the error in each of the following sentences.

- Write the letter of the correct answer choice on the line marked "Answer."

- Correct the error on the lines marked "Correction."

- Explain the reason for your answer choice and correction on the lines marked "Reason."

You will not need to write out steps 2 and 3 on the real test, but you cannot pick the correct answer without recognizing the error. Having to write out all three steps here will help you become accustomed to recognizing the error.

1. Most citizens would not be surprised if
                         A
   their income taxes are even higher next
    B   C
   year than last year. No error
        D   E

   Answer _____

   Correction _____

   _____

   Reason _____

   _____

   _____

2. I thought *Galaxy Quest* was the best of
       A   B   C
   the two films we rented Saturday.
             D
   No error
    E

   Answer _____

   Correction _____

   _____

   Reason _____

   _____

3. Greg is more funny than his brother Alan
          A   B C
   who won the comedy award. No error
            D   E

   Answer _____

   Correction _____

   _____

   Reason _____

   _____

   _____

4. I have painted the largest of the houses
             A   B
   on the block by the end of summer.
       C   D
   No error
    E

   Answer _____

   Correction _____

   _____

   Reason _____

   _____

   _____

179

5. Of the people in Raquel's class,
                            A
red-headed Peter is the tallest. No error
     B   C   D   E

Answer _____

Correction _____

_____

Reason _____

_____

_____

IDIOMS

An *idiom* is an expression that seems to defy the rules of grammar. One of the greatest difficulties with idioms involves the use of prepositions. For example, we agree *with* a person but *to* a proposal. We are angry *at* or *about* an act but *at* or *with* a person. Idioms usually do not cause a problem for native English speakers, but some idioms are so odd that they must be memorized.

Common Idioms	
Hit the hay	Compare to, with
Hit the rack	Concur with, in
You gave me a fright.	Confide in, to
In appreciation of	Conform to, with
With regard to	Connected by, with
A kind of	Differ about, from, with
Interest in	Different from
Comply with	Enter into, on, upon
Burn up	Free from, of
Burn down	Identical with
Independent from, of	Join in, to, with
In pursuit of	Live at, in, on
Arguing with	Necessity for, of
Help see	Need for, of
Capable of	Object to
With respect to	Oblivious of
In connection with	Overcome by, with
Absolved by, from	Parallel between, to, with
Accede to	Preferable to
Accompany by, with	Reason about, with
Acquitted of	Reward by, for, with
Adapted to, from	Variance with
Admit to, of	Vary from, in, with
Agree to, with, in	Wait for, on
Angry with, at, about	Worth of
Charge for, with	

CHECK YOUR WRITING SKILLS

Find the error in each of the following sentences.

- Write the letter of the correct answer choice on the line marked "Answer."

- Correct the error on the lines marked "Correction."

- Explain the reason for your answer choice and correction on the lines marked "Reason."

You will not need to write out steps 2 and 3 on the real test, but you cannot pick the correct answer without recognizing the error. Having to write out all three steps here will help you become accustomed to recognizing the error.

1. I have lived in both places, and I can tell
         A   B
   you that summers in southern California
                  C
   are different than summers in Connecti-
          D
   cut. No error
        E

   Answer _____

   Correction _____

   _____

   Reason _____

   _____

2. In the military, trainees need to
             A
   conform about everything, from what they
         B
   wear to when they awaken in the
     C   D
   morning. No error
        E

   Answer _____

   Correction _____

   _____

   Reason _____

   _____

3. I was <u>kind of</u> happy <u>to be</u> in the Friday
    A   B
    morning biology lab <u>even though</u> the class
    C
    <u>was not</u> my first choice. <u>No error</u>
    D   E

    Answer _____

    Correction _____

    _____

    Reason _____

    _____

    _____

4. Your report about the accident is <u>at</u>
    A
    <u>variance to</u> the <u>one</u> given by the
    B   C
    <u>investigating</u> officers. <u>No error</u>
    D   E

    Answer _____

    Correction _____

    _____

    Reason _____

    _____

    _____

5. Neither <u>the pins</u> nor the <u>needle</u> <u>were</u>
    A   B
    <u>successful in keeping</u> the tent <u>flaps</u> closed.
    C   D
    <u>No error</u>
    E

    Answer _____

    Correction _____

    _____

    Reason _____

    _____

    _____

CONTRACTIONS AND POSSESSIVES

You may find a sentence with an error in the use of an apostrophe. Most probably, this results from the misuse of a possessive or a contraction.

- Do not confuse the contractions *who's, it's* and *they're* with the possessive pronouns *whose, its,* and *their.*

- Remember that possessive forms of personal pronouns do not have apostrophes.

- Remember that if something belongs to two or more people, the *'s* is added to the last person in the series.

For more about the use of apostrophes, see Chapter 5.

Contractions are used sparingly in formal written English. It is acceptable to use contractions when writing dialogue, but in other cases, replace the contraction with an entire word.

CHECK YOUR WRITING SKILLS

Find the error in each of the following sentences.

- Write the letter of the correct answer choice on the line marked "Answer."

- Correct the error on the lines marked "Correction."

- Explain the reason for your answer choice and correction on the lines marked "Reason."

You will not need to write out steps 2 and 3 on the real test, but you cannot pick the correct answer without recognizing the error. Having to write out all three steps here will help you become accustomed to recognizing the error.

1. Rick's and Alexandra's
   A   B
   dog, a golden retriever, could catch and
                              C
   carry two balls in her mouth. No error
                        D   E

   Answer _____

   Correction _____

   _____

   Reason _____

   _____

2. Originally, I wanted to borrow they're
   A   B
   generator, but I decided to buy one of
                    C
   my own instead. No error
        D   E

   Answer _____

   Correction _____

   _____

   Reason _____

   _____

3. Don't forget to dot your *i*'s and cross your
       A   B   C   D
t's. No error
      E

Answer _____

Correction _____

_____

Reason _____

_____

_____

4. Someone else's suitcase was stolen, not
       A   B   C
mine. No error
 D   E

Answer _____

Correction _____

_____

Reason _____

_____

_____

5. His family's parakeet always perched
     A   B
on the top of it's cage and watched
         C   D
television. No error
        E

Answer _____

Correction _____

_____

Reason _____

_____

_____

USAGE PROBLEMS

You will encounter some problems on the SAT I Writing test that do not fall into a specific category of grammar or usage. Many of these result from a conflict between standard and nonstandard English.

DOUBLE NEGATIVES

In modern English, a sentence needs only one negative to express a negative idea. More than one negative can make a sentence confusing and positive in meaning rather than negative. There are three correct ways to form a negative sentence.

- The most common method of writing sentence negatives is to use a single negative word such as *never, no, nobody, nothing,* or *not*.

  Flawed: I did not like none of the new television comedies.

  Improved: I did not like any of the new television comedies.

- Likewise, if a sentence includes the words *barely, hardly,* or *scarcely* with another negative word, the sentence is incorrect.

Flawed: I couldn't hardly drive because the fog was so thick.

Improved: I could hardly drive because the fog was so thick.

- Negatives can be formed by using *only*. However, if *but* is used to mean *only*, the sentence is faulty.

    Flawed: Suzanna had but one pair of sneakers.

    Improved: Suzanna had only one pair of sneakers.

THE TOP 100 COMMON USAGE PROBLEMS

You will almost certainly be tested on usage and diction in the Identifying Sentence Errors section. Many usage errors result from using colloquialisms, or the language we use every day, in formal written English. Others occur because words that are similar in meaning or spelling are confused. The following is a list of 100 usage problems that you may encounter on the SAT I Writing test.

1. *a, an*
   Use the article *a* before consonant sounds and the article *an* before vowel sounds. Words beginning with *h*, *o*, and *u* can have either sound.

2. *accept, except*
   Accept is a verb meaning "to receive," and *except* is a preposition meaning "other than" or "leaving out."

3. *accuse, allege*
   Accuse means "to blame," whereas *allege* means "to state as fact something that has not been proved."

4. *adapt, adopt*
   Adapt means "to change," but *adopt* means "to take as one's own."

5. *advice, advise*
   Advice, a noun, means "an opinion." *Advise* is a verb that means "to express an opinion to."

6. *affect, effect*
   Affect is normally a verb meaning "to influence." *Effect* is usually a noun that means "result." Sometimes, *effect* is a verb that means "to cause."

7. *aggravate*
   Aggravate means "to make something worse;" it should not be used to refer to an annoyance.

THE TOP 100 COMMON USAGE PROBLEMS—*continued*

8. *ain't*
   Ain't is nonstandard English.

9. *allot, a lot, alot*
   The verb *allot* means "to divide in parts" or "to give out shares." *A lot* is an informal phrase meaning "a great many," so you should not use it in formal writing. *Alot* is nonstandard spelling. It should never be used.

10. *all ready, already*
    All ready, which functions as an adjective, is an expression meaning "ready." *Already,* an adverb, means "by or before this time" or "even now."

11. *all right, alright.*
    Alright is a nonstandard spelling. Use the two-word version.

12. *all together, altogether*
    All together means "all at once." *Altogether* means "completely."

13. *a.m., p.m.*
    a.m. refers to hours before noon, *p.m.* to hours after noon. Numbers are not spelled out when you use these abbreviations nor should you use phrases such as "in the morning" or "in the evening" with them.

14. *among, between*
    Among and *between* are prepositions. *Among* is used with three or more items. *Between* is generally used with only two items.

15. *amount, number*
    Amount is used with quantities that cannot be counted. Use *number* when items can be counted.

16. *anxious*
    Anxious means "worried" or "uneasy." It should not be used to mean "eager."

17. *anyone, any one, everyone, every one*
    Anyone and *everyone* mean "any person" and "every person." *Any one* means "any single person or thing," and *every one* means "every single person or thing."

THE TOP 100 COMMON USAGE PROBLEMS—*continued*

18. *anyway, anywhere, everywhere, nowhere, somewhere*
These adverbs should never end in *s*.

19. *as*
As should not be used to mean "because" or "since."

20. *as to*
As to is awkward. Substitute *about*.

21. *at*
Eliminate *at* when used after *where*.

22. *at about*
Eliminate *at* or *about* if you find them used together.

23. *awful, awfully, awesome*
Awful is used informally to mean "extremely bad." *Awfully* is also informal, meaning "very." In formal writing, *awful* should be used to mean only "inspiring fear or awe." *Awesome* is used informally to mean "amazing," whereas it really means "inspiring awe or wonder."

24. *awhile, a while*
Awhile is an adverb, meaning "for a while." *A while* is an article and a noun and is usually used after the preposition *for*.

25. *bad, badly*
Bad is an adjective and, therefore, must not be used as an adverb after an action verb. *Badly* is an adverb and, therefore, must not be used as an adjective after a linking verb, that is, "feel bad," not "feel badly."

26. *beat, win*
Beat means "to overcome." *Win* means "to achieve victory in." Replace *win* if the sentence sense is *beat*.

27. *because*
Eliminate *because* if it follows "the reason," or rephrase the sentence.

28. *being as, being that*
Replace either phrase with *since* or *because*.

29. *beside, besides*
Beside means "at the side of" or "close to." *Besides* means "in addition to." They are not interchangeable.

THE TOP 100 COMMON USAGE PROBLEMS—*continued*

30. *bring, take*
    Bring means "to carry from a distant place to a nearer one." *Take* means the opposite, "to carry from a near place to a more distant place."

31. *bunch*
    Bunch means "a number of things of the same kind." Do not use *bunch* to mean "group."

32. *burst, bust, busted*
    Burst is the present, past, and past participle of the verb *to burst*. *Bust* and *busted* are nonstandard English.

33. *but what*
    But what is nonstandard English. Use *that*.

34. *can, may*
    Use *can* to mean "to have the ability to." Use *may* to mean "to have permission to."

35. *can't help but*
    Use *can't help* plus a gerund instead of *can't help but;* for example, *can't help crying*.

36. *condemn, condone*
    These words have nearly opposite meanings. *Condemn* means "to express disapproval of." *Condone* means "to pardon" or "excuse."

37. *continual, continuous*
    Continual means "occurring over and over in succession," but *continuous* means "occurring without stopping."

38. *different from, different than*
    The expression *different from* is more accepted.

39. *doesn't, don't*
    Use *doesn't* with third-person singular subjects.

40. *done*
    Done, the past participle of the verb *to do*, follows a helping verb.

41. *dove*
    Use *dived* instead of *dove* for the past tense of the verb *dive*.

THE TOP 100 COMMON USAGE PROBLEMS—*continued*

42. *due to*
    Use *due to* only when the words *caused by* can be substituted.

43. *due to the fact that*
    Use *since* or *because* instead.

44. *each other, one another*
    Most of the time these expressions are interchangeable. Sometimes *each other* is used when only two people or things are involved, and *one another* is used when more than two are involved.

45. *emigrate, immigrate*
    These are opposites. *Emigrate* means "to leave a country," and *immigrate* means "to enter a country." In both cases, it is a reference to establishing a residency.

46. *enthused, enthusiastic*
    Enthused is nonstandard English; therefore, use *enthusiastic*.

47. *farther, further*
    Farther is a reference to distance, but *further* means "to a greater degree."

48. *fewer, less*
    Fewer is properly used with things that are counted, and *less* is used with qualities or quantities that are not counted.

49. *former, latter*
    In referring to two items, *former* designates the first and *latter*, the second.

50. *get, got, gotten*
    Although these verbs are acceptable, it is better to select different verbs if possible, such as *become, became, have become*.

51. *gone, went*
    Gone, the past participle of the verb *to go*, requires a helping verb. *Went* is the past tense of *go*, and no helping verb is required.

52. *good, lovely, nice*
    Try to use more specific adjectives in their place.

THE TOP 100 COMMON USAGE PROBLEMS—*continued*

53. *good, well*
Good is an adjective and must not be used as an adverb after an action verb. *Well* is usually an adverb and can be used after an action verb. *Well* can also be an adjective when it is used to mean "healthy." Therefore, it can be used after a linking verb, for example, "I feel well."

54. *hanged, hung*
Hanged means "executed," and *hung* means "suspended."

55. *healthful, healthy*
Healthful is used with things (*healthful diet*), and *healthy* refers to people.

56. *if, whether*
These conjunctions are interchangeable, except when the intention is to give equal stress to alternatives, in which case *if* won't work, and *whether* must be used with *or not*. "I'll go whether you come with me or not" is not the same as "I'll go if you come with me."

57. *in, into*
In is a position reference (*the kitten drank the milk in the bowl*), but *into* implies movement (*the kitten stepped into the bowl of milk*).

58. *irregardless*
This is nonstandard English. Use *regardless* instead.

59. *judicial, judicious*
Judicial refers to a legal system. *Judicious* means "to show wisdom."

60. *just*
Place *just*, when it is used as an adverb meaning "no more than," immediately before the word it modifies.

61. *kind of, sort of*
Do not use these words to mean "rather" or "somewhat."

62. *kind of a, sort of a*
Do not use *a* following *kind of* or *sort of*.

THE TOP 100 COMMON USAGE PROBLEMS—*continued*

63. *lay, lie*
The principal parts of *lay* are *lay, laying, laid, laid.* The principal parts of *lie* are *lie, lying, lay, lain. Lay* means "to set or put something down," and it is usually followed by a direct object. *Lie* means "to recline," and it is never followed by a direct object.

64. *learn, teach*
Learn refers to "gaining knowledge," whereas *teach* means "to give knowledge."

65. *leave, let*
Leave means "to allow to remain," and *let* means "to permit."

66. *like*
Like is a preposition and should not be used in place of *as.*

67. *loose, lose*
Loose is commonly an adjective. *Lose* is always a verb meaning "to miss from one's possession."

68. *mad*
When used in formal language, *mad* means "insane." When it is used in informal language, it means "angry."

69. *maybe, may be*
Maybe is an adverb that means "perhaps." *May be* is a verb.

70. *number, numeral*
Use *number* to mean quantity and *numeral* to mean the figure representing the number, that is, *the numeral that comes after 3 is 4.*

71. *of*
Do not use *of* after the verbs *should, would, could,* or *must.* Use *have* instead. Also eliminate *of* after the words *outside, inside, off,* and *atop.*

72. *OK, O.K., okay*
Do not use these words in formal writing.

73. *only*
Make sure to place *only* immediately preceding the word it logically modifies. *You only say you love me,* that is, you say it but you don't mean it; *You say you love only me,* that is, I am the only one you love.

THE TOP 100 COMMON USAGE PROBLEMS—*continued*

74. *ought*
Do not use *have* or *had* with *ought. Ought* is used with an infinitive; for example, *ought to wash, ought not to cry.*

75. *outside of*
Do not use *outside of* to mean "besides" or "except."

76. *parameter*
Use *parameter* only in mathematical contexts to designate a variable.

77. *persecute, prosecute*
Persecute means "to subject to ill treatment," whereas *prosecute* means "to bring a lawsuit against."

78. *plurals that don't end in* s
If a word ends in an *a* or *i*, be careful; it may be plural. Some nouns are made plural in the same way that they were in their original language. For example, *criteria* and *phenomena* are plural. Make sure that you treat them as plural, not singular, nouns. That means that their predicate must be plural for correct subject-verb agreement.

79. *poorly*
Do not use *poorly* to mean "ill" in formal writing.

80. *precede, proceed*
Precede means "to go before," and *proceed* means "to go forward."

81. *principal, principle*
Principal can be a noun or an adjective. As a noun, it means "a person who has controlling authority," and as an adjective, it means "most important." *Principle* is always a noun, and it means "a basic law." You can remember the difference by thinking of "your princiPAL as your PAL."

82. *raise, rise*
Raise normally takes a direct object, but *rise* never takes a direct object, as in "I *raised* the flag," but "I *rise* every morning at 6."

83. *real*
Do not use *real* to mean "very" or "really" in formal language.

THE TOP 100 COMMON USAGE PROBLEMS—*continued*

84. *says*

Do not use *says* in place of *said*.

85. *seen*

Seen requires a helping verb, as in "I was *seen* at the movies," not "I *seen* him at the movies."

86. *set, sit*

Set is usually followed by a direct object and means "to put something in a specific place." *Sit* means "to be seated," and it is never followed by a direct object.

87. *shape*

In formal language, do not use the word *shape* to mean "condition," as in *The boxer was in good shape*.

88. *since, because*

Use *since* when time is involved and *because* when a reason is involved. *Since I last saw them, I read a book*, but *Because they came last Saturday, I did not finish the book I was reading*.

89. *slow, slowly*

It is preferable to use *slow* as the adjective and *slowly* as the adverb.

90. *than, then*

Than is a comparative and is not to be confused with *then*, which refers to time.

91. *that, which, who*

These pronouns refer to the following: *that*—people and things, *which*—only things, and *who*—only people.

92. *their, there, they're*

Their is a possessive pronoun. *There* is an expletive or an adverb. *They're* is a contraction of *they are*.

93. *them, them there, these here, this here, that there*

Replace with *these* or *those* if an adjective is required.

94. *till, until*

These words are interchangeable, but they are often misspelled.

THE TOP 100 COMMON USAGE PROBLEMS—*continued*

95. *to, too, two*
To is a preposition. *Too* is an adverb used to modify adjectives and adverbs. *Two* is a number.

96. *unique*
Unique means "one of a kind"; therefore, it should not be modified by words such as *very* or *most*.

97. *want in, want out*
These are nonstandard expressions and should be avoided.

98. *ways*
Ways is plural. Do not use the article *a* immediately preceding *ways*.

99. *when, where*
Do not use these words directly after a linking verb. Also, do not use *where* as a substitute for *that*.

100. *-wise*
Do not use this suffix to create new words.

CHECK YOUR WRITING SKILLS

Find the error in each of the following sentences.

- Write the letter of the correct answer choice on the line marked "Answer."

- Correct the error on the lines marked "Correction."

- Explain the reason for your answer choice and correction on the lines marked "Reason."

You will not need to write out steps 2 and 3 on the real test, but you cannot pick the correct answer without recognizing the error. Having to write out all three steps here will help you become accustomed to recognizing the error.

1. Carol, who does a great deal of importing
    A
   in her business, was adversely effected by
                                      B
   the increased taxes on foreign goods.
            C   D
   No error
      E

   Answer _____

   Correction _____

   _____

   Reason _____

   _____

   _____

2. As soon as the conductor raised his baton,
         A   B
   the soloist and the chorus began singing
                                C
   all together. No error
       D   E

   Answer _____

   Correction _____

   _____

   Reason _____

   _____

   _____

3. Beside swollen glands, Alicia also had a
    A   B
   sore throat and a high fever. No error
        C   D   E

   Answer _____

   Correction _____

   _____

   Reason _____

   _____

   _____

4. In many Mid-Western states, one of the
                A
principal agricultural products is soybeans.
  B   C D
No error
  E

Answer _____

Correction _____

_____

Reason _____

_____

_____

5. Today, a great many people are interested
      A   B
in the preparation and consumption of
                       C
healthful foods. No error
  D   E

Answer _____

Correction _____

_____

Reason _____

_____

_____

ANSWERS AND EXPLANATIONS

Quick-Score Answers									
1.	B	**2.**	B	**3.**	C	**4.**	D	**5.**	B
1.	D	**2.**	C	**3.**	D	**4.**	B	**5.**	C
1.	D	**2.**	C	**3.**	A	**4.**	A	**5.**	E
1.	D	**2.**	B	**3.**	A	**4.**	B	**5.**	B
1.	A	**2.**	B	**3.**	E	**4.**	E	**5.**	C
1.	B	**2.**	E	**3.**	A	**4.**	E	**5.**	E

CHECK YOUR WRITING SKILLS: VERBS, PAGE 172

1. **The correct answer is (B).** *Teach* is an irregular verb. The correct form of the past tense is *taught.*

2. **The correct answer is (B).** The sequence of tenses is incorrect. The verb should be *talked.*

3. **The correct answer is (C).** The verb should be subjunctive, *stand,* because the sentence is a statement contrary to fact.

4. **The correct answer is (D).** The error is in subject-verb agreement. The antecedent of *who* is *classmates,* so the verb must be *enjoy.*

5. **The correct answer is (B).** Any title is singular, even if it sounds plural. The verb should be *was*.

CHECK YOUR WRITING SKILLS: PRONOUNS, PAGE 176

1. **The correct answer is (D).** The *neither . . . nor* construction calls for a singular pronoun. The error in pronoun antecedent agreement can be corrected by replacing *their* with *his*.

2. **The correct answer is (C).** Again, a singular form of the possessive pronoun is necessary.

3. **The correct answer is (D).** A reflexive pronoun should not be used when a personal pronoun can be substituted. Use *me*.

4. **The correct answer is (B).** *You* has a vague or nonexistent antecedent. The sentence needs to be rewritten.

5. **The correct answer is (C).** The ambiguous pronoun should be replaced with *the outfit*.

CHECK YOUR WRITING SKILLS: MODIFIERS AND COMPARISONS, PAGE 179

1. **The correct answer is (D).** This unbalanced comparison can be corrected by adding *they were* to the underlined phrase to read *than they were last year*.

2. **The correct answer is (C).** Since two films are compared, use the comparative form, *better*.

3. **The correct answer is (A).** Most two-syllable adjectives form the comparative by adding *-er*.

4. **The correct answer is (A).** The sentence requires a future perfect verb, *I will have painted*. We were just making sure you were paying attention.

5. **The correct answer is (E).** Since you can assume that there are more than two people in the class, the superlative adjective is correct.

CHECK YOUR WRITING SKILLS: IDIOMS, PAGE 181

1. **The correct answer is (D).** The idiom is *different from*.

2. **The correct answer is (B).** The idiom is *conform to* or *conform with*.

3. **The correct answer is (A).** *Kind of* is nonstandard English.

4. **The correct answer is (B).** The idiom is *at variance with*. However, a better revision would be *Your report about the accident varies from. . . .*

5. **The correct answer is (B).** Remember the subject-verb agreement rule: When a compound subject is joined by *nor* or *or*, the subject that is closer to the verb determines the verb form.

CHECK YOUR WRITING SKILLS: CONTRACTIONS AND POSSESSIVES, PAGE 183

1. **The correct answer is (A).** Since Rick and Alexandra own one dog together, only the second noun, *Alexandra*, takes the apostrophe.

2. **The correct answer is (B).** The possessive pronoun *their*, not the contraction *they're*, is the correct choice here.

3. **The correct answer is (E).** The sentence is correct.

4. **The correct answer is (E).** The sentence is correct. Rewriting the phrase can help you decide whether *else's* is a possessive, *the suitcase of someone else*.

5. **The correct answer is (C).** The possessive form of *it* is *its*. *It's* is a contraction of *it is*.

CHECK YOUR WRITING SKILLS: COMMON USAGE, PAGE 195

1. **The correct answer is (B).** The correct word is *affected*.

2. **The correct answer is (E).** In this sentence, you need the phrase that means *all at once*, which is *all together*.

3. **The correct answer is (A).** The correct word is *besides*.

4. **The correct answer is (E).** *Principal*, meaning *one of the most important*, is correct.

5. **The correct answer is (E).** The adjective modifies *food*, which is a thing, so you need *healthful*.

MORE PRACTICE

Review your answers from the Check Your Writing Skills sections. Do you see any pattern of missed errors? Are there specific areas of grammar and usage that you repeatedly failed to identify? If so, write them here.

_____

_____

_____

You will need to spend additional time reviewing these rules.

Choose one of the practice essays you wrote when working through Chapter 4. Review it against the sentence errors listed in this chapter. Have you made any of the common errors related to

- Verbs?

Write the correction here.

_____

_____

- Pronouns?

Write the correction here.

_____

_____

- Modifiers and comparisons?

Write the correction here.

_____

_____

- Idioms?

Write the correction here.

_____

_____

- Contractions and possessives?

Write the correction here.

_____

_____

- Usage?

Write the correction here.

_____

_____

Choose another one of your practice essays. Review it against the sentence errors listed in this chapter. Have you made any of the common errors related to

- Verbs?

Write the correction here.

_____

_____

- Pronouns?

Write the correction here.

_____

_____

- Modifiers and comparisons?

Write the correction here.

_____

_____

- Idioms?

Write the correction here.

_____

_____

- Contractions and possessives?

Write the correction here.

_____

_____

- Usage?

Write the correction here.

_____

_____

Choose a third essay and repeat the process. Have you made any of the common errors related to

- Verbs?

Write the correction here.

_____

_____

- Pronouns?

Write the correction here.

_____

_____

- Modifiers and comparisons?

Write the correction here.

_____

_____

- Idioms?

Write the correction here.

_____

_____

- Contractions and possessives?

Write the correction here.

_____

_____

- Usage?

Write the correction here.

_____

_____

Can you see a pattern of areas emerging where you need to improve your understanding of common grammar and usage rules? List any areas that you need to improve in your own writing.

_____

_____

_____

CHECK OFF

Before you move on to the next chapter, can you

- Identify common errors that you missed in answering the Identifying Sentence Errors multiple-choice questions?

- Identify common sentence errors that you make repeatedly in your own writing?

- Develop a plan to identify and correct these errors as you answer the multiple-choice questions and write practice essays?

Chapter 8

ABOUT IMPROVING SENTENCES

Your goals for this chapter are to
- Learn how to recognize different problems with sentences and how to improve sentences
- Practice identifying and improving sentences

The Sentence Improvement section on the SAT I Writing test evaluates you on many of the problem areas already discussed in earlier chapters. You will find sentences with errors in usage, style and expression, or structure. This chapter concentrates on problems with sentence structure. However, the questions in the Sentence Improvement section will ask you to revise many different kinds of flaws in addition to problems with sentence structure. Be sure to review the other chapters about style and grammar to help you with improving sentences.

The questions about sentence improvement ask you to choose the best of five answers. Because answer choice (A) always repeats the original sentence or sentence part, choose it if you think that no change is needed. Some of the sentences will have one clearly right answer, but other may have several grammatically correct answer choices. In those cases, you must decide which is the most effective restatement of the original sentence. There may also be sentences that contain several errors, but you only need to be concerned about errors that are underlined. There will only be one *underlined* error per sentence, and you will have to read the sentences carefully to identify and correct it.

Never pick an answer that changes the meaning of the sentence, even if the choice is grammatically correct and elegantly written. Your answer will be marked wrong. The correct answer has to retain all the information in the original sentence and the same meaning.

USING THE PRACTICE ITEMS

After the explanations of potential sentence problems, there are sets of Check Your Writing Skills exercises. Complete each set. If you are unsure of how to improve a sentence, you may look at the explanations. Be sure to read all explanations in the Answers and Explanations sections. You may find a piece of information that will help you on test day with a real question.

REVISING INCOMPLETE AND RUN-ON SENTENCES

In most languages, the basic unit of thought used to express meaning is the sentence. You will recall that, in English, a sentence is a group of words with two main parts: a complete subject and a complete predicate. Jointly, the subject and the predicate express a complete thought. In some sentences, the subject *you* may be understood as in "Do your homework now."

FRAGMENTS

If a group of words does not contain a complete subject and predicate, it is a *sentence fragment*. A fragment does not and cannot express a complete thought. Do not be deluded into thinking that a long series of words and phrases is a sentence. Always check to see that the series has a subject (which may be implied) and a verb. You will most certainly encounter a question about sentence fragments on the test.

To correct an item that involves a sentence fragment, you must choose the answer that rewrites the fragment, adding the missing part. Notice how the fragments below have been corrected.

Correcting Sentence Fragments		
Fragment	**Error**	**Complete Sentence**
The tall man wearing the colorful aloha shirt.	Noun fragment	The tall man wearing the colorful aloha shirt <u>has traveled to many South American countries.</u> (predicate added)
In spite of all the road blocks to her success has finished her course work and will graduate in June.	Verb fragment	In spite of all the road blocks to her success, <u>Eleanor</u> has finished her course work and will graduate in June. (subject added)
In the alpine meadow, full of sunlight, inhaled the fragrance of wildflowers.	Gerund fragment	In the alpine meadow, full of sunlight, <u>the backpackers</u> inhaled the fragrance of wildflowers. (subject added)
Peeling the vegetable, broiling the steak, and preparing the sauce.	Participial fragment	<u>All of us pitched in with the tasks of</u> peeling the vegetable, broiling the steak, and preparing the sauce. (subject and predicate added)
On a hot, humid evening on the island of Molokai.	Prepositional fragment	On a hot, humid evening on the island of Molokai, <u>everyone was plagued</u> by biting insects. (subject and predicate added)
When I departed, looking at my family's faces and seeing the tears.	Clause fragment	When I departed, looking at my family's faces and seeing the tears, <u>I almost returned then and there.</u> (independent clause added)

RUN-ONS

A *run-on sentence* is two or more sentences punctuated as one. To correct a run-on sentence, you will need to choose the answer that uses punctuation, conjunctions, or other means to join or separate its parts.

Fused Sentences

One kind of run-on, called a *fused sentence*, consists of two or more sentences that are not separated or joined by any punctuation at all.

Flawed: The storm surf crashed against the rocks gulls squawking flew into the gray skies.

Improved: The storm surf crashed against the rocks, and squawking gulls flew into the gray skies.

Comma Splices

Another kind of run-on, the *comma splice*, consists of several sentences separated only by commas.

> **Flawed:** Alexandra finished her homework early, after that she drove to Maria's house.
>
> **Improved:** Alexandra finished her homework early; after that, she drove to Maria's house.
>
> **Improved:** After finishing her homework early, Alexandra drove to Maria's house.

When you are asked to correct a run-on, look for the choice that adds punctuation and conjunctions or that rewrites the sentence.

> **Flawed:** My uncle and aunt vacationed with our family, my cousins also joined us.
>
> **Improved with capitals and end mark:** My uncle and aunt vacationed with our family. My cousins also joined us.
>
> **Improved with comma and conjunction:** My uncle and aunt vacationed with our family, and my cousins also joined us.
>
> **Improved with semicolon:** My uncle and aunt vacationed with our family; my cousins also joined us.
>
> **Improved by rewriting:** When my uncle and aunt vacationed with our family, my cousins also joined us.

A Word about Semicolon Errors

The SAT I Writing test may have an item about semicolon misuse. A *semicolon* can be substituted for a period to connect two independent clauses that contain similar or contrasting ideas. Generally, a semicolon must not be substituted for a comma.

> **Flawed:** During his final physical fitness test, Mateo scored an amazing 97 percent; which was the best in the class.
>
> **Improved:** During his final physical fitness test, Mateo scored an amazing 97 percent, which was the best in the class. (The clause *which was the best in the class* is not an independent clause.)

Remember, a semicolon can be used to avoid confusion when independent clauses or items in a series already contain commas.

> **Example:** His concerts took place in Austin, Texas; Little Rock, Arkansas; Augusta, Georgia; and Oxford, Mississippi.

CHECK YOUR WRITING SKILLS

Find the error in each of the following sentences.

- Write the letter of the correct answer choice on the line marked "Answer."

- Correct the error on the lines marked "Correction."

- Explain the reason for the your answer choice and correction on the lines marked "Reason."

You will not need to write out steps 2 and 3 on the real test, but you cannot pick the correct answer without recognizing the error. Having to write out all three steps here will help you become accustomed to recognizing the error.

1. This year's legislative committee <u>being more involved than last year's.</u>

  (A) being more involved than last year's
  (B) was more involved than last year's.
  (C) which was more involved than last year's.
  (D) that was more involved than last year's.
  (E) having been more involved than last year's.

  Answer _____

  Correction _____

  _____

  Reason _____

  _____

  _____

2. Writing a novel takes nine to twelve <u>months; depending</u> upon the author's experience, knowledge, and speed.

  (A) months; depending
  (B) and depending
  (C) months, depending
  (D) months depending
  (E) months. Depending

  Answer _____

  Correction _____

  _____

  Reason _____

  _____

  _____

3. George played football with power; Hakeem finesse.

   (A) George played football with power; Hakeem finesse.
   (B) George played football with power; Hakeem, finesse.
   (C) George played football with power, and Hakeem played it with finesse.
   (D) George played football with power Hakeem finesse.
   (E) George played football with power— Hakeem finesse.

   Answer _____

   Correction _____

   _____

   Reason _____

   _____

   _____

4. The moon cast silver light on the beach the storm had finally passed the island.

   (A) on the beach the storm had finally passed
   (B) on the beach, the storm had finally passed
   (C) on the beach and the storm had finally passed
   (D) on the beach the storm was finally passed
   (E) on the beach; the storm had finally passed

   Answer _____

   Correction _____

   _____

   Reason _____

   _____

   _____

5. Rarely did Lilliana come to work late, on Saturday she arrived late because her car broke down.

   (A) come to work late, on Saturday she arrived late
   (B) come to work late but on Saturday she arrived late
   (C) come to work late on Saturday she arrived late
   (D) come to work late, but on Saturday she arrived late
   (E) come to work late on Saturday she had arrived late

   Answer _____

   Correction _____

   _____

   Reason _____

   _____

   _____

REVISING AMBIGUOUS AND CONFUSING SENTENCES

There are a number of different types of ambiguous and confusing sentence structures that you may find on the test. You may be asked to correct mixed and illogical constructions such as faulty parallelism, faulty coordination and subordination, and a variety of faulty modifier problems.

MIXED AND ILLOGICAL CONSTRUCTIONS

Correctness and clarity are essential elements in good writing. Illogical sentence structure can obstruct clarity of expression.

Faulty Parallel Structure

Parallel structure is the placement of equal ideas in words, phrases, or clauses. Parallel grammatical structures can be two or more words of the same part of speech, two or more phrases of the same type, or two or more clauses of the same type. (This last sentence is an example of parallel nouns modified by prepositional phrases.) Faulty parallelism occurs when a sentence does not employ equal grammatical structures to express related ideas. Faulty parallel structures can involve words, phrases, and clauses in a series as well as in comparisons. You correct faulty parallelism by ensuring that a series contains like elements—all nouns, all adjectives, all prepositional phrases, and so forth—or some combination of nouns, adjectives, and so on, that are equal. The second sentence in this paragraph repeats nouns and prepositional phrases in the same construction.

Notice in the table how errors in parallel structure not only disrupt the natural flow of sentences but also make the meaning of the sentence difficult to understand.

Correcting Faulty Parallel Structure		
Sentences with Nonparallel Structure	**Nonparallel Elements**	**Improved Sentence**
The musical was unique, exciting, and kept us laughing.	Adjectives and a prepositional phrase in a series	The musical was unique, exciting, and <u>funny.</u>
The rabbit hopped across the grass, under the tree, and its hole was the final stop.	Prepositional phrases and a clause in series	The rabbit hopped across the grass, under the tree, and <u>into its hole.</u>
My piano teacher says that I make few mistakes, but I play without feeling.	A noun clause and an independent clause in series	My piano teacher says that I make few mistakes but <u>that</u> I play without feeling.

Coordinating conjunctions such as *and*, *but*, *nor*, and *or* often connect items in a series. When you see them in a question item on the test, check for errors in parallel structure.

Faulty Coordination and Subordination

When two or more independent clauses that are not related or that are of unequal importance are connected by *and*, the result is *faulty coordination*. To be joined by *and* or another coordinating conjunction, two independent clauses must contain related ideas of equal importance. Faulty coordination is easily corrected by

- Putting unrelated ideas into separate sentences

  Flawed: The junior class built a homecoming float, and it had lights and a sound system that worked amazingly well.

  Improved: The junior class built a homecoming float. It had lights and a sound system that worked amazingly well.

- Putting a less important or subordinate idea into a subordinate clause or phrase

  Flawed: Denee is one of our school's most popular actors, and she starred in last year's spring musical.

  Improved: Denee, one of our school's most popular actors, starred in last year's spring musical.

- Reducing an unimportant idea to a phrase by changing the compound sentence into a simple sentence

  Flawed: The *Dune* books are my favorite science-fiction series, and I have read them all three times.

  Improved: I have read all of the *Dune* books, my favorite science-fiction series, three times.

The main device for showing the difference between major and minor ideas is *subordination*. When a sentence contains proper subordinate coordination, the independent clause includes the main idea while the dependent clauses, phrases, or single words convey the subordinate idea. Faulty subordination can happen in two ways:

- Two ideas of equal rank are joined by a subordinate conjunction.

  Flawed: Alan Brown is a professor, and he is the dean of the science department, while he teaches at the local junior college, too.

  Improved: Alan Brown is a professor who is the dean of the science department at a local junior college.

- When there is upside-down subordination—the independent clause containing the minor idea and the dependent clause, the main idea.

> **Flawed:** Although he easily finished the Iron Man Triathlon, he showed some signs of exhaustion.
>
> **Improved:** Although he showed some signs of exhaustion, he easily finished the Iron Man Triathlon.

Sentence Shifts

Mixed constructions are frequently the result of some sort of shift in a sentence. This occurs when a sentence begins with one type of structure and then changes to another. Usually, a sentence with mixed construction may be improved in several ways. To correct sentence shifts, you must either rewrite or rearrange the sentence. Let's look at some examples:

> **Flawed:** By attending the party as a guest rather than as a maid was a new experience for her.
>
> **Improved:** By attending the party as a guest rather than as a maid, she enjoyed a new experience.
>
> **Improved:** Attending the party as a guest rather than as a maid was a new experience for her.

The preposition *by* introduces a modifying phrase, as shown in the flawed sentence. A modifying phrase cannot be the subject of a sentence.

Here is another example:

> **Flawed:** Rick realized that during the company meeting how inattentive he had been.
>
> **Improved:** Rick realized that during the company meeting he had been inattentive.
>
> **Improved:** Rick realized how inattentive he had been during the company meeting.

This sentence is confusing because *that* as used in the flawed sentence is a subordinating conjunction and should introduce a noun clause. However, the *that* construction is incomplete. Further in the sentence, another subordinating conjunction, *how*, introduces a noun clause. Thus, the sentence contains two words that introduce a noun clause, but only one word is required.

Other types of sentence shifts have been discussed in earlier chapters. Go back and review them now: shifts in verb tense, pronouns shifts, subject shifts, and passive or active voice shifts.

FAULTY MODIFIER PLACEMENT

Generally, modifiers should be placed as close as possible to the words they modify. If a modifier is misplaced or left dangling, it will seem to be modifying the wrong word or no word.

Misplaced Modifiers

A *misplaced modifier* seems to modify the wrong word in a sentence. Any phrase or clause functioning as an adjective or adverb can be misplaced in a sentence. When a modifier is placed too far from the word it should modify, the sentence can become confusing. To correct the flaw, place the modifier close to the word it modifies or restructure the sentence.

> **Flawed:** George and Liam argued about football while I tried to study loudly.
>
> **Improved:** George and Liam argued loudly about football while I tried to study.

A *relative clause*—a clause introduced by a relative pronoun—should normally follow the word that it modifies.

> **Flawed:** The composition was played at the concert which was composed of dissonant chords.
>
> **Improved:** The composition, which was composed of dissonant chords, was played at the concert.

Ambiguous Modifiers

When a modifier is placed between two elements of a sentence so that it could modify either item, the modifier is *ambiguous*. The meaning of the sentence is, therefore, unclear. To correct an ambiguous modifier, choose the answer that places the modifier as close as possible to the word it modifies.

> **Flawed:** The automobile that had been driving south erratically entered the intersection.
>
> **Improved:** The automobile that had been driving south entered the intersection erratically.
>
> **Improved:** The automobile that had been erratically driving south entered the intersection.

Dangling Modifiers

The meaning of a sentence can become clouded when the word that a phrase or clause logically modifies does not appear in the sentence. Such modifiers are said to *dangle*. Correct a dangling modifier by choosing the answer that adds the modifier right before or right after the word the phrase should modify.

Flawed: Wrapped in my towel, the sun was not a problem.

Improved: Wrapped in my towel, I found that the sun was not a problem.

Awkward Constructions

Awkwardness is an umbrella category of writing flaws that includes incorrect grammar, faulty sentence structure, and misplaced modifiers. In other words, awkwardness can result from the errors discussed throughout these pages. Most often, however, awkwardness occurs when a sentence is clumsily or carelessly constructed. The words do not seem to make much sense, and there is no flow to the sentence. Poor diction or flawed use of idiom may produce an *awkward* sentence. Although your own sense of correctness is your best tool for identifying and correcting awkward sentences, the following rules review good diction:

- Choose the simple word over the long word if the simple word says the right thing.

- Choose the precise and concise word to eliminate wordiness and redundancies.

- Replace a worn-out phrase (trite expression or cliché) with a fresh restatement.

- Replace excessive, preachy, or illogical statements with reasonable ones.

- Replace jargon or slang with standard words.

- Choose vigorous action verbs to improve force and clarity.

Review the 10 rules of effective writing in Chapter 5. You will find that the same rules that apply to making your writing effective help you improve sentences in the multiple-choice section.

CHECK YOUR WRITING SKILLS

Find the error in each of the following sentences.

- Write the letter of the correct answer choice on the line marked "Answer."

- Correct the error on the lines marked "Correction."

- Explain the reason for your answer choice and correction on the lines marked "Reason."

You will not need to write out steps 2 and 3 on the real test, but you cannot pick the correct answer without recognizing the error. Having to write out all three steps here will help you become accustomed to recognizing the error.

1. At her brother's birthday party, Rosa's job was to set the table, to vacuum the living room carpet, and running errands for her dad.

   (A) to set the table, to vacuum the living room carpet, and running errands

   (B) to set the table to vacuum the living room carpet and running errands

   (C) to set the table, to vacuum the living room carpet, and to run errands

   (D) setting the table, vacuuming the living room carpet, and to run errands

   (E) to set the table, to vacuum the living room carpet, and having run errands

   Answer _____

   Correction _____
   _____

   Reason _____
   _____
   _____

2. The islands out at sea from the ship looked very small.

   (A) The islands out at sea from the ship looked very small.

   (B) Out at sea the islands from the ship looked very small.

   (C) Very small were the way the islands out at sea looked from the ship.

   (D) Out at sea from the ship the islands looked very small.

   (E) The islands out at sea looked very small from the ship.

   Answer _____

   Correction _____
   _____

   Reason _____
   _____
   _____

3. <u>Martha did not do well on the exam, and it was very easy.</u>

- (A) Martha did not do well on the exam, and it was very easy.
- (B) Martha did not do well on the exam even though it was very easy.
- (C) Martha did not do well on the exam, but it was very easy.
- (D) Martha did not do well on the exam; it was very easy.
- (E) It was a very easy exam and Martha did not do well.

Answer _____

Correction _____

_____

Reason _____

_____

_____

4. <u>The students sought to matriculate at the forums of higher education, for they realized the inherent value of education.</u>

- (A) The students sought to matriculate at the forums of higher education, for they realized the inherent value of education.
- (B) The students sought to matriculate at the forums of higher education realizing the inherent value of education.
- (C) Because the students realized the inherent value of education, they sought to matriculate at the forums of higher education.
- (D) The students tried to get into college because they knew the value of education.
- (E) Matriculating at their choice of college was important to the students.

Answer _____

Correction _____

_____

Reason _____

_____

_____

5. Because of accepting more responsibility at work was a stressful time for Jeremy.

(A) Because of accepting more responsibility at work was a stressful time for Jeremy.

(B) Accepting more responsibility at work caused stress for Jeremy.

(C) By accepting more responsibility at work, was a stressful time for Jeremy.

(D) Accepting more responsibility at work totally stressed Jeremy out.

(E) A stressful time for Jeremy because he accepted more responsibility at work was.

Answer _____

Correction _____

_____

Reason _____

_____

_____

6. Ling hopes to visit Peru this summer, and she has not applied for her visa yet.

(A) Ling hopes to visit Peru this summer, and she has not applied for her visa yet.

(B) Ling hopes to visit Peru this summer; she has not applied for her visa yet.

(C) Ling hopes to visit Peru this summer, and she hasn't yet applied for her visa.

(D) Ling hopes to visit Peru this summer, but a visa has not been applied for by her.

(E) Ling hopes to visit Peru this summer, but she has not applied for her visa yet.

Answer _____

Correction _____

_____

Reason _____

_____

_____

7. When he was 85 years old, Mr. Combs' son taught him to fly.

(A) When he was 85 years old, Mr. Combs' son taught him to fly.

(B) Mr. Combs' son taught him to fly when he was 85 years old.

(C) When Mr. Combs was 85 years old, his son taught him to fly.

(D) At 85 years old, Mr. Combs' son taught him to fly.

(E) When he was 85 years old, his son taught him to fly.

Answer _____

Correction _____

_____

Reason _____

_____

_____

8. To go to the premier of the new film, seats must be reserved.

(A) To go to the premier of the new film, seats must be reserved.

(B) Going to the premier of the new film, seats must be reserved.

(C) To attend the premier of the new film, seats must be reserved.

(D) To go to the premier of the new film, you must reserve seats.

(E) To go to the premier of the new film, seats must be reserved ahead of time.

Answer _____

Correction _____

_____

Reason _____

_____

_____

9. I relaxed while lying in the shade, and soon I fell asleep.

(A) I relaxed while lying in the shade, and soon I fell asleep.

(B) I relaxed while lying in the shade, falling asleep.

(C) I relaxed while lying in the shade, soon I fell asleep.

(D) Lying in the shade, soon I fell asleep.

(E) I relaxed while lying in the shade, yet soon I fell asleep.

Answer _____

Correction _____

_____

Reason _____

_____

_____

10. Although she is a young, vigorous female, my dog Murphy is a golden retriever.

(A) Although she is a young, vigorous female, my dog Murphy is a golden retriever.

(B) My dog Murphy, a golden retriever, she being young and vigorous and female.

(C) Young, vigorous female, I have a golden retriever, Murphy.

(D) My dog Murphy is a golden retriever, and she is a young, vigorous female.

(E) Being a young, vigorous female, my dog Murphy is a golden retriever.

Answer _____

Correction _____

_____

Reason _____

_____

_____

ANSWERS AND EXPLANATIONS

Quick-Score Answers									
1.	B	**2.**	D	**3.**	C	**4.**	E	**5.**	D
1.	C	**2.**	E	**3.**	B	**4.**	D	**5.**	B
6.	E	**7.**	C	**8.**	D	**9.**	A	**10.**	D

CHECK YOUR WRITING SKILLS: INCOMPLETE AND RUN-ON SENTENCES, PAGE 207

1. **The correct answer is (B).** This is the only choice that corrects the problem of a sentence fragment.

    Choice (A) The selection is a sentence fragment.

    Choice (C) The use of the pronoun *which* does not correct the sentence fragment.

    Choice (D) The use of the pronoun *that* does not correct the sentence fragment.

    Choice (E) The shift in the verb tense to *having been involved* neither corrects the sentence fragment nor makes the author's thought complete.

2. **The correct answer is (D).** The prepositional phrase requires no punctuation to separate it from the balance of the sentence.

    Choice (A) A semicolon should not be used to separate an independent clause from a prepositional phrase.

    Choice (B) The use of a conjunction reduces clarity and makes the sentence meaningless.

    Choice (C) A comma should not be used to separate an independent clause from a prepositional phrase.

    Choice (E) The prepositional phrase is a sentence fragment and cannot be separated from the independent clause.

3. **The correct answer is (C).** Elliptical sentences should be avoided.

    Choice (A) This is an elliptical sentence and should be avoided.

    Choice (B) The comma is used properly to designate the missing words; however, choice (C) is better because it makes the sentence nonelliptical.

    Choice (D) Improper punctuation is the problem with this sentence.

    Choice (E) The use of the dash is incorrect. To punctuate the sentence properly, a semicolon and comma are required as shown in choice (B).

4. **The correct answer is (E).** The semicolon corrects the fused or run-on sentence.

    Choice (A)   The run-on sentence needs to be corrected with a semicolon or a comma and conjunction.

    Choice (B)   The comma without a conjunction does not correct the run-on sentence.

    Choice (C)   The conjunction without a comma does not correct the run-on sentence.

    Choice (D)   The change in the verb fails to correct the run-on sentence.

5. **The correct answer is (D).** The sentence has a comma splice. It is best corrected by the insertion of the conjunction *but*.

    Choice (A)   The sentence has a comma splice.

    Choice (B)   The insertion of the conjunction requires a comma.

    Choice (C)   The sentence requires a semicolon if there is no conjunction.

    Choice (E)   The change in the verb does not correct the comma splice.

Check Your Writing Skills: Ambiguous and Confusing Sentences, page 214

1. **The correct answer is (C).** The sentence lacks parallel construction. The change from *running* to *to run* corrects the problem.

    Choice (A)   The sentence does not have parallel construction.

    Choice (B)   Commas are needed to separate items in a series.

    Choice (D)   This is the reverse of choice (A); it also lacks parallel construction.

    Choice (E)   The change in the tense of the verb does not correct the lack of parallel construction.

2. **The correct answer is (E).** This choice creates a coherent sentence by placing the modifiers near the words that they modify.

    Choice (A)   The modifiers are misplaced, making the sentence unclear.

    Choice (B)   The modifiers are misplaced, making the sentence unclear.

    Choice (C)   The modifiers are misplaced, making the sentence unclear.

    Choice (D)   The modifiers are misplaced, making the sentence unclear.

3. **The correct answer is (B).** To correct faulty coordination, the second clause is properly subordinated.

   Choice (A) The second clause is not subordinated as it should be.

   Choice (C) The change in the conjunction does not correct the problem with coordination.

   Choice (D) The elimination of the conjunction and insertion of the semicolon does not correct the coordination problem.

   Choice (E) The sentence lacks coordination, and a comma is required before *and*.

4. **The correct answer is (D).** The sentence is awkwardly worded, but it is correct in this choice. Choice (D) uses simple words to convey the author's meaning without losing any of the key points.

   Choice (A) The sentence has very awkward wording.

   Choice (B) The sentence has very awkward wording.

   Choice (C) The sentence has very awkward wording.

   Choice (E) The sentence is not as awkward; however, it sacrifices some of the author's points.

5. **The correct answer is (B).** This alternative eliminates the sentence shift.

   Choice (A) The original sentence has a severe sentence shift, almost to the point of making the sentence incomprehensible.

   Choice (C) This alternative does not correct the shift and exacerbates the problems by incorrectly adding a comma.

   Choice (D) While this answer corrects the shift, it contains slang, *totally stressed out.*

   Choice (E) This one makes more sense, but unfortunately it is not a complete sentence.

6. **The correct answer is (E).** This answer corrects the problem created by the faulty use of the coordinating conjunction *and*.

   Choice (A) In the original sentence, the clauses are related in content, but the relation between them is incorrectly expressed.

   Choice (B) The use of the semicolon does not correct the faulty coordination of the original.

   Choice (C) Not only is a contraction not acceptable in formal English, but this alternative also does not correct the faulty coordination.

   Choice (D) This choice corrects the coordination problem, but the awkwardly worded subordinate clause is in the passive voice.

7. **The correct answer is (C).** This choice corrects the ambiguous modifier. Now you know who is 85 years old—Mr. Combs, not his son.

   Choice (A) In the original sentence it is not clear who is 85 years old.

   Choice (B) This alternative rearranges the clauses but does not rectify the ambiguousness of the sentence.

   Choice (D) The question here is the same. The change to a prepositional phrase still does not make clear who is 85 years old.

   Choice (E) This alternative makes the sentence worse. The pronouns have no antecedents.

8. **The correct answer is (D).** This choice corrects the dangling infinitive phrase.

   Choice (A) The problem here is with the main verb. Correct it by adding a pronoun and the active voice of the verb: *To go to the premier of the new film, one must reserve tickets.*

   Choice (B) This alternative makes the sentence even more confusing because it now has a sentence shift.

   Choice (C) Changing *go* to *attend* does not correct the dangling modifier.

   Choice (E) This alternative does not correct the dangling infinitive phrase, and it creates a redundancy. *Reserve* and *ahead of time* mean the same thing.

9. **The correct answer is (A).** The sentence is correct.

   Choice (B) This version contains a dangling participle, *falling asleep*.

   Choice (C) This alternative is marred by a comma splice.

   Choice (D) While grammatically correct, this choice changes the meaning of the sentence.

   Choice (E) This alternative contains faulty subordination.

10. **The correct answer is (D).** This response corrects the faulty subordination.

    Choice (A) Being a young vigorous female and a golden retriever are of equal weight, so the sentence should have a coordinating conjunction.

    Choice (B) This alternative is not a complete sentence.

    Choice (C) This version contains an ambiguity. It is unclear who is a young, vigorous female. Is it the owner or the dog?

    Choice (E) This alternative is illogical. Being a young, vigorous female does not make the dog any special breed.

MORE PRACTICE

After you have corrected your answers, see if you can find any pattern in the kinds of mistakes that you made. If you can, then you need to work on your area(s) of weakness as you study for the SAT I.

Choose one of the practice essays you wrote when working through Chapter 4. Check it for incomplete and run-on sentences. Underline any you find.

• What kind of sentence error(s) have you made?

_____

• Did you make the same error repeatedly in the essay?

_____

• Rewrite any incomplete or run-on sentences below.

_____

_____

_____

_____

Choose another one of your practice essays. Check it for incomplete and run-on sentences. Underline any you find.

- What kind of sentence error(s) have you made?

  _____

- Did you make the same error repeatedly in the essay?

  _____

- Rewrite any incomplete or run-on sentences below.

  _____

  _____

  _____

  _____

Choose another one of your practice essays. Check it for ambiguous and confusing sentences. Underline any you find.

- What kind of sentence error(s) have you made?

  _____

- Did you make the same error repeatedly in the essay?

  _____

- Rewrite any ambiguous or confusing sentences below. When you rework sentences, always make sure that you are not losing some of your original meaning. This is true in choosing answers for the multiple-choice questions, too.

  _____

  _____

  _____

  _____

  _____

Choose another one of your practice essays. Check it for ambiguous and confusing sentences. Underline any you find.

- What kind of sentence error(s) have you made?

_____

- Did you make the same error repeatedly in the essay?

_____

- Rewrite any ambiguous or confusing sentences below. When you rework sentences, always make sure that you are not losing some of your original meaning. This is true in choosing answers for the multiple-choice questions, too.

_____

_____

_____

_____

_____

Do you see any pattern in your writing in regard to problems with sentence structure? If so, describe it here. Then, decide how you can keep from continuing to make the same errors in your own writing.

_____

_____

_____

_____

CHECK OFF

Before you move on to the next chapter, can you

- Identify ways to improve sentences that you missed in answering the Improving Sentences multiple-choice questions?

- Identify ways to improve sentences in your own writing that you repeatedly overlook?

- Develop a plan to identify and correct these areas of weakness as you answer the multiple-choice questions and write practice essays?

Chapter 9
ABOUT IMPROVING PARAGRAPHS

> Your goals for this chapter are to
> - Learn how to recognize different problems with paragraphs and how to improve paragraphs
> - Practice identifying and improving paragraphs

The Paragraph Improvement section of the SAT I Writing test assesses your knowledge of writing more extensively than the other multiple-choice sections. You may be tested on aspects of sentence structure and on errors in style, expression, and diction, or word choice. Many of the test items focus on the same problems as the usage and sentence sections. Other questions will test your knowledge of author's purpose, paragraph structure, development, function, and sentence and paragraph relationships.

USING THE PRACTICE ESSAYS

At the end of this chapter, you will find two essays with practice questions, the Check Your Writing Skills sets. Complete each set without looking at the answers, if possible. Once you have answered the questions for the first essay, review the explanations of the answers before going on to the second essay. Be sure to read all the Answers and Explanations.

THE ANATOMY OF AN ESSAY

An essay is simply a piece of writing that is built with paragraphs. The paragraphs work together to present a main point. The Paragraph Improvement questions examine paragraphs and their relationships in an essay.

THE PURPOSE OF THE ESSAY

After you have finished reading the essay, decide on its purpose. The writer of the essay has chosen to inform you, to entertain you, to convince you, or to persuade you to take action. When you have established the writer's purpose, you will be able to determine how effectively the essay accomplishes its goal. Ask yourself what the writer is trying to tell you. Writing style hints at the writer's purpose. Use the following clues to help you determine the reason for writing:

- If the style is impersonal and formal, the purpose may be to inform or instruct the audience. Often, these essays are written in the third person.

- If the style is personal and informal, the purpose may be to entertain or amuse. These essays may be written in the first person. Subjects for this style may be a narration of an experience or a description of a special place.

- If the style is direct, the purpose may be to instruct or persuade. These essays may be written in the second person and include many imperative sentences.

Remember that the essays on the SAT I Writing test are intended to be revised. Because of that, the essays are short, simple, and straight-forward. If, as you read, you discover any material that is outside the parameters of the writer's purpose, you most probably will find a question asking you to revise that part.

ORGANIZATION OF AN ESSAY

Very likely, you will be asked about the role a paragraph or part of a paragraph plays within the essay. Since you may be asked to identify a paragraph's function or decide which of the five alternatives is preferable, you need to have a good command of the function of paragraphs within an essay. Chapter 3 contains an extensive discussion of the organization of an essay.

To review briefly, an essay has three parts. The first paragraph (or first several paragraphs in a long essay) forms the introduction; body paragraphs develop support for the thesis; and a concluding paragraph summarizes what has been said, the points that have been made.

- In a well-written essay, the *introduction* catches the reader's attention, establishes the writer's purpose and tone, and presents the thesis statement. The introduction usually begins with some general remarks providing background. Then it focuses on the topic, leading the reader from a broad view to a more specific point—the thesis statement or controlling idea.

- The *central portion* of the essay, consisting of two or more paragraphs, develops the thesis statement with relevant examples, details, facts, or reasons. The number of paragraphs can vary depending on the number of subtopics and the amount of supporting information the writer wants to convey.

- The *conclusion*, usually one paragraph, brings the essay to a satisfying close while reminding readers of the controlling idea. It may also include any final remarks that help the reader understand and appreciate the essay, that help unify the essay, or that provide a solution to a problem. The final sentence or so of the conclusion is particularly effective when it acts as a clincher, presenting an especially forceful, eloquent, or witty statement.

Organizational errors may occur for several reasons. If the writer loses focus and wanders from the main idea, distracting or irrelevant information may be added. If a writer concentrates on one point, other ideas may receive little attention, and the essay will seem unbalanced.

To answer questions about organization, look at the opening paragraph. You should find the purpose and any limitations that the writer puts on the essay. On the SAT I Writing test, you will not find elaborate or clever introductions. Most will be direct and to the point. If you are asked about the introductory paragraph, look for any material that does not narrow the topic. Such information may need revision or elimination.

When dealing with the body paragraphs, be aware of their function. Body paragraphs on the SAT I Writing test may serve one or more of the following purposes:

- Provide background information

- Evaluate an opinion occurring earlier in the essay

- Add new ideas or thoughts

- Strengthen support by using an example

- Persuade the reader to act or to believe as the writer wishes

- Explain in detail an idea expressed earlier in the essay

- Provide a comparison or a contrast

- Explain a relationship among ideas given earlier

- Ask a rhetorical question about the topic

- Summarize information or arguments made previously

The concluding paragraph restates the thesis, probably summarizes major points, and brings the essay to a satisfactory close. Since the essays you will read on the exam are short, you will probably not find an elaborate conclusion. One flaw you may encounter is an abrupt ending. You may also be asked to revise a conclusion that wanders from the thesis or that has little to do with the essay.

ANALYZING AN ESSAY FOR PARAGRAPH ORGANIZATION AND FUNCTION

Read the essay and answer the questions that follow.

As Americans search for alternative methods of transportation, many people are turning to the bicycle. Riding a bicycle, however, is not always safe on today's crowded roadways. Cyclists often compete with motorists and pedestrians for space. If cities and towns built designated bike routes for cyclists only, this problem could be remedied.

Designated bike routes—paths set up and clearly indicated for cyclists only—are needed for the safety of all who travel. Most roads were not built with bicycles in mind. If a cyclist has to move into the car lane because of an inadequate shoulder, motorists are forced into other lanes. Accidents can result. However, if a cyclist must ride on the sidewalk, pedestrians are endangered.

Some might argue that special bike lanes are too expensive. However, reducing accidents and saving lives are worth the cost. Often the cost is less than people think. Not all cities and communities would need to construct entirely new bike paths. In some places where sidewalks are wide or pedestrian traffic is light, a part of the sidewalk can become a designated bike lane. Ramps at corners must be built, but that has been done for wheelchair traffic. By combining already existing spaces with new construction, a total bicycle route can be inexpensively constructed and safety achieved.

Designated bicycle paths are not a luxury but a necessity for bicyclists, motorists, and pedestrians alike. By providing specific routes for cyclists, cities and towns will make the roads safer for everyone. Designated bike routes would benefit the entire community.

1. What is the purpose of this essay?

_____

_____

2. Which paragraphs are the introduction, body, and conclusion?

_____

_____

3. Write the thesis statement here.

_____

_____

4. What function do the body paragraphs serve? How are these paragraphs developed?

_____

_____

5. What type of essay is this?

_____

_____

6. Do the body paragraphs have topic sentences? If so, where are they found?

_____

_____

7. Which sentence in the conclusion offers a reminder of the thesis statement?

_____

_____

8. Which sentence is a clincher?

_____

_____

Review the explanations of the answers.

1. Did you recognize that the writer wants to convince you that designated bicycle routes should be constructed? Good. Hopefully, you also recognized that the style was formal and impersonal, since it does not use the second-person pronoun.

2. This essay follows the classic format, so the answer to this question is straightforward. The first paragraph is the introduction; the last paragraph is the conclusion. The middle two paragraphs form the body.

3. The thesis statement is the last sentence in the first paragraph. It expresses the opinion that bike routes can help solve the problems of overcrowded streets and road safety.

4. The purpose of the body paragraphs in this essay is to persuade readers to accept bike lanes. The first body paragraph is

developed with examples. The second body paragraph contains solutions. The essay is built on descriptive order.

5. It is a persuasive essay, and we already mentioned that it is formal and impersonal in style.

6. Both body paragraphs have topic sentences. Paragraph 2 places the topic sentence at the beginning. The topic sentence in paragraph 3 is the third sentence.

7. The first sentence of the final paragraph reiterates the thesis statement.

8. While the final sentence is not the most exciting example of a clincher, it attempts to leave you, the reader, with a strong impression of the benefits of bike lanes to everyone.

PARAGRAPHS AND ESSAYS

Many of the features found in good paragraphs are also found in good essays. For the test, you must know how paragraphs function in an essay as well as the characteristics of good paragraphs. Understanding what makes a good paragraph and identifying faults within paragraphs will help you to score well on the Paragraph Improvement section.

STRUCTURE OF A PARAGRAPH

Like an essay, a paragraph follows a three-part model. First, it has a topic sentence indicating the subject of the paragraph and expressing an attitude toward that subject. The second part is the development, or body. The development pulls together supporting information. The third part concludes the paragraph, although this element may be missing in a paragraph that is part of an essay.

The topic sentence expresses the main idea of the paragraph and defines the scope of the paragraph. The topic sentence can be located at the beginning, in the middle, or at the end of a paragraph. A topic sentence at the beginning of a paragraph prepares you for the information that follows.

If you find that a paragraph begins with information that helps you understand an important point, you most probably have a paragraph with the topic sentence in the middle. In this case, the topic sentence acts as a bridge between introductory statements and specific supporting information.

You will find that some paragraphs present ideas and thoughts first. In this type of paragraph, the topic sentence serves as a summary. It may serve as the climax to which the supporting paragraphs lead.

Some paragraphs do not have a topic sentence. The main idea is implied. You, the reader, are to draw your own conclusions from the supporting information that you are given. This is most frequent in narrative or descriptive writing.

In addition to the topic sentence, a well-constructed paragraph should contain enough specific information to explain the main idea. Support may consist of examples, details, facts, reasons, or incidents. You may find a question on the test asking you to revise a paragraph that does not have enough supporting information to meet the expectations set up by the topic sentence and to make the paragraph complete.

Keep in mind these seven principles of paragraph construction when answering the Paragraph Improvement section of the SAT I Writing test:

- Most paragraphs have two types of sentences, a topic sentence and supporting sentences.

- The paragraph's intent is stated by the topic sentence. It is sometimes stated directly, and sometimes it is implied.

- The supporting sentences explain or illustrate the topic sentence.

- The relationships among sentences in a paragraph are demonstrated by employing styles such as argument and proof, cause and effect, classification and analysis, and definition. These are also known as common patterns of paragraph development.

- Unified paragraphs present only one major idea.

- Coherent paragraphs contain no irrelevant material.

- Coherence is enhanced by transitions and logical linkage.

ANALYZING THE FUNCTION OF TOPIC SENTENCES

Work with the following paragraphs and questions to strengthen your understanding of topic sentences. Identify the topic sentences in the following paragraphs. If the topic sentence is implied, write it on the lines below the paragraph.

1. *(1) Smoke curled from under the eaves and rose from the roof. (2) Flames shooting from the window shot up toward the sky. (3) Many of the walls and ceilings crashed downward, shooting sparks and red-hot cinders through lower windows and doors. (4) The building could not be saved.*

Topic Sentence:_____

_____

2. *(1) For humans, the world seems stocked with harmful pests—insects, sharks, and snakes to name a few. (2) Of all of these nuisances, the greatest pest is the rat. (3) According to statistics, rats in the United States do more than $200,000,000 worth of damage each year. (4) The rat is an animal well adapted to living anywhere human beings live. (5) It steals human food. (6) Since rats are attracted to phosphorous in matches, they cause damaging fires by lighting the matches while dragging or chewing them. (7) They cause short circuits by gnawing on electric wires. (8) Worst of all, rats provide a home for various disease-carrying insects. (9) The flea that carries typhus fever lives on rats. (10) Another flea that is the carrier of bubonic plague also lives on rats.*

Topic Sentence:_____

_____

3. *(1) In the late twentieth century, Italians have made an effort to stop the deterioration of Venice. (2) Over the years, soot, smoke, and other pollutants have discolored and eroded the city's marble palaces and public buildings. (3) Now, factories filter their smoggy output, reducing the pollution. (4) Citizens have switched their home heating systems to cleaner-burning natural gas. (5) To save Venice from its most serious threat, the sinking of the city into the Adriatic, officials have taken action to maintain the water table. (6) By building aqueducts to import water, Venice can keep the water table at a safe level.*

Topic Sentence:_____

_____

4. *(1) Chanting and swaying to the beat of gourds and bamboo, the students at the Polynesian Cultural Center in Honolulu give you a sense of Hawaii's history. (2) In its exhibits and performances, the Center presents the many aspects of Hawaiian culture and history to those that come to visit. (3) There, you will discover the contributions of the original colonists, the Polynesians. (4) Using life-sized models, the Center shows you the similarities between Polynesian and Hawaiian villages. (5) In addition, the Center performs dramatizations of Hawaiian legends telling of the dangerous voyages of ancestors crossing the ocean in great canoes. (6) Also, gardens full of sweet potato, taro, bananas, and breadfruit plants exhibit the food carried by those ancient immigrants to their new home.*

Topic Sentence:_____

_____

Review the explanations of the answers.

1. The topic sentence is the last one of the paragraph. This style builds emotions that reach a peak with the topic sentence.

2. Sentence 2 is the topic sentence. Sentence 1 is introductory. Did you recognize the order of importance development? You will review it a little later in this chapter.

3. This is the classic topic sentence as the first sentence of the paragraph. Do you see the cause-and-effect nature of this paragraph?

4. Sentence 2 is the topic sentence, but if you said it was the first sentence you would not be far off. Sentence 1 hints at the topic.

UNITY AND COHERENCE IN PARAGRAPHS

Two characteristics of well-written paragraphs are *unity* and *coherence*. If a paragraph includes more than one main idea, it is not unified. If the supporting sentences do not relate to one another, it does not have coherence. You may be asked to revise sentences that detract from a paragraph's unity or damage its coherence.

Unity

In a unified paragraph, all the sentences and pieces of information are related to the main idea and to each other. When one or more sentences wander from the topic, the unity suffers. In the following paragraph, for example, the fourth and fifth sentences do not fit.

(1) Every adult and every child should learn to swim. (2) Knowing how to swim builds confidence when near water. (3) Good swimming ability adds to life's enjoyment because recreational avenues such as waterskiing and surfing open up. (4) Recreation can also lead to better mental and physical health. (5) Sports like running build stamina, while basketball burns a lot of calories. (6) Some enjoyable summer jobs, such as lifeguard, recreation aide, or camp counselor, may require the ability to swim. (7) Finally, the ability to swim can save a life—that of the swimmer or that of another individual who may be drowning.

Coherence and Development

Paragraphs must contain enough information to fully develop an idea. In most cases, a paragraph should be longer than one or two sentences. On the other hand, paragraphs should not be extremely lengthy. Four to eight sentences is standard. On the SAT I Writing test, any paragraph that varies a good deal from this standard most probably will need revision.

In a coherent paragraph, the topic sentence and all supporting ideas follow a logical order, while transitions and other devices clarify connections between ideas. Supporting information should be logically arranged to help the reader. Support can follow chronological order, spatial order, order of importance, comparison-and-contrast order, or developmental order. The following chart will help you review the types of logical order.

Ways to Logically Order the Development of Paragraphs	
Order	**Explanation**
Chronological order	Information and details presented in a time sequence
Spatial order	Support arranged by position: from near to far, outside to inside, left to right, and so on
Order of importance	Information and arguments arranged from the least important to the most important, least interesting to most interesting, least powerful to most powerful, or vice versa
Comparison-and-contrast order	Facts and details grouped by similarities and differences by presenting one item completely and then comparing and contrasting a second with the first or by comparing and contrasting two or more items point by point
Descriptive order	Information arranged in the most logical order for the particular topic sentence and support

235

Transitions can smooth the flow of ideas. Transitions connect ideas and point out the direction of ideas. A few well-placed transitions strengthen a paragraph because transitions clarify relationships among ideas in a paragraph.

Coherence can also be achieved by combining sentences. If you are asked to revise a paragraph for coherence, look for the answer choice that combines several short, disjointed sentences. Repeated main words, synonyms, and consistent pronouns help make a paragraph coherent. Parallelism and a concluding sentence tie ideas together. While concluding sentences do not belong in every paragraph, a concluding sentence can summarize the information, remind the reader of the topic sentence, or indicate the completion of the thought of the paragraph. When a concluding sentence creates a powerful impression, it is called a clincher, as you already know.

ANALYZING PARAGRAPHS FOR UNITY AND COHERENCE

Identify the logical development order, the kind of supporting information, and any transitional words in each of these paragraphs.

1. *The German shepherd, a breed of dog that originated in northern Europe, has served human beings for hundreds of years. Once used mainly for herding sheep, the shepherd today helps police in tracking and capturing criminals. Police have used shepherds to locate drugs and other contraband. In addition, these dogs can function as guards for homes, stores, and factories. German shepherds have earned respect because of their keen, careful work as guide dogs for the blind. Intelligent, versatile, and loyal, German shepherds have earned their popularity with their usefulness.*

Order:_____

Supporting information:_____

_____

_____

_____

Transitions:_____

_____

_____

_____

2. *Scientists and others search for answers to the problem of alarming damage done to our environment. Their suspect, in the cases of dying trees, barren lakes, and eroded architectural treasures, is acid rain. Acid rain forms as a result of the burning of fossil fuels such as coal, oil, and natural gas. When these fuels burn, pollutants are released into the atmosphere, combining with water vapor to form acid-laden chemicals. This acidic mixture falls to earth in precipitation known as acid rain. Scientists believe that the abnormally high levels of acid in the rains wreak havoc on plants, animals, and buildings. The problem is widespread because the rain has no respect for national boundaries. Problems exist in such diverse places as Germany, Japan, China, Canada, and the United States. The international character of this environmental demon has caused many nations around the world to join together to combat it. Over two dozen countries have agreed to restrictive measures to reduce dioxide emissions, the major component of acid rain.*

Order:_____

Supporting information:_____

_____

_____

_____

Transitions:_____

_____

_____

_____

3. *I prefer swimming in the ocean to swimming in a pool. I find the cool salt water refreshing. Diving through the waves invigorates me. Also, the ocean has no chlorine or other chemicals that can burn my eyes and smell horrible. Most of all, I love to snorkel or scuba dive to see the underwater world of fish, coral, and invertebrates. The ocean is more refreshing, cleaner, and more interesting than a swimming pool.*

Order:_____

Supporting information:_____

_____

_____

_____

Transitions:_____

_____

_____

_____

4. *Although most people think that horses are beautiful but stupid, I know better. Molly, a strawberry roan, and I were learning some tricks—counting with her hoof, rearing on command, dancing sideways, and kneeling down—to perform at our local rodeo. Molly was doing very well, but she was still my saddle horse. On a mid-winter's evening I rode over to a friend's house to deliver a birthday present. Once I was there, we began talking and joking around. Time sped by, and I soon realized that it was dark and snow had begun to fall. I had to hurry home, because my boyfriend was taking me to dinner that night and I, of course, wanted to look my best. I thought if I took a shortcut through the canyon, I could cut about 5 miles from the trip. I turned off the trail and rode on through the snow alone with Molly. How beautiful it looked in the moonlight! Down the sloping canyon wall we traveled. Then, crash, Molly stumbled on a snow-covered rock. Molly struggled to her feet, but I was down, helpless and unable to stand up. Something important was broken. I felt panic rise in me. No one knew where I was, and snow was filling Molly's hoof prints—the only clue that could lead searchers to me. I called to my horse. She came and nuzzled me gently. Then, I ordered her to*

kneel. Yes, she could do that in the ring, but would she out here in the snow? Over and over I repeated the command. She did it! Slowly and painfully, I dragged myself over the saddle. On command Molly rose and, sensing my predicament, gently headed home. Yes, horses are beautiful, but they are not stupid. Molly proved it that night.

Order:_____

Supporting information:_____

_____

_____

_____

Transitions:_____

_____

_____

_____

Review the explanations of the answers.

1. Paragraph 1 is organized by order of importance. In other words, the writer saves the best information for last. The supporting information is made up of examples that support the idea that German shepherds have benefited humankind. The writer uses several transitions and logical links, in the second sentence *once* and *today*, and *in addition* in the following sentence. The last sentence is a good clincher.

2. The order in paragraph 2 is chronological. The paragraph begins with the formation of acid rain and then describes the damage it causes. Facts support the idea that acid rain is destroying parts of the environment. The transitional devise is repetition of words or synonyms for important words.

3. Paragraph 3 is developed by order of importance. Supporting information gives the reasons for preferring swimming in the ocean to swimming in a pool. There is little transition in this paragraph, but the writer does use *also* and *most of all*. Notice that the last sentence reminds the reader of the topic sentence.

4. Paragraph 4 is developed chronologically, a logical choice for supporting information about an incident. The transitions show time—*evening, once, then*. The last two sentences create a

heartwarming conclusion. The final sentence is an effective clincher.

PATTERNS OF PARAGRAPH DEVELOPMENT

The Paragraph Improvement questions may also ask you to make decisions about paragraph development. Knowing various common patterns of development can help you identify problems within paragraphs.

- **Cause and effect:** Supporting information developed by cause and effect explains or shows how one set of circumstances causes, or leads to, another outcome, the effect.

- **Definition:** The details of the paragraph define or explain a general idea, term, or word. Usually these are not simply dictionary definitions but examples or descriptions.

- **Argument and proof:** Support comes from persuasive examples and arguments that are intended to validate the topic sentence.

- **Classification and analysis:** Very commonly used to explain a process or a classification system, this method of development divides the topic into its components. Then the supporting information explains the procedure or classification system step by step.

CHECK YOUR WRITING SKILLS

Read Practice Essay A and then answer the questions. Write your answers in the margin or on a separate sheet of paper. If you do not remember the directions for Improving Paragraphs, review the instructions.

(1) *In Egyptian culture and society, painting is its people's history.* (2) *It makes its first appearance in prehistory; its last phase belongs to the Greco-Roman period.* (3) *The paintings of Fayum, for instance, came under Egyptian, Greek, and Roman influences, and are described in many art books under all three different civilizations.*

(4) *As is also true in Greek painting, much Egyptian painting is on reliefs.* (5) *These are almost always made of hard limestone rather than the harder marble.* (6) *Art from the tomb of Seti at Thebes serves as examples.* (7) *Examples of Greek friezes are found in Athens and at the British Museum in London.* (8) *More common are the paintings on papyrus, especially in* The Book of the Dead; *these were placed in tombs where they have been discovered in great numbers.*

(9) *The Egyptians had a remarkable, lively sense of color.* (10) *They loved to juxtapose contrasting color.* (11) *Egyptian paintings were unique in color and that was a reflection of their vivid environment.* (12) *They demon-*

strated an understanding of color. (13) *The artists succeeded in painting works of art that had both original character and creative character.*

(14) *Apart from their artistic value, the paintings provide an almost inexhaustible variety of scenes from the life of the Egyptian people.* (15) *In minute detail the paintings capture the humble activities of workmen, brick layers, and peasants, as well as the ceremonies and actions of the Pharaohs and other dignitaries in peace and war.* (16) *Taken together, these paintings provide a visual history of this long-lasting civilization.*

(17) *All this indicates that Egyptian painters truly understood their mission.* (18) *The artists adapted their work to the demands made upon them by their individual environment, sensitivity, race, culture, and historical and geographical situation.* (19) *The result was paintings of great beauty and historical relevance.*

1. Considering the main idea of the whole essay, which of the following is the best revision of sentence 1?

    (A) Egyptian painting and culture is as great as its people's history.
    (B) Egyptian art and culture, so totally cool, is as impressive as its people's history.
    (C) Egyptian painting follows the sweep of its people's history.
    (D) Some experts may argue that Egyptian painting is the most sweepingly impressive in history.
    (E) Egyptian painting follows its people's history, but we know that some will be destroyed because of flood control on the Nile River.

2. Which is the best revision of the under-lined segment of sentence 8 below?

    More common are the paintings on papyrus, especially in The Book of the Dead; *these were placed in tombs where they have been discovered in great numbers.*

    (A) these pictures were placed in tombs where they have been discovered in great numbers.
    (B) these were placed in tombs where they have been discovered in great numbers. More common are the paintings on papyrus.
    (C) they placed them in tombs where they have been discovered in great numbers.
    (D) placed in tombs where they have been discovered in great numbers.
    (E) archaeologists found them in tombs where they have been discovered in great numbers.

3. To improve the coherence of paragraph 2, which of the following is the best sentence to delete?

    (A) Sentence 4
    (B) Sentence 5
    (C) Sentence 6
    (D) Sentence 7
    (E) Sentence 8

4. With regard to the entire essay, which of the following best explains the writer's intention in paragraphs 2, 3, and 4?

(A) To compare and contrast Egyptian and Greek art

(B) To provide evidence that there is a relationship between Egyptian painting and Egyptian history

(C) To convince the reader that Egyptian painting is timeless

(D) To describe the beauty and the expertise of Egyptian paintings

(E) To analyze the subtle changes in Egyptian painting throughout history

5. In the context of the essay, which is the best combination of sentences 11, 12, and 13 in paragraph 3?

(A) Egyptian painters were unique, they demonstrated an understanding of color that reflected their environment, and succeeded in painting works of art that had both original character and creative character.

(B) Unique Egyptian painters demonstrated an understanding of color, which succeeded, through the efforts and talents of the artists, as works of art that had both original character and creative character, while reflecting the colors of the environment.

(C) Egyptian painters were unique with an understanding of color that reflected their environment. This allowed the artists to be successful painting works of art that had both original character and creative character.

(D) Egyptian painters demonstrated uniqueness in their understanding of environmental color, and thus succeeding in painting works of art that had both original character and creative character.

(E) With their unique understanding of the colors of their environment, artists succeeded in painting works of art with original and creative character.

6. What purpose does the underlined section of the following sentence serve?

Apart from their artistic value, the paintings provide an almost inexhaustible variety of scenes from the life of the Egyptian people.

(A) It serves as a transitional phrase, changing the direction of the essay.
(B) It introduces the subject.
(C) It is the thesis statement.
(D) It establishes the spatial nature of the organizational development.
(E) It serves as a conclusion to the previous paragraph.

ANSWERS AND EXPLANATIONS

Quick-Score Answers					
1. C	**2.** A	**3.** D	**4.** B	**5.** E	**6.** A

1. **The correct answer is (C).** This is the most succinct and elegant sentence.

   Choice (A)   The essay is about painting, not about culture.
   Choice (B)   Not only does this have the same flaw as choice (A), but it also incorporates slang.
   Choice (D)   Nothing in the essay says that Egyptian painting is the most impressive in history.
   Choice (E)   The second clause is irrelevant.

2. **The correct answer is (A).** This choice corrects the ambiguous pronoun reference.

   Choice (B)   This revision changes the meaning of the sentence.
   Choice (C)   This choice exacerbates the ambiguous pronoun reference flaw.
   Choice (D)   This changes an independent clause into a participial phrase. Therefore, the use of the semicolon is incorrect.
   Choice (E)   While this does change the voice from passive to active, pronoun reference remains a problem.

3. **The correct answer is (D).** Information about the location of Greek friezes is irrelevant.

   Choice (A) This information is important to the paragraph and essay.

   Choice (B) This information is important to the paragraph and essay.

   Choice (C) This information is important to the paragraph and essay.

   Choice (E) This information is important to the paragraph and essay.

4. **The correct answer is (B).** This is the controlling idea of the essay.

   Choice (A) There is little about Greek art in this essay.

   Choice (C) This is not a persuasive essay. The writer's intention is to inform.

   Choice (D) There is little description of pieces of art per se, and not much is said about beauty.

   Choice (E) Virtually nothing is said about changes in the art.

5. **The correct answer is (E).** The sentence is succinct and grammatically correct.

   Choice (A) The sentence lacks parallel structure; the third clause does not have a subject.

   Choice (B) The artists are not unique; the paintings' colors are.

   Choice (C) This is too wordy.

   Choice (D) This awkward run-on sentence is difficult to understand.

6. **The correct answer is (A).** The phrase is a transition that changes the focus from technique to subject.

   Choice (B) The thesis statement is in paragraph 1, so it is impossible for an introduction to come after the thesis.

   Choice (C) Sentence 1 is the thesis statement.

   Choice (D) The essay is organized by order of importance, not spatial order.

   Choice (E) A conclusion occurs at the end of a paragraph or essay, not at the beginning.

CHECK YOUR WRITING SKILLS

Read Practice Essay B and then answer the questions. Write your answers in the margin or on a separate sheet of paper.

(1) *For hundreds, even thousands, of years the Kazakh people of central Asia have hunted with golden eagles.* (2) *These huge birds, with a wing span of up to 10 feet, can weigh approximately 14 pounds.* (3) *A bird's grip can break the bones of a human hand.* (4) *Eagles in Kazakhstan are not flown for sport.* (5) *This is because of the fact that the Kazakhs live in a harsh land where falconry, the practice of hunting with birds, serves a practical purpose which is feeding the family.*

(6) *Eagles are valuable to Kazakhs.* (7) *They serve as partners, and help provide a livelihood.* (8) *Thus, eagles ensure survival.* (9) *They can catch rabbits, which are good to eat.* (10) *The birds can also hunt foxes.* (11) *Until recently, Kazakhs could trade a fox skin for a sheep.* (12) *Since an eagle can capture twenty to forty foxes in one season, a successful bird could feed a family for more than a year.*

(13) *Surprisingly, Kazakh eagles hunt wolves.* (14) *Common in central Asia, wolves prey on sheep and goats.* (15) *While a wolf often kills the eagle instead, wolves are actually caught by some strong eagles.* (16) *This seems unbelievable because a wolf can weigh 100 pounds, yet eagles never weigh more than 15 pounds.* (17) *Like other birds, their bones are hollow so they are light enough to fly.* (18) *However, an eagle can exert hundreds of pounds of pressure with its powerful feet and sharp talons, enough to hold or even kill a wolf.* (19) *Not only found in central Asia, the endangered eagle inhabits a few wilderness areas of North America.*

(20) *Kazakh eagles, some of whom live forty years, are highly valued by hunters.* (21) *After ten or eleven hunting seasons, the birds are retired, but not forgotten.* (22) *Hunters attach little white streamers to the eagle's wings so they can recognize their bird if they see it again.* (23) *In fact, eagles are so important to the Kazakhs that they call themselves the eagle people.*

1. Given the context of paragraph 1, which is the best revision of sentence 4?

    (A) This is why—the Kazakhs live in a harsh land where falconry, the practice of hunting with birds, serves a practical purpose and the birds help with feeding the family.

    (B) In fact, the Kazakhs live in a harsh land where falconry, (the practice of hunting with birds), serves a practical purpose which is feeding the family.

    (C) This is because Kazakhs live in a harsh land where falconry, the practice of hunting with birds, serves a practical purpose which is feeding the family.

    (D) The Kazakhs live in a harsh land where falconry, the practice of hunting with birds, serves a practical purpose—feeding the family.

    (E) The Kazakhs live in a harsh land where they practice falconry which serves a practical purpose and that is, of course, feeding the family.

245

2. Given the context of paragraph 2, which is the best revision of sentences 6, 7, and 8?

  (A) Eagles are valuable to Kazakhs, they serve as partners, and help provide a livelihood, and thus, eagles ensure survival.

  (B) Because they serve as partners, eagles are valuable to Kazakhs and help provide a livelihood to ensure survival.

  (C) Eagles ensure their survival by serving the Kazakhs as partners and helping to provide a livelihood.

  (D) The valuable eagles serve as partners and help provide a livelihood so the eagles ensure survival.

  (E) Valuable partners in providing a livelihood, eagles ensure survival.

3. Which of the following is the best revision of the underlined segment of sentence 15 below?

While a wolf often kills the eagle instead, wolves are actually caught by some strong eagles.

  (A) While a wolf often kills the eagle instead, some strong eagles can actually catch a wolf.

  (B) While a wolf often kills the eagle instead, some wolves are actually caught by strong eagles.

  (C) While a wolf often kills the eagle instead, wolves are sometimes caught by strong eagles.

  (D) Often the wolf sometimes kills the eagle, but wolves are actually caught by some strong eagles.

  (E) Often, wolves are actually caught, killing the eagle instead, by some strong eagles.

4. To improve the unity of paragraph 3, which of the following sentences would be the best to delete?

  (A) Sentence 13
  (B) Sentence 14
  (C) Sentence 15
  (D) Sentence 17
  (E) Sentence 18

5. In an effort to provide a better transition between paragraphs 3 and 4, which of the following is the best revision of sentence 13?

  (A) Although catching foxes is amazing enough, even more surprising is that Kazakh eagles hunt wolves.

  (B) Kazakh eagles also hunt wolves.

  (C) Kazakh eagles catch foxes and hunt wolves.

  (D) While they can catch foxes, wolves are hunted by Kazakh eagles.

  (E) On the other hand, Kazakh eagles hunt wolves in addition to catching foxes.

6. Considering the essay as a whole, which one of the following least accurately describes the function of paragraph 4?

  (A) It summarizes the main idea of the essay.

  (B) It serves to satisfactorily conclude the essay.

  (C) It proves the validity of the essay's thesis statement.

  (D) It serves to unify the essay.

  (E) It redefines the purpose of the essay.

ANSWERS AND EXPLANATIONS

Quick-Score Answers					
1. D	2. E	3. A	4. E	5. A	6. C

1. **The correct answer is (D).** This sentence is grammatically correct and succinct.

   Choice (A)   This sentence is awkwardly worded. Also, the first three words are unnecessary, and the use of the dash is questionable.

   Choice (B)   Parentheses should not surround information that is an essential appositive, and the commas are redundant.

   Choice (C)   Using the phrase *this is because* is nonstandard diction.

   Choice (E)   This choice is very wordy.

2. **The correct answer is (E).** The sentence captures the essence of the paragraph.

   Choice (A)   This choice lacks parallel construction.

   Choice (B)   This sentence is awkward.

   Choice (C)   The survival relates to the humans, not the birds.

   Choice (D)   This is another awkwardly worded sentence.

3. **The correct answer is (A).** The active voice is almost always a better choice than passive construction.

   Choice (B)   The independent clause is in the passive voice.

   Choice (C)   This version is also passive.

   Choice (D)   Also passive, this version contains a contradiction. Do the wolves sometimes or often kill eagles?

   Choice (E)   Passive again, and the modifier is misplaced.

4. **The correct answer is (E).** Where other eagles live is irrelevant to the golden eagle's importance to the Kazakhs.

   Choice (A)   Sentence 12 is the topic sentence of this paragraph.

   Choice (B)   This sentence adds support to the topic sentence.

   Choice (C)   This helps explain why eagles hunting wolves is surprising.

   Choice (D)   This continues the explanation of the eagle's strength.

5. **The correct answer is (A).** This sentence is well worded and connects fox hunting in the previous paragraph to wolf hunting in this paragraph.

Choice (B)   There is little transition in this choice, and it is dull.
Choice (C)   While correct, it lacks the impact of choice (A).
Choice (D)   This has a problem with the pronoun antecedent for *they,* and it is passive.
Choice (E)   The transition *On the other hand* implies a contrast. The paragraph does not compare or contrast wolves and foxes.

6. **The correct answer is (C).** The choice does not describe the function of the last paragraph.

Choice (A)   The final paragraph does summarize the main idea of the essay.
Choice (B)   The conclusion does satisfactorily end the essay.
Choice (D)   It does unify the essay.
Choice (E)   It does redefine the purpose of the essay.

MORE PRACTICE

1. Reread your answers to the two practice essays and compare them with the answers and explanations in this book. Do you see any pattern in the kinds of mistakes that you made? Were you confused by Paragraph Structure questions or did you continue to have problems with sentence structure and usage? Develop a plan to review the specific areas that you need to improve.

2. Choose one of the essays you wrote when working through Chapter 4. Evaluate it for the following topics:

- Is your purpose clear? If not, what could you do to make it clearer?

_____

_____

_____

- Is your essay well organized? If not, what could you do to better organize your ideas?

  _____

  _____

  _____

- Choose any one paragraph. Is it unified, that is, built around one idea? Is it coherent, that is, do all the supporting details relate to one another? If not, how could you revise the paragraph to be unified and coherent?

  _____

  _____

  _____

- Choose another paragraph and evaluate it for unity and coherence. If it is not, how could you revise the paragraph to make it unified and coherent?

  _____

  _____

  _____

- What method of organization did you use in developing your essay? Cause and effect, definition, argument and proof, or classification and analysis?

- How could you make your organization stronger?

  _____

  _____

  _____

3. Choose another one of the essays you wrote when working through Chapter 4. Evaluate it for the following topics:

- Is your purpose clear? If not, what could you do to make it clearer?

_____

_____

_____

- Is your essay well organized? If not, what could you do to better organize your ideas?

_____

_____

_____

- Choose any one paragraph. Is it unified, that is, built around one idea? Is it coherent, that is, do all the supporting details relate to one another? If not, how could you revise the paragraph to be unified and coherent?

_____

_____

_____

- Choose another paragraph and evaluate it for unity and coherence. If it is not, how could you revise the paragraph to make it unified and coherent?

_____

_____

_____

- What method of organization did you use in developing your essay? Cause and effect, definition, argument and proof, or classification and analysis?

_____

- How could you make your organization stronger?

_____

_____

_____

4. Choose another one of the essays you wrote when working through Chapter 4. Evaluate it for the following topics:

- Is your purpose clear? If not, what could you do to make it clearer?

_____

_____

- Is your essay well organized? If not, what could you do to better organize your ideas?

_____

_____

_____

- Choose any one paragraph. Is it unified, that is, built around one idea? Is it coherent, that is, do all the supporting details relate to one another? If not, how could you revise the paragraph to be unified and coherent?

_____

_____

_____

- Choose another paragraph and evaluate it for unity and coherence. If it is not, how could you revise the paragraph to make it unified and coherent?

_____

_____

_____

- What method of organization did you use in developing your essay? Cause and effect, definition, argument and proof, or classification and analysis?

  _____

- How could you make your organization stronger?

  _____

  _____

  _____

5. Reread all your practice essays. Are there any specific areas that you need to work on in your writing? Make a list and each time you write a practice essay, choose one area and consciously work on it in your drafting and revision stages. Concentrating on effective essay writing will help you recognize areas of improvement in the essays on the SAT I Writing test.

CHECK OFF

Before you move on to take the Practice Exercise Sets, can you

- Identify ways to improve paragraphs that you missed in answering the Improving Paragraphs multiple-choice questions?

- Identify ways to improve paragraphs in your own writing that you repeatedly overlook?

- Develop a plan to identify and correct these areas of weakness as you answer the multiple-choice questions and write practice essays?

Part III
Putting It All Together

- In Part I, you reviewed what makes an essay effective and practiced your essay writing skills.

- In Part II, you reviewed conventions of standard written English and practiced applying those rules to multiple-choice questions similar to those on the SAT I Writing test. You also looked at how those same rules apply to your own writing.

- In Part III, you will put your essay writing, grammar, usage, and mechanics skills together to work through simulated SAT I Writing exercises.

Practice Exercise Set 1

PRACTICAL ADVICE

Before you begin this Practice Set, review the

- Timing guide for writing the essay

- Top 10 rules of effective writing

- System for working the multiple-choice test questions

- Strategies for answering the different types of multiple-choice questions

You will find these reviews compiled for you in a handy Quick Reference Guide on pages 372–373.

Answers and Explanations are provided immediately after the set of practice exercises, but do not look at them until you have finished all the exercises in the set. Time this Practice Set as though it were the real test; that means allotting 20 minutes to write the essay and 25 minutes to answer the multiple-choice questions.

WRITING THE ESSAY

Directions: Think carefully about the issue described in the excerpt below and about the assignment that follows it.

To paraphrase Elie Wiesel, "More dangerous than anger and hatred is indifference. Indifference is not a beginning, it is an end—and it is always the friend to the enemy."

Assignment: Do you believe that Wiesel's view is valid? Plan and write an essay that develops your point of view on the issue. Support your opinion with reasoning and examples from your reading, your classwork, your personal experiences, or your observations.

Write your essay on separate sheets of paper or go to www.petersons.com/satessayedge.

ANSWER SHEET:
PRACTICE EXERCISE SET 1

1 Ⓐ Ⓑ Ⓒ Ⓓ Ⓔ	21 Ⓐ Ⓑ Ⓒ Ⓓ Ⓔ	41 Ⓐ Ⓑ Ⓒ Ⓓ Ⓔ
2 Ⓐ Ⓑ Ⓒ Ⓓ Ⓔ	22 Ⓐ Ⓑ Ⓒ Ⓓ Ⓔ	42 Ⓐ Ⓑ Ⓒ Ⓓ Ⓔ
3 Ⓐ Ⓑ Ⓒ Ⓓ Ⓔ	23 Ⓐ Ⓑ Ⓒ Ⓓ Ⓔ	43 Ⓐ Ⓑ Ⓒ Ⓓ Ⓔ
4 Ⓐ Ⓑ Ⓒ Ⓓ Ⓔ	24 Ⓐ Ⓑ Ⓒ Ⓓ Ⓔ	44 Ⓐ Ⓑ Ⓒ Ⓓ Ⓔ
5 Ⓐ Ⓑ Ⓒ Ⓓ Ⓔ	25 Ⓐ Ⓑ Ⓒ Ⓓ Ⓔ	45 Ⓐ Ⓑ Ⓒ Ⓓ Ⓔ
6 Ⓐ Ⓑ Ⓒ Ⓓ Ⓔ	26 Ⓐ Ⓑ Ⓒ Ⓓ Ⓔ	46 Ⓐ Ⓑ Ⓒ Ⓓ Ⓔ
7 Ⓐ Ⓑ Ⓒ Ⓓ Ⓔ	27 Ⓐ Ⓑ Ⓒ Ⓓ Ⓔ	47 Ⓐ Ⓑ Ⓒ Ⓓ Ⓔ
8 Ⓐ Ⓑ Ⓒ Ⓓ Ⓔ	28 Ⓐ Ⓑ Ⓒ Ⓓ Ⓔ	48 Ⓐ Ⓑ Ⓒ Ⓓ Ⓔ
9 Ⓐ Ⓑ Ⓒ Ⓓ Ⓔ	29 Ⓐ Ⓑ Ⓒ Ⓓ Ⓔ	49 Ⓐ Ⓑ Ⓒ Ⓓ Ⓔ
10 Ⓐ Ⓑ Ⓒ Ⓓ Ⓔ	30 Ⓐ Ⓑ Ⓒ Ⓓ Ⓔ	50 Ⓐ Ⓑ Ⓒ Ⓓ Ⓔ
11 Ⓐ Ⓑ Ⓒ Ⓓ Ⓔ	31 Ⓐ Ⓑ Ⓒ Ⓓ Ⓔ	
12 Ⓐ Ⓑ Ⓒ Ⓓ Ⓔ	32 Ⓐ Ⓑ Ⓒ Ⓓ Ⓔ	
13 Ⓐ Ⓑ Ⓒ Ⓓ Ⓔ	33 Ⓐ Ⓑ Ⓒ Ⓓ Ⓔ	
14 Ⓐ Ⓑ Ⓒ Ⓓ Ⓔ	34 Ⓐ Ⓑ Ⓒ Ⓓ Ⓔ	
15 Ⓐ Ⓑ Ⓒ Ⓓ Ⓔ	35 Ⓐ Ⓑ Ⓒ Ⓓ Ⓔ	
16 Ⓐ Ⓑ Ⓒ Ⓓ Ⓔ	36 Ⓐ Ⓑ Ⓒ Ⓓ Ⓔ	
17 Ⓐ Ⓑ Ⓒ Ⓓ Ⓔ	37 Ⓐ Ⓑ Ⓒ Ⓓ Ⓔ	
18 Ⓐ Ⓑ Ⓒ Ⓓ Ⓔ	38 Ⓐ Ⓑ Ⓒ Ⓓ Ⓔ	
19 Ⓐ Ⓑ Ⓒ Ⓓ Ⓔ	39 Ⓐ Ⓑ Ⓒ Ⓓ Ⓔ	
20 Ⓐ Ⓑ Ⓒ Ⓓ Ⓔ	40 Ⓐ Ⓑ Ⓒ Ⓓ Ⓔ	

IDENTIFYING SENTENCE ERRORS

Instructions: The sentences in this section test your knowledge of grammar, usage, diction (choice of words), and idiom.

Some sentences are correct.

No sentence contains more than one error.

The underlined and lettered parts of each sentence below may contain an error in grammar, usage, word choice, or expression. Read each sentence carefully, and identify the item that contains the error according to standard written English.

Indicate your choice by filling in the corresponding oval on your answer sheet. Only the underlined parts contain errors. Assume that the balance of the sentence is correct. No sentence contains more than one error.

Some sentences may contain no error. In those cases, the correct answer will always be No error (E).

SAMPLE QUESTION

The meteor showers <u>attracted</u>
                         A
astronomers from all over the world, <u>for</u>
                                        B
there <u>had never been</u> such a brilliant <u>one</u>
          C   D
in recent times. <u>No error</u>
                      E

SAMPLE ANSWER

(A) (B) (C) ● (E)

---

1. There is <u>no one</u> <u>who</u> denies <u>that</u>
              A   B   C
<u>they work</u> hard to make a good living.
    D
<u>No error</u>
    E

2. The second test in algebra <u>was</u> the
                                  A
<u>toughest</u> <u>when</u> <u>compared</u> with the first
    B   C   D
exam. <u>No error</u>
         E

3. The <u>butterfly's</u> wing <u>made</u> whispering
          A   B
sounds as the creature <u>rose</u> <u>beautiful</u> to
                          C   D
the blue sky. <u>No error</u>
                  E

4. When Ann and Megan <u>went</u> to the store
                         A
to find food for <u>their</u> party, they <u>find</u> that
                    B   C
<u>nothing</u> was available. <u>No error</u>
    D   E

5. <u>Its'</u> true that hope <u>springs</u> eternal, but it
      A   B
<u>doesn't always seem</u> to be <u>that</u> way.
    C   D
<u>No error</u>
    E

6. It is difficult <u>to repeat as champions</u> in
   A   B
any <u>sport;</u> but the New York Yankees
        C
have won the World Series <u>more than</u>
                              D
twenty times. <u>No error</u>
                  E

7. When people moved

   from the <u>Atlantic coast of the United</u>
                          A
   States to the <u>Pacific coast</u>, <u>they</u> encoun-
                        B   **C**
   tered <u>many new things</u>. <u>No error</u>
              D   **E**

8. <u>In politics</u>, the variance of opinions <u>are</u>
        A   **B**
   often a source of conflict <u>among</u> <u>members</u>
                                  C   **D**
   of the same political party. <u>No error</u>
                                       E

9. My father <u>will understand</u> that I
                      A
   <u>will not clean</u> the <u>yard</u> if I <u>went</u> to the
         B   **C**   **D**
   basketball game. <u>No error</u>
                          E

10. <u>Most of the actors agreed</u> that
              A
    <u>his performances</u> <u>were</u> <u>better</u> in the
           B   **C**   **D**
    second act. <u>No error</u>
                     E

11. It hurt Jenny <u>that</u> her friends laughed
    A   **B**
    <u>so cruel</u> about the Halloween costume
        C
    <u>that she had made</u>. <u>No error</u>
           D   **E**

12. Rose took the teasing from <u>her</u> classmates
              A   **B**
    without <u>making</u> <u>no</u> scene about their
                C   **D**
    comments. <u>No error</u>
                    E

13. When all the lights <u>are turned off</u> on
                              A
    Christmas Eve, <u>many little children</u> still
                          B
    <u>cannot get to sleep</u> because <u>they are too</u>
             C   **D**
    excited. <u>No error</u>
                  E

14. Getting to school early in the morning,
                                        A
    they start teaching the <u>students</u> about
    A   **B**   **C**
    <u>history, math, and science</u>. <u>No error</u>
                D   **E**

15. The dorymen <u>who travel offshore</u> every
                          A
    morning <u>catches</u> the <u>fish used in</u>
                B   **C**
    New England's <u>famous chowder</u>. <u>No error</u>
                        D   **E**

16. It is the <u>responsibility</u> of a <u>sports agent</u>
                    A   **B**
    <u>to obtain</u> the biggest salary for each
        C
    <u>players' contract</u>. <u>No error</u>
           D   **E**

17. Kyra and Piper <u>heard that</u> the dance
                          A
    decorations <u>were</u> completed, so they went
                    B
    <u>in</u> the gym <u>to see them</u>. <u>No error</u>
     C   **D**   **E**

18. The process of <u>making chocolate bars</u>
                              A
    involves <u>melting</u> the cocoa beans,
                  B
    adding milk, and <u>the refrigeration</u> of <u>the</u>
                            C   **D**
    candy. <u>No error</u>
                E

19. When <u>the winds blow</u> from the
           <u>   </u>
                A
    <u>Arctic Ocean sailors</u> and landsmen alike
              B
    hope that <u>the cold will not impact</u>
                         C
    <u>their ability</u> to make a living. <u>No error</u>
         D   E

20. Dalton and Josh felt <u>badly</u> that
                          A
    <u>they knocked over</u> the computer <u>when</u>
             B   C
    they <u>were playing catch</u> in the library.
              D
    <u>No error</u>
        E

IMPROVING SENTENCES

Instructions: The underlined sections of the sentences below may contain errors in standard written English, including awkward or ambiguous expressions, poor word choice, incorrect sentence structure, or faulty grammar, usage, and punctuation. In some items, the entire sentence may be underlined.

Read each sentence carefully. Identify which of the five alternative choices is most effective in correctly conveying the meaning of the original statement. Choice (A) always repeats the original. Select (A) if none of the other choices improves the original sentence.

Indicate your choice by filling in the corresponding oval on the answer sheet. Your choice should make the most effective sentence—clear and precise, with no ambiguity or awkwardness.

SAMPLE QUESTION

Ansel Adams photographed landscapes <u>and they communicate</u> the essence of Yosemite and other mountainous regions.

(A) and they communicate
(B) landscapes, they communicate
(C) landscapes, and communicating
(D) which communicate
(E) that communicate

SAMPLE ANSWER

 Ⓐ Ⓑ Ⓒ Ⓓ ⬤

21. As we traveled around the country, we saw natural wonders, watched movies, <u>and were fishing in various lakes.</u>

   (A) and were fishing in various lakes.
   (B) and go fishing in various lakes.
   (C) but were fishing in various lakes.
   (D) but fished in various lakes.
   (E) and fished in various lakes.

22. <u>Kelly is the type of person that everybody likes.</u>

   (A) Kelly is the type of person that everybody likes.
   (B) Kelly was liked by everybody, because she is that type of person.
   (C) Kelly was the type of person whom everybody likes.
   (D) Kelly is the type of person whom everybody likes.
   (E) Kelly is the type of person who everybody likes.

23. When we search our thoughts, <u>we often realize that we have the opportunity to improve our lives.</u>

   (A) we often realize that we have the opportunity to improve our lives.

   (B) we often realize that we have the opportunity to improve our life.

   (C) we realize often that we have the opportunity to improve our lives.

   (D) we often realize that we have the opportunities to improve our lives.

   (E) we often realized that we have the opportunity to improve our lives.

24. Long exploratory trips to the sea floor are not expected in the near future <u>because it is too costly.</u>

   (A) because it is too costly.

   (B) because they are too costly.

   (C) it is too costly.

   (D) because it costs too much.

   (E) since they are needing too much money.

25. <u>The homecoming game is the event in high school that is most remembered by me.</u>

   (A) The homecoming game is the event in high school that is most remembered by me.

   (B) The event in high school most remembered by me is the homecoming game.

   (C) The homecoming game is the event in high school that I remember the most.

   (D) I will remember the homecoming game as the event in high school.

   (E) Of the events in high school the homecoming game is the one that is remembered the most by me.

26. <u>If we decide to go on the trip today, we</u> would have gotten first-class seats on the airplane.

   (A) If we decide to go on the trip today,

   (B) If we were deciding to go on the trip today,

   (C) If we will decide to go on the trip today,

   (D) If deciding to go on the trip today,

   (E) If we had decided to go on the trip today,

27. <u>The development of new employees giving</u> the greatest satisfaction to managers in most companies.

   (A) The development of new employees giving

   (B) New employee development gives

   (C) The development of new employees having given

   (D) It is the development of new employees giving

   (E) Having given new employee development

28. There are many characteristics that are found with the athlete in any sport, but one that is common is their passion for success.

    (A) There are many characteristics that are found with the athlete in any sport, but one that is common is their passion for success.
    (B) There are many characteristics that are found with the athlete in any sport, but they commonly have a passion for success.
    (C) There are many characteristics that are found with the athlete in any sport, but, commonly, have a passion for success.
    (D) Athletes in any sport share common characteristics, especially a passion for success.
    (E) There are many characteristics that are found with the athlete in any sport, but success is a passion.

29. Claire and Ali played well against their opponents, and their serves were hit beautiful.

    (A) and their serves were hit beautiful.
    (B) and their serves were hit beautifully.
    (C) and they hit their serves beautifully.
    (D) and each of their serves were hit beautifully.
    (E) and they hit beautifully serves.

30. Many of the people we come into contact with on a daily basis become lifelong friends.

    (A) Many of the people we come into contact with on a daily basis
    (B) Many of the people we have come into contact with on a daily basis
    (C) Many of the people, we come into contact with on a daily basis
    (D) Many of the people we contact with on a daily basis
    (E) Many of the people we will come into contact with on a daily basis

31. Rose and Jean were ready to perform, they had rehearsed their piano recital for weeks.

    (A) Rose and Jean were ready to perform, they had rehearsed
    (B) Rose and Jean were ready to perform; they had rehearsed
    (C) Their rehearsing had made them ready for
    (D) They had rehearsed and Rose and Jean were ready for
    (E) Rose and Jean were ready to perform; they rehearsed

32. It is a mistake of the kind no one but him would make.

    (A) a mistake of the kind no one but him would make.
    (B) a mistake of the kind no one but he would make.
    (C) a mistake of the kind none but him would make.
    (D) a kind of mistake only he would make.
    (E) a mistake of the kind only he would make.

33. Patrons came to give money while the Getty Museum was being built, and see the progress of the construction.

- (A) Patrons came to give money while the Getty Museum was being built, and see the progress of the construction.
- (B) Patrons were coming to give money while the Getty Museum was built, and saw the progress of the construction.
- (C) Patrons came to give money and saw the progress of construction while the Getty Museum was built.
- (D) While the Getty Museum was being built, patrons came to give money and saw the progress of the construction.
- (E) While the Getty Museum was being built, patrons came to give money and to see the progress of the construction.

34. Having practiced for days, losing to Rick's team in the tournament was startling to Tom's team.

- (A) losing to Rick's team in the tournament was startling to Tom's team.
- (B) startling to Tom's team was losing to Rick's team in the tournament.
- (C) Tom's team was startled to lose to Rick's team in the tournament.
- (D) Tom's teams' losing to Rick's team in the tournament was startling.
- (E) the loss to Rick's team in the tournament was startling to Tom's team.

35. During the Constitutional Convention, the framers of the United States Constitution were confronted with many controversial issues, but they were to be resolved in time.

- (A) but they were to be resolved in time.
- (B) but the framers resolved these items in time.
- (C) but they were resolved in time.
- (D) but the framers were to resolve these items in time.
- (E) but they were resolved by the framers in time.

36. Should approved construction plans be required, one should expect to spend a great deal of time with city employees.

- (A) Should approved construction plans be required,
- (B) Should you need approved construction plans,
- (C) In those cases that you need approved construction plans,
- (D) If you need to get approved construction plans,
- (E) If approved construction plans are needed to be obtained by you,

37. Hillary paints beautiful landscapes although not being able to draw portraits.

- (A) although not being able to draw portraits.
- (B) although drawing portraits she is not able to do.
- (C) although to draw portraits she has not been able to do.
- (D) although she cannot draw portraits.
- (E) although portrait drawing she has not been able to do.

38. Driving down the freeway, <u>there blew the</u> <u>most noisy car horns</u> that I had ever encountered.

   (A)   there blew the most noisy car horns
   (B)   I heard the most noisy car horns
   (C)   there were the noisiest car horns
   (D)   the most noisy car horns blew
   (E)   I heard the noisiest car horns

IMPROVING PARAGRAPHS

Instructions: The selections below are unedited drafts of students' essays. Carefully read each essay. Sections of each essay need to be rewritten to make the meaning clearer and more precise.

Each essay is followed by a series of questions about changes that might improve all or part of its organization, development, sentence structure, language usage (diction), audience focus, or use of the conventions of standard written English.

Choose the answer that most clearly and effectively expresses the writer's intended meaning. Indicate your choice by filling in the appropriate oval on the answer sheet.

Questions 39 through 44 are based on the following first draft of an essay, which is a response to an assignment discussing foreign language.

(1) *You are in a foreign country and your money is stolen.* (2) *You go to the police, but they do not speak English.* (3) *You lose your belongings in a Chinese railroad station.* (4) *You complain to the authorities, but they don't understand English.* (5) *In Paris you order veal for dinner but get sweetbreads instead.* (6) *All of these unfortunate events can be eliminated by the knowledge of the applicable foreign language.*

(7) *This type of verbal mistake is not isolated to the ordinary American citizen.* (8) *A former United States Department of State official went to Japan.* (9) *She intended to say, "Your country is beautiful."* (10) *It came out as "Your country smells like a horse."* (11) *American companies are not immune from language mistakes.* (12) *One of the most publicized corporate language errors involved General Motors.* (13) *When the company introduced its Nova car in Latin America, it did not sell up to expectations.* (14) *The company eventually learned that one of the reasons was Nova means "no go" in Spanish.*

(15) *These and other fiascoes point out the lack of understanding of foreign languages by Americans.* (16) *In Europe most students learn two foreign languages.* (17) *In the United States it is likely that students have not learned any foreign language when they graduate from their high school.* (18) *Admission to college does not require a foreign language for 90 percent of the colleges.* (19) *Of the students who do learn a foreign language less than 20 percent can speak it well.*

(20) *In today's global marketplace most business executives recognize the need to communicate with their customers in a language that they understand.* (21) *Non-English speaking customers are more comfortable talking in their own language.* (22) *Problems can develop when important elements of a contract need to be translated.* (23) *The bottom-line benefit to an employee who can speak a foreign language is greater pay and opportunity.*

39. Taking into account paragraph 1 in its entirety, which of the following is the best revision of sentence 6?

(A) Knowledge of the applicable foreign language could eliminate all of these unfortunate events.

(B) Having knowledge of the applicable foreign language can eliminate all of these unfortunate events.

(C) Knowledge of the applicable foreign language can eliminate all of these unfortunate events.

(D) A way to eliminate these unfortunate events is through the knowledge of the applicable foreign language.

(E) Elimination of these unfortunate events is through the knowledge of the applicable foreign language.

40. As the introductory sentence of paragraph 2, which of the following is the best revision of sentence 7?

(A) Mistakes of the verbal kind are not only for the ordinary American citizen.

(B) Ordinary American citizens are not the only ones who make verbal mistakes.

(C) The making of verbal mistakes can be seen in American citizens who are not ordinary.

(D) American government and business officials also make verbal mistakes.

(E) Verbal mistakes can be found with Americans other than the ordinary ones.

41. In the context of paragraph 2, which is the best condensation of sentences 12, 13, and 14?

(A) When selling Nova cars in Latin America, General Motors did not sell many because "no go" is nova in the Spanish language.

(B) General Motor's Nova car did not sell well in Latin America because the car's name means "no go" in Spanish.

(C) In Spanish, "nova" means "no go" so the General Motors car with the same name did not sell well in Latin America.

(D) Meaning "no go" in Spanish, the General Motors car having the same name sold poorly in Latin America.

(E) Latin American sales of a General Motors car Nova had not been selling well because the name means, "no go" in Spanish.

42. Which of the following is the best revision of sentence 18 in paragraph 3?

(A) Knowledge of a foreign language is not required for admission to 90 percent of colleges.

(B) 90 percent of colleges do not require that you know a foreign language.

(C) Getting admitted to college hasn't a requirement of a foreign language 90 percent of the time.

(D) College admission does not require that you know how to speak a foreign language 90 percent of the time.

(E) Having a knowledge of a foreign language doesn't help getting admitted to colleges 90 percent of the time.

43. Which of the following is the best revision for the underlined portion of the following sentence?

In today's global marketplace most business executives recognize <u>the need to communicate with their customers in a language that they understand.</u>

(A) the need to communicate with one's customers in a language that they understand.

(B) the necessity of language in communicating their ideas.

(C) the ability to communicate with their customers in a language that they understand.

(D) that their communication with their customers is related to understanding a foreign language.

(E) the need to communicate in a language that their customers understand.

44. Based upon the essay in its entirety, which of the following best summarizes the writer's comments in the last paragraph?

(A) The goal of business is to improve communications with their customers. As a result, bilingual employees will be paid more money than those who don't speak a foreign language.

(B) Foreign language is important to business.

(C) Most foreigners prefer communicating in their own language.

(D) Employees can make more money if they understand a foreign language. They can do this because their companies focus on communications.

(E) Companies that have employees who can communicate in foreign languages have an advantage. These employees can personally benefit from their foreign language skills.

Questions 45 through 50 are based on the following first draft of an essay, which is a response to an assignment discussing health.

(1) *"My grandfather lived to be a hundred and one. (2) What do I have to worry about?" says one of my friends. (3) Another is a junk food addict who advocates the position "So what if I get sick! I have sick days and good insurance." (4) There is a young smoker who says, "By the time I've smoked long enough to get lung cancer, they will have found a cure for cancer." (5) All these people they have optimistic outlooks on life. (6) The problem is that they are not taking responsibility for their own health. (7) Our choices and our lifestyles have a significant impact on our health.*

(8) *There are a number of myths that exist about our health. (9) What about heredity? (10) It is true that genetics and heredity play a key role in our health. (11) For example, children of long-lived parents are statistically more likely to live longer than those of early dying parents. (12) There is, however, no way to tell if the genes that are passed along from parent to child are the specific ones that will yield a long life for the child. (13) The view of some that medicines will be discovered to correct all diseases is an equally unfounded myth. (14) The mere fact that medicines have been found to combat illnesses in the past is not a predictor of future medical discoveries.*

(15) *The real question becomes—why rely on someone else's actions rather than taking control of your own life? (16) It is within our control to create a healthy lifestyle. (17) So what can we do to get a long healthy life? (18) The first thing to consider is the recommendations of experts.*

(19) *One of the first things told to us by the experts is to maintain lifelong activity. (20) Regular exercise not only stimulates the cardiovascular and pulmonary functions, but also it has been found to improve the strength of our bones.*

(21) *The second thing to focus on according to the experts is diet. (22) We should work to reduce our consumption of fatty and processed foods. (23) High intake of these foods increases the risk of heart disease and some forms of cancer.*

(24) *The last area to address covers the avoidance of those lifestyle choices that are known causes of death. (25) The most obvious of these is smoking. (26) The relationship between smoking and disease, particularly coronary heart disease and cancer, is extremely well documented. (27) The decision not to smoke is ours, and ours alone. (28) We can take control of our lives by making that one healthy choice.*

45. Which of the following is the best revision of sentence 5?

   (A) All these people have optimistic attitudes about life.
   (B) The people have something in common—optimistic attitudes.
   (C) All these many people share optimistic, cheerful attitudes about their existence in the world.
   (D) Optimistic attitudes are shared by all of these people.
   (E) What do these people have in common? Totally optimistic attitudes!

46. What is the most effective way to combine sentences 8, 9, and 10?

   (A) Heredity and genetics are not a myth, they play a key role in our health.
   (B) While many myths exist about our health, heredity and genetics play a key role.
   (C) Heredity and genetics play a key role.
   (D) Health myths are not true, because heredity and genetics play a role in our health.
   (E) Heredity and genetics, not myths play a key role in our health.

47. Which is the thesis statement of this essay?

   (A) Sentence 1
   (B) Sentence 4
   (C) Sentence 5
   (D) Sentence 7
   (E) Sentence 28

48. What is the best way to revise the following sentence?

   For example, children of long-lived parents are statistically more likely to live longer than those of early dying parents.

   (A) For example, children of long-lived parents are statistically more likely to live longer than those of early-dying parents.
   (B) For example, children of long-lived parents are statistically more likely to live longer than children of early dying parents.
   (C) For example, children of long-lived parents are statistically more likely to live longer than children of short-lived parents.
   (D) For example, children whose parents lived a long time are statistically more likely to live longer than those who's parents die young.
   (E) For example, children whose parents lived a long time are statistically more likely to live longer than children whose parents die young.

49. The writer used which of the following types of development in this essay?

   (A) Definition
   (B) Spatial
   (C) Compare and contrast
   (D) Argument and proof
   (E) Chronological

50. Which of the following best describes the purpose of paragraph 4?

   (A) Develop the main idea of the essay's second paragraph
   (B) Develop the idea introduced in sentence 18
   (C) Illustrate sentence 5
   (D) Provide background material for the next paragraph
   (E) Clarify the thesis

Practice Exercise Set 1

ANSWERS AND EXPLANATIONS

SELF-EVALUATION RUBRIC

	6	5	4	3	2	1
Overall Impression	Demonstrates excellent command of the conventions of English; outstanding competence; thorough and effective; incisive	Demonstrates good command of the conventions of English; good writing competence; less thorough and incisive than the highest essays	Demonstrates adequate command of the conventions of English; competent writing	Demonstrates fair command of the conventions of English; some writing competency	Demonstrates little command of the conventions of English; poor writing skills; unacceptably brief; fails to respond to the question	Lacking skill and competence
Thesis and Purpose	Exhibits excellent perception and clarity; original, interesting, or unique approach; includes apt and specific references, facts, and/or examples	Exhibits good perception and clarity; engaging approach; includes specific references, facts, and/or examples	Clear and perceptive; somewhat interesting; includes references, facts, and/or examples	Somewhat clear but exhibits incomplete or confused thinking; dull, mechanical, overgeneralized	Very little clarity; confusing; flawed logic	Very confusing or completely off the topic
Organization and Development	Meticulously organized and thoroughly developed; coherent and unified	Well organized and developed; coherent and unified	Reasonably organized and developed; generally coherent and unified	Moderately organized and developed; some incoherence and lack of unity	Little or no organization and development; incoherent and void of unity	No apparent organization or development; incoherent
Use of Sentences	Effectively varied and engaging; virtually error free	Varied and interesting; a few errors	Adequately varied; some errors	Moderately varied and marginally interesting; one or more major errors	Little or no variation; dull and uninteresting; some major errors	Numerous major errors
Word Choice	Interesting and effective; virtually error free	Generally interesting and effective; a few errors	Occasionally interesting and effective; several errors	Moderately dull and ordinary; some errors in diction	Mostly dull and conventional; numerous errors	Numerous major errors; extremely immature
Grammar and Usage	Virtually error free	Occasional minor errors	Some minor errors	Some major errors	Severely flawed; frequent major errors	Extremely flawed

Instructions: Rate yourself in each of the categories on the rubric. Circle the description in each category that most accurately reflects your performance. Enter the numbers on the lines below. Then, calculate the average of the six numbers to determine your final score. On the SAT I, at least two readers will rate your essay on a scale of 1 to 6, with 6 being the highest. Because it is difficult to score yourself objectively, you may wish to ask a respected friend or teacher to assess your writing to reflect more accurately its effectiveness.

SELF-EVALUATION

Each category is rated 6 (high) to 1 (low)

Overall Impression _____

Thesis and Purpose _____

Organization and Development _____

Use of Sentences _____

Word Choice _____

Grammar and Usage _____

TOTAL _____

Divide by 6 for final score _____

OBJECTIVE EVALUATION

Each category is rated 6 (high) to 1 (low)

Overall Impression _____

Thesis and Purpose _____

Organization and Development _____

Use of Sentences _____

Word Choice _____

Grammar and Usage _____

TOTAL _____

Divide by 6 for final score _____

Quick-Score Answers

1. D	11. C	21. E	31. B	41. B
2. B	12. D	22. D	32. D	42. A
3. D	13. E	23. A	33. E	43. E
4. C	14. A	24. B	34. C	44. E
5. A	15. B	25. C	35. B	45. A
6. C	16. D	26. E	36. A	46. B
7. E	17. C	27. B	37. D	47. D
8. B	18. D	28. D	38. E	48. E
9. D	19. B	29. C	39. C	49. D
10. B	20. A	30. A	40. D	50. B

MULTIPLE-CHOICE SELF-EVALUATION

SCORING

	Number Correct	Number Incorrect
Identifying Sentence Errors, Questions 1–20		
Improving Sentences, Questions 21–38		
Improving Paragraphs, Questions 39–50		
Subtotal		
Penalty Points	N/A	.25 × number incorrect =

Total Score

Number Correct _____

Subtract Penalty Points _____

Equals _____

Where do you need to improve? _____

_____

Spend more time working on that area. See Chapters 7 through 9 for help with grammar, mechanics, punctuation, usage, and sentence and paragraph structure.

ANSWERS AND EXPLANATIONS
IDENTIFYING SENTENCE ERRORS

1. **The correct answer is (D).** The pronoun reference should be to the singular *no one*.

2. **The correct answer is (B).** The comparative *tougher* should be used.

3. **The correct answer is (D).** Use the adverb *beautifully* to modify the verb. Adverbs modify verbs. Adding *-ly* usually turns an adjective into an adverb.

4. **The correct answer is (C).** The verb should be past tense *found*.

5. **The correct answer is (A).** The correct contraction for the expression *it is* is *it's*.

6. **The correct answer is (C).** The punctuation is incorrect. A comma, not a semicolon, should be used with a conjunction.

7. **The correct answer is (E).** Verb tenses, pronoun antecedent, and the *from-to* construction are all correct.

8. **The correct answer is (B).** The verb should be the singular *is* since the subject is singular *variance*.

9. **The correct answer is (D).** The verb should be in the present tense, *go*. See Chapter 7 for a list of irregular verbs to learn.

10. **The correct answer is (B).** The pronoun should agree with the plural noun *most*.

11. **The correct answer is (C).** The adverb for *cruelly* should modify the verb *laughed*.

12. **The correct answer is (D).** This sentence contains a double negative. To eliminate it, use *a* instead of *no*.

13. **The correct answer is (E).** All punctuation is correct. The subordinate clauses correctly modify elements in the main clause.

14. **The correct answer is (A).** The wording creates a dangling participle because it lacks a noun or pronoun to modify.

15. **The correct answer is (B).** The verb must match the plural subject of the sentence *dorymen*.

16. **The correct answer is (D).** The possessive should be the singular *player's*.

17. **The correct answer is (C).** This is an error in diction. Use *into* when referring to going from the outside to the inside.

18. **The correct answer is (D).** The sentence does not have parallel construction. Use *refrigerating* instead of *the refrigeration of*.

19. **The correct answer is (B).** A comma is required to set off any introductory subordinate clause.

20. **The correct answer is (A).** The linking verb *felt* needs a predicate adjective, *bad*, as a modifier for the subject. Linking verbs are modified by predicate adjectives, not adverbs.

IMPROVING SENTENCES

Note: Although some choices may have more than one error, only one error is listed for each incorrect response.

21. **The correct answer is (E).**

Choice (A)   The verb does not have parallel construction.
Choice (B)   The verb has the incorrect tense.
Choice (C)   The verb does not have parallel construction.
Choice (D)   The use of the conjunction *but* changes the meaning of the sentence.

22. **The correct answer is (D).**

Choice (A)   The pronoun *that* should not be used when referring to a person.
Choice (B)   The active form of the verb is preferred.
Choice (C)   The verbs are not in parallel construction.
Choice (E)   The objective pronoun *whom* is required.

23. **The correct answer is (A).**

Choice (B)   Parallel construction requires the plural noun *lives*.
Choice (C)   The standard idiom is *often realize*.
Choice (D)   The use of the plural *opportunities* incorrectly suggests multiple occasions. That is not consistent with the original sentence.
Choice (E)   The use of the past tense *realized* is incorrect.

24. The correct answer is (B).

    Choice (A)   The antecedent of the pronoun *it* is plural *trips*. The plural pronoun *they* is needed.

    Choice (C)   Punctuation is required to separate two independent clauses.

    Choice (D)   The antecedent of the pronoun *it* is plural *trips*. The plural pronoun *they* is needed.

    Choice (E)   The sentence is referring to something in the future. The verb *are needing* is present tense.

25. The correct answer is (C).

Active voice makes stronger writing.

    Choice (A)   The use of active construction is preferred to passive construction.

    Choice (B)   The use of active construction is preferred to passive construction.

    Choice (D)   The sentence does not make sense.

    Choice (E)   The sentence is wordy.

26. The correct answer is (E).

    Choice (A)   The tense of the verb is incorrect. *If we decide* identifies future action, but the principle clause has action that has already been completed.

    Choice (B)   The tense of the verb is incorrect.

    Choice (C)   The tense of the verb is incorrect.

    Choice (D)   The use of the gerund *deciding* is incorrect.

27. The correct answer is (B).

    Choice (A)   The verb form *giving* is a gerund. The sentence needs a verb.

    Choice (C)   The form of the verb is incorrect.

    Choice (D)   The form of the verb is incorrect.

    Choice (E)   The form of the verb is incorrect.

28. The correct answer is (D).

    Choice (A)   The antecedent of *their* is the singular *athlete*. Use *his* or *her*.

    Choice (B)   The construction is not parallel because the antecedent of *they* is the singular noun *athlete*.

    Choice (C)   There is no subject; therefore, this phrase is a fragment.

    Choice (E)   The second clause does not link with the thought in the first clause.

29. **The correct answer is (C).**

Choice (A) The clause requires the adverb *beautifully*.

Choice (B) Changing the subject from *Claire and Ali* to *their serves* is a stylistic error.

Choice (D) Changing the subject from *Claire and Ali* to *each* is a stylistic error.

Choice (E) The adjective *beautiful* is used incorrectly to modify the noun *serves*.

30. **The correct answer is (A).**

Choice (B) The tense of the verb is incorrect. The action of the sentence is set in the present, not in the past.

Choice (C) The use of a comma is unnecessary.

Choice (D) The common idiom is *come into contact with*.

Choice (E) The tense of the verb is incorrect. The action of the sentence is set in the present, not in the future.

31. **The correct answer is (B).**

Choice (A) These are two independent clauses. They require a semicolon to separate them.

Choice (C) There is no pronoun antecedent, and the sentence is in passive, not active, voice.

Choice (D) A comma is required after *rehearsed* to separate the two independent clauses.

Choice (E) The past perfect tense of the verb *had rehearsed* is needed.

32. **The correct answer is (D).**

Choice (A) The standard idiom is *kind of mistake*.

Choice (B) The objective case pronoun *him* is used after the conjunction *but*.

Choice (C) The standard idiom is *kind of mistake*. The use of *none* does not change the construction of the sentence.

Choice (E) The standard idiom is *kind of mistake*.

33. **The correct answer is (E).**

Choice (A) The tense of the verb *see* is incorrect.

Choice (B) The tenses of the verbs are incorrect.

Choice (C) The modifier *while the Getty Museum was built* is improperly modifying *construction*.

Choice (D) Turning *saw* into an infinitive and changing the clause to read "patrons came to give money and to see the progress of the construction" is a smoother construction than using *patrons* as the subject of both *came* and *saw*.

34. The correct answer is (C).

To correct a dangling participle, ask yourself who or what did the acting. Then, revise the sentence to make the reference clear. Add words if that will make the meaning clear.

Choice (A)   The phrase *having practiced for days* is a dangling participle with nothing to modify.

Choice (B)   The phrase *having practiced for days* is a dangling participle with nothing to modify.

Choice (D)   The phrase *having practiced for days* is a dangling participle with nothing to modify.

Choice (E)   The phrase *having practiced for days* is a dangling participle with nothing to modify.

35. The correct answer is (B).

Choice (A)   The verb is an incorrect use of a subjunctive mood.

Choice (C)   The subject is shifted incorrectly from *framers* to *items*.

Choice (D)   The verb's action is in the future. It should be past tense.

Choice (E)   The subject is shifted from *framers* to *items*.

36. The correct answer is (A).

Choice (B)   The second person *you* is incorrect because the sentence is in the third person *one*.

Choice (C)   The second person *you* is incorrect because the sentence is in the third person *one*.

Choice (D)   The second person *you* is incorrect because the sentence is in the third person *one*.

Choice (E)   The construction of the sentence is awkward. Wording such as *to be obtained by you* should be avoided.

37. The correct answer is (D).

Choice (A)   The clause lacks parallel construction with the verbs *paints* and *not being able*.

Choice (B)   The clause has awkward phrasing.

Choice (C)   The clause has awkward phrasing.

Choice (E)   The clause has awkward phrasing.

38. The correct answer is (E).

Choice (A)   The phrase *driving down the freeway* is a dangling participle. It should modify *I*.

Choice (B)   The superlative form of the adjective is *noisiest*.

Choice (C)   The phrase *driving down the freeway* is a dangling participle. It should modify *I*.

Choice (D)   The superlative form of the adjective is *noisiest*.

IMPROVING PARAGRAPHS

39. The correct answer is (C). The sentence presents a clear statement and is grammatically correct.

Choice (A) The tense of the verb is changed incorrectly.

Choice (B) The use of active voice is preferable to passive voice.

Choice (D) This is not a bad response, but it is wordier and lacks the stronger active voice of response (C).

Choice (E) This is a more definitive statement than the original sentence.

40. The correct answer is (D). The sentence states the main idea of the paragraph, so that the rest of the sentences provide supporting details.

Choice (A) Parallel construction makes the subject of the sentence *citizens,* not *mistakes.*

Choice (B) The reference with *ones* is too broad. This could refer to a citizen of any country. The essay is focused on United States citizens.

Choice (C) The phrase *The making of* is superfluous.

Choice (E) The phrasing is awkward. The phrase *other than the ordinary ones* is very cumbersome.

41. The correct answer is (B). The sentence is clear and grammatically correct.

Choice (A) The response is wordy and redundant. The use of *selling* and *sells* in the same sentence is awkward. *Language* after *Spanish* is superfluous.

Choice (C) The reference of the word *name* is unclear. Does it refer to *General Motors* or *Nova?*

Choice (D) The phrase *meaning "no go" in Spanish* is a dangling participle.

Choice (E) The verb *had not been selling* is not the correct tense.

42. The correct answer is (A). The revision eliminates the redundancy.

Choice (B) A sentence should not begin with numerals.

Choice (C) This is very awkwardly phrased. It is also passive construction that should be avoided.

Choice (D) This response suggests that the ability to speak a foreign language is not required. The context of the paragraph does not distinguish between speaking, reading, and writing a language.

Choice (E) This is also passive-voice construction.

43. **The correct answer is (E).** The revision replaces the vague pronoun antecedent *they* with *their customers* to make the reference clear.

Choice (A)   The antecedent of the singular pronoun *one's* is incorrectly the plural pronoun *executives*.

Choice (B)   This changes the meaning of the sentence and misses the core element of a foreign language.

Choice (C)   The antecedent of the pronoun *they* is uncertain. Does it refer to *executives* or *customers*?

Choice (D)   This sentence is vague. It is not clear whether the customers or the executives should have knowledge of a foreign language.

44. **The correct answer is (E).** The sentence restates the ideas in the last paragraph correctly.

Choice (A)   The goal of business is not *to improve communications*.

Choice (B)   Although foreign language is important to business, this covers only a portion of the thoughts of the concluding paragraph.

Choice (C)   This response is similar to the previous one in that it covers only a portion of the content of the paragraph.

Choice (D)   The paragraph does suggest that employees can make more money if they know a foreign language. On the other hand, the paragraph does not say that companies focus on communications.

45. **The correct answer is (A).** The sentence corrects the incorrect subject *people they*.

Choice (B)   The answer contains a dash which is best avoided in formal writing.

Choice (C)   The choice is wordy.

Choice (D)   This is grammatically correct, but it is preferable to use the active voice.

Choice (E)   Slang words such as *totally* are to be avoided.

46. **The correct answer is (B).** The sentence combines all the pertinent information while eliminating the redundancy in sentence 9.

Choice (A)   This choice contains a comma splice.

Choice (C)   This choice is too brief.

Choice (D)   This choice has faulty logic.

Choice (E)   This sentence needs another comma after *myths* to be correct.

47. **The correct answer is (D).** It contains the main idea of the essay.

Choice (A)   Sentence 1 is a quotation included to interest the reader.

Choice (B)   Sentence 4 continues the introduction but does not include the main idea.

Choice (C)   Sentence 5 serves as a transition to the thesis.

Choice (E)   Sentence 28 is part of the concluding paragraph and restates the thesis.

48. **The correct answer is (E).**

Choice (A)   This sentence has an unclear pronoun antecedent. *Those* should be *children.*

Choice (B)   There is a punctuation error. A hyphen is used to connect two or more words that are used as one word, known as a unit modifier. Therefore, *early dying* becomes *early-dying.*

Choice (C)   This is grammatically correct but awkwardly worded.

Choice (D)   This sentence contains an incorrect pronoun. The contraction *who's* should be the possessive *whose.* To test the apostrophe, ask yourself, "Who is parents die young?" If the question doesn't make sense, try the possessive pronoun.

49. **The correct answer is (D).** The writer presents a theory (thesis) and then sets out proof (support) to make his/her points.

Choice (A)   This answer is incorrect because terms are not defined.

Choice (B)   This choice is incorrect because the essay does not discuss location.

Choice (C)   This answer is incorrect because nothing is being compared to health.

Choice (E)   This choice is incorrect because time is not involved.

50.   **The correct answer is (B).** Sentence 18 introduces the role of experts, and paragraph 4 develops one of the recommendations of experts.

Choice (A)	This is unacceptable because paragraph 2 discusses the role of heredity, whereas paragraph 4 argues the importance of exercise.
Choice (C)	This is incorrect because paragraph 4 does not illustrate the sentence.
Choice (D)	This is unacceptable because the next paragraph is about diet.
Choice (E)	This answer is incorrect because the body paragraphs develop the thesis, but they do not clarify it.

Practice Exercise Set 2

PRACTICAL ADVICE

Before you begin this Practice Set, review the

- Timing guide for writing the essay
- Top 10 rules of effective writing
- System for working the multiple-choice test questions
- Strategies for answering the different types of multiple-choice questions

You will find these reviews compiled for you in a handy Quick Reference Guide on pages 372–373.

Answers and Explanations are provided immediately after the set of practice exercises, but do not look at them until you have finished all the exercises in the set. Time this Practice Set as though it were the real test; that means allotting 20 minutes to write the essay and 25 minutes to answer the multiple-choice questions.

WRITING THE ESSAY

Directions: Think carefully about the issue described in the excerpt below and about the assignment that follows it.

Difficulty is a nurse of greatness—a harsh nurse who rocks her foster children roughly but rocks them into strength and athletic proportions.
—William Cullen Bryant

Assignment: What is your opinion of the idea that difficult times and hardship create strength of character and greatness? Plan and write an essay that develops your point of view on the issue. Support your opinion with reasoning and examples from your reading, your classwork, your personal experiences, or your observations.

Write your essay on separate sheets of paper or go to www.petersons.com/satessayedge.

ANSWER SHEET:
PRACTICE EXERCISE SET 2

1 Ⓐ Ⓑ Ⓒ Ⓓ Ⓔ	21 Ⓐ Ⓑ Ⓒ Ⓓ Ⓔ	41 Ⓐ Ⓑ Ⓒ Ⓓ Ⓔ
2 Ⓐ Ⓑ Ⓒ Ⓓ Ⓔ	22 Ⓐ Ⓑ Ⓒ Ⓓ Ⓔ	42 Ⓐ Ⓑ Ⓒ Ⓓ Ⓔ
3 Ⓐ Ⓑ Ⓒ Ⓓ Ⓔ	23 Ⓐ Ⓑ Ⓒ Ⓓ Ⓔ	43 Ⓐ Ⓑ Ⓒ Ⓓ Ⓔ
4 Ⓐ Ⓑ Ⓒ Ⓓ Ⓔ	24 Ⓐ Ⓑ Ⓒ Ⓓ Ⓔ	44 Ⓐ Ⓑ Ⓒ Ⓓ Ⓔ
5 Ⓐ Ⓑ Ⓒ Ⓓ Ⓔ	25 Ⓐ Ⓑ Ⓒ Ⓓ Ⓔ	45 Ⓐ Ⓑ Ⓒ Ⓓ Ⓔ
6 Ⓐ Ⓑ Ⓒ Ⓓ Ⓔ	26 Ⓐ Ⓑ Ⓒ Ⓓ Ⓔ	46 Ⓐ Ⓑ Ⓒ Ⓓ Ⓔ
7 Ⓐ Ⓑ Ⓒ Ⓓ Ⓔ	27 Ⓐ Ⓑ Ⓒ Ⓓ Ⓔ	47 Ⓐ Ⓑ Ⓒ Ⓓ Ⓔ
8 Ⓐ Ⓑ Ⓒ Ⓓ Ⓔ	28 Ⓐ Ⓑ Ⓒ Ⓓ Ⓔ	48 Ⓐ Ⓑ Ⓒ Ⓓ Ⓔ
9 Ⓐ Ⓑ Ⓒ Ⓓ Ⓔ	29 Ⓐ Ⓑ Ⓒ Ⓓ Ⓔ	49 Ⓐ Ⓑ Ⓒ Ⓓ Ⓔ
10 Ⓐ Ⓑ Ⓒ Ⓓ Ⓔ	30 Ⓐ Ⓑ Ⓒ Ⓓ Ⓔ	50 Ⓐ Ⓑ Ⓒ Ⓓ Ⓔ
11 Ⓐ Ⓑ Ⓒ Ⓓ Ⓔ	31 Ⓐ Ⓑ Ⓒ Ⓓ Ⓔ	
12 Ⓐ Ⓑ Ⓒ Ⓓ Ⓔ	32 Ⓐ Ⓑ Ⓒ Ⓓ Ⓔ	
13 Ⓐ Ⓑ Ⓒ Ⓓ Ⓔ	33 Ⓐ Ⓑ Ⓒ Ⓓ Ⓔ	
14 Ⓐ Ⓑ Ⓒ Ⓓ Ⓔ	34 Ⓐ Ⓑ Ⓒ Ⓓ Ⓔ	
15 Ⓐ Ⓑ Ⓒ Ⓓ Ⓔ	35 Ⓐ Ⓑ Ⓒ Ⓓ Ⓔ	
16 Ⓐ Ⓑ Ⓒ Ⓓ Ⓔ	36 Ⓐ Ⓑ Ⓒ Ⓓ Ⓔ	
17 Ⓐ Ⓑ Ⓒ Ⓓ Ⓔ	37 Ⓐ Ⓑ Ⓒ Ⓓ Ⓔ	
18 Ⓐ Ⓑ Ⓒ Ⓓ Ⓔ	38 Ⓐ Ⓑ Ⓒ Ⓓ Ⓔ	
19 Ⓐ Ⓑ Ⓒ Ⓓ Ⓔ	39 Ⓐ Ⓑ Ⓒ Ⓓ Ⓔ	
20 Ⓐ Ⓑ Ⓒ Ⓓ Ⓔ	40 Ⓐ Ⓑ Ⓒ Ⓓ Ⓔ	

IDENTIFYING SENTENCE ERRORS

Instructions: The sentences in this section test your knowledge of grammar, usage, diction (choice of words), and idiom.

Some sentences are correct.

No sentence contains more than one error.

The underlined and lettered parts of each sentence below may contain an error in grammar, usage, word choice, or expression. Read each sentence carefully, and identify the item that contains the error according to standard written English.

Indicate your choice by filling in the corresponding oval on your answer sheet. Only the underlined parts contain errors. Assume that the balance of the sentence is correct. No sentence contains more than one error.

Some sentences may contain no error. In those cases, the correct answer will always be No error Ⓔ.

SAMPLE QUESTION

The meteor showers attracted
                A

astronomers from all over the world, for
                               B

there had never been such a brilliant one
      C   D

in recent times. No error
          E

SAMPLE ANSWER

Ⓐ   Ⓑ   Ⓒ   ●   Ⓔ

---

1. On a camping trip with

   an established outfitter, a tent and a
                A

   sleeping bag, a down water-proof model,
                       B

   is the equipment you need. No error
   C   D   E

2. Outside of the janitors and Penny,
         A   B

   hardly anyone helped clean the gymna-
         C   D

   sium. No error
        E

3. Well before the evening concert began,
       A   B

   the audience had became
             C

   restless, rude, and hostile. No error
         D   E

4. The older chef claims to cook as well or
        A   B   C

   better than his young protégé. No error
   D   E

5. Before the party was over, all the soda
                A

   and coffee had been drank, so the guests
               B   C

   left unsatisfied. No error
        D   E

6. The ship came loose from its moorings,
            A

   and then it gently floated out of the dock
        B   C   D

   and into the harbor. No error
            E

7. When Richard asked his father if he
   $\overline{}$
   $\underset{A}{}$
   could borrow the car, he said he needed
   $\underset{B}{}\underset{C}{}\underset{D}{}$
   it to go to work. No error
   $\underset{E}{}$

8. I will arrive on Flight 714 to Miami well
   $\underset{A}{}\underset{B}{}\underset{C}{}$
   before the rest of you returned to the
   $\underset{D}{}$
   restaurant. No error
   $\underset{E}{}$

9. You can be served a subpoena if you
   $\underset{A}{}\underset{B}{}$
   do not cooperate fully with
   $\underset{C}{}$
   the district attorney and the police
   $\underset{D}{}$
   No error
   $\underset{E}{}$

10. Ann hadn't but one request, take
    $\underset{A}{}\underset{B}{}$
    her daughter Allie to lunch sometime
    $\underset{C}{}$
    during the vacation week. No error
    $\underset{D}{}\underset{E}{}$

11. My aunt, who was ten years old at the
    $\underset{A}{}\underset{B}{}$
    time, immigrated from Hong Kong after
    $\underset{C}{}$
    World War II ended. No error
    $\underset{D}{}\underset{E}{}$

12. *The Merry Wives of Windsor*,
    $\underset{A}{}$
    an amusing comedy by Shakespeare,
    $\underset{B}{}$
    will be playing at the
    $\underset{C}{}$
    Performing Arts Center during the month
    $\underset{D}{}$
    of August. No error
    $\underset{E}{}$

13. With bulging pockets the child entered
    $\underset{A}{}$
    the room and tried to make it to the stairs
    $\underset{B}{}$
    unobserved, but Mr. Baez stopped the
    $\underset{C}{}$
    child and asked what was in them.
    $\underset{D}{}$
    No error
    $\underset{E}{}$

14. Between you and I, I think that the new
    $\underset{A}{}$
    football coach of the Spartans
    $\underset{B}{}$
    does not know enough about the game
    $\underset{C}{}$
    to build a winning team. No error
    $\underset{D}{}\underset{E}{}$

15. When the Trojans lost the bowl game,
    $\underset{A}{}$
    Rick felt so badly that he moped during
    $\underset{B}{}\underset{C}{}\underset{D}{}$
    the entire evening. No error
    $\underset{E}{}$

16. The damage from yesterday's severe
    $\underset{A}{}$
    hurricane was considerably more than
    $\underset{B}{}$
    the one that destroyed
    $\underset{C}{}$
    downtown Laguna Beach last year.
    $\underset{D}{}$
    No error
    $\underset{E}{}$

17. Although Tomas had been severely injured
    $\underset{A}{}$
    when his sports utility vehicle was hit by
    $\underset{B}{}$
    a sixteen-wheel truck, the doctors told his
    $\underset{C}{}$
    family that he would be alright. No error
    $\underset{D}{}\underset{E}{}$

18. This season Kurt was more inspired than
 $\underline{\text{A}}$ $\underline{\text{B}}$
any member of the hockey team. No error
 $\underline{\text{C}}$ $\underline{\text{D}}$ $\underline{\text{E}}$

19. We should invite
 $\underline{\text{A}}$
people with whom you work and your
 $\underline{\text{B}}$ $\underline{\text{C}}$
friends from the tennis club. No error
 $\underline{\text{D}}$ $\underline{\text{E}}$

20. I have been jogging and working out
 $\underline{\text{A}}$ $\underline{\text{B}}$
in order to stay fit. No error
 $\underline{\text{C}}$ $\underline{\text{D}}$ $\underline{\text{E}}$

IMPROVING SENTENCES

Instructions: The underlined sections of the sentences below may contain errors in standard written English, including awkward or ambiguous expressions, poor word choice, incorrect sentence structure, or faulty grammar, usage, and punctuation. In some items, the entire sentence may be underlined.

Read each sentence carefully. Identify which of the five alternative choices is most effective in correctly conveying the meaning of the original statement. Choice (A) always repeats the original. Select (A) if none of the other choices improves the original sentence.

Indicate your choice by filling in the corresponding oval on the answer sheet. Your choice should make the most effective sentence—clear and precise, with no ambiguity or awkwardness.

SAMPLE QUESTION

Ansel Adams photographed landscapes <u>and they communicate</u> the essence of Yosemite and other mountainous regions.

- (A) and they communicate
- (B) landscapes, they communicate
- (C) landscapes, and communicating
- (D) which communicate
- (E) that communicate

SAMPLE ANSWER

---

21. The individuals in the government <u>explored the options—legal, moral, scholarly—which lay before their community.</u>

- (A) The individuals in the government explored the options—legal, moral, scholarly—that lay before their community.
- (B) The community's legal, moral, and scholarly options were reviewed by government individuals.
- (C) Government individuals reviewed the community's legal, moral, and scholarly options.
- (D) Government individuals explored the options—legal, moral, scholarly—laying before the community.
- (E) The community's options—legal, moral, scholarly—were reviewed by government individuals.

22. *The Little Prince*, a wonderful book by Antoine de Saint-Exupéry, is <u>a story that everyone should be reading at least once.</u>

- (A) a story that everyone should be reading at least once.
- (B) that everyone has read.
- (C) a story that everyone should read at least once.
- (D) a story which everyone should read.
- (E) that should be read by everyone at least once.

23. <u>A black cloth hung over the bird cage, where it had been placed many evenings ago.</u>

(A) A black cloth hung over the bird cage, where it had been placed many evenings ago.

(B) A black cloth had been placed over the bird cage many evenings ago.

(C) Many evenings ago, a black cloth had been placed over the bird cage.

(D) Having been placed there many years ago, a black cloth hung over the bird cage.

(E) A black cloth had been hanging over the bird cage, where it had been placed many evenings ago.

24. Suddenly Theo spotted a brilliant hum-mingbird <u>that is hovering near the fuchsias.</u>

(A) Suddenly Theo spotted a brilliant hummingbird that is hovering near the fuchsias.

(B) Suddenly Theo spotted a brilliant hummingbird which is hovering near the fuchsias.

(C) Suddenly Theo spotted a brilliant hummingbird that was hovering near the fuchsias.

(D) Suddenly Theo spotted a brilliant hummingbird which was hovering near the fuchsias.

(E) A brilliant hummingbird which hovered near the fuchsias was spotted suddenly by Theo.

25. <u>Every decade, every man, woman, and child in the United States is counted, tabulated, and translated into statistics, they tell us the average income of Americans, the percentage of female graduates, the typical life span, and many other interesting pieces of information.</u>

(A) Every decade, every man, woman, and child in the United States is counted, tabulated, and translated into statistics, they tell us the average income of Americans, the percentage of female graduates, the typical life span, and many other interesting pieces of information.

(B) Every decade, the Census Bureau counts, tabulates, and translates every man, woman, and child in the United States into statistics, they tell us the average income of Americans, the percentage of female graduates, the typical life span, and many other interesting pieces of information.

(C) Every decade, every man, woman, and child in the United States is counted, tabulated, and translated into statistics, the numbers tell us the average income of Americans, the percentage of female graduates, the typical life span, and many other interesting pieces of information.

(D) Every decade, every man, woman, and child in the United States is counted, tabulated, and translated into statistics that tell us the average income of Americans, the percentage of female graduates, the typical life span, and many other interesting pieces of information.

(E) Every decade, every man, woman, and child in the United States is counted, tabulated, and translated into statistics: they tell us the average income of Americans, the percentage of female graduates, the typical life span, and many other interesting pieces of information.

26. To knit a sweater, <u>all the yarn must be bought at once to ensure consistent colors.</u>

   (A) all the yarn must be bought at once to ensure consistent colors.
   (B) you must buy all the yarn at once to ensure consistent colors.
   (C) all the yarns must be bought at once to ensure consistent colors.
   (D) buy all the yarn at once to ensure consistent colors.
   (E) all the yarn must have been bought at once to ensure consistent colors.

27. The battle of Gettysburg <u>featured a cast of characters admired, revered, and despised by Civil War aficionados.</u>

   (A) The battle of Gettysburg featured a cast of characters admired, revered, and despised by Civil War aficionados.
   (B) The battle of Gettysburg had a cast of characters admired, revered, and despised by Civil War aficionados.
   (C) The cast of the battle of Gettysburg is admired, revered, and despised by Civil War aficionados.
   (D) Admired, revered, and despised by Civil War aficionados, the battle of Gettysburg featured a cast of characters.
   (E) Gettysburg's cast of characters admired, revered, and despised by Civil War aficionados for their actions in the battle.

28. <u>In the coming elections, we citizens are asked to vote on the sale of state bonds, for more state parks, and to have the state cut property taxes.</u>

   (A) In the coming elections, we citizens are asked to vote on the sale of state bonds, for more state parks, and to have the state cut property taxes.
   (B) The sale of state bonds, more state parks, and cutting state property taxes are issues us citizens are being asked to vote on.
   (C) In the coming elections, we citizens are being asked to vote on the sale of state bonds, for more state parks, and to have the state cut property taxes.
   (D) In the coming elections, us citizens are asked to vote on the sale of state bonds, for more state parks, and to have the state cut property taxes.
   (E) In the coming elections, we citizens are asked to vote on the sale of state bonds, for more state parks, and for a cut in property taxes.

29. The general would be given leave, <u>with instructions that his staff would accompany them.</u>

   (A) with instructions that his staff would accompany them.
   (B) with instructions that his staff would accompany him.
   (C) with instructions that their staff would accompany them.
   (D) and instructing his staff would accompany the man.
   (E) instructing his staff to accompany them.

30. Here was a person <u>who wanted to write a book about fitness, yet whom was extremely obese.</u>

   (A) who wanted to write a book about fitness, yet whom was extremely obese.

   (B) who wanted to write a book about fitness, yet who's body was extremely obese.

   (C) who wanted to write a book about fitness, but whom was extremely obese.

   (D) whom wanted to write a book about fitness, yet whom was extremely obese.

   (E) who wanted to write a book about fitness, yet who was extremely obese.

31. Amazed by the panorama, <u>Geraldo advanced to the edge of the lake, which stretches before him for miles.</u>

   (A) Geraldo advanced to the edge of the lake which stretches before him for miles.

   (B) Geraldo advancing to the edge of the lake which stretches before him for miles.

   (C) Geraldo advanced to the edge of the lake which stretched before him for miles.

   (D) Geraldo advanced to the lake's edge which stretches before him for miles.

   (E) Geraldo advanced to the edge of the lake that stretches before him for miles.

32. Claire and the other students would joke among themselves about Halloween or nights of the full moon, <u>but never seeming to explain the strangeness that sometimes occurred.</u>

   (A) but never seeming to explain the strangeness that sometimes occurred.

   (B) but never explaining the strangeness that sometimes occurred.

   (C) but that never seemed to explain the strangeness that sometimes occurred.

   (D) yet never seemingly explaining that strangeness that sometimes occurred.

   (E) but never did they seemingly explain the strangeness that occurred sometimes.

33. All candidates for admission must answer difficult <u>questions, college professors have prepared the questions.</u>

   (A) questions, college professors have prepared the questions.

   (B) questions; college professors having prepared the questions.

   (C) questions prepared by college professors.

   (D) questions college professors have prepared them.

   (E) questions to be asked by college professors.

34. In the eighth chapter, <u>it shows very clearly that his</u> motivation is greed.

   (A) it shows very clearly that his

   (B) it very clearly shows that his

   (C) the author shows very clearly that his

   (D) it is showed very clearly how his

   (E) the author showed how his

35. I saw a hawk diving for prey while driving past the bird sanctuary.

  (A) I saw a hawk diving for prey while driving past the bird sanctuary.

  (B) Diving for prey, I saw a hawk while driving past the bird sanctuary.

  (C) While driving past the bird sanctuary, I saw a hawk diving for prey.

  (D) While driving past the bird sanctuary, I saw a diving-for-prey hawk.

  (E) Seeing a hawk diving for prey while driving past the bird sanctuary.

36. Samuel Clemens is a famous American writer, and he used the pen name Mark Twain.

  (A) Samuel Clemens is a famous American writer, and he used the pen name Mark Twain.

  (B) Samuel Clemens is a famous American writer and used the pen name Mark Twain.

  (C) Using the pen name Mark Twain, Samuel Clemens was a famous American writer.

  (D) Samuel Clemens, a famous American writer, used the pen name Mark Twain.

  (E) Samuel Clemens is a famous American writer, he used the pen name Mark Twain.

37. The enormous, red-eyed hound was the fearfulest thing Charlotte had ever saw on the moors.

  (A) was the fearfulest thing Charlotte had ever saw on the moors.

  (B) was the most scary thing Charlotte had ever seen on the moors.

  (C) was the most fearfulest thing Charlotte had ever seen on the moors.

  (D) Charlotte saw the most frightening sight on the moors, an enormous, red eyed hound.

  (E) was the most frightening thing Charlotte had ever seen on the moors.

38. When the students finished a long day at the car wash fundraiser, they all wringed the soapy water out of their clothes and hair.

  (A) they all wringed the soapy water out of their clothes and hair.

  (B) they all were wringing the soapy water out of their clothes and hair.

  (C) they wringed all the soapy water out of their clothes and hair.

  (D) they all wrung the soapy water out of their clothes and hair.

  (E) they all wringed out of their clothes and hair the soapy water.

IMPROVING PARAGRAPHS

Instructions: The selections below are unedited drafts of students' essays. Carefully read each essay. Sections of each essay need to be rewritten to make the meaning clearer and more precise.

Each essay is followed by a series of questions about changes that might improve all or part of its organization, development, sentence structure, language usage (diction), audience focus, or use of the conventions of standard written English.

Choose the answer that most clearly and effectively expresses the writer's intended meaning. Indicate your choice by filling in the appropriate oval on the answer sheet.

Questions 39 through 44 are based on the following first draft of an essay, which is a response to an assignment discussing foreign language.

(1) *Different periods are singled out by movie buffs as the "Golden Age of Films."* (2) *For some, Hollywood has never equaled the great movies of the silent era.* (3) *Others prefer the brilliant comedies and romances of the 1930s.* (4) *An all time favorite is* It Happened One Night. (5) *However, few people pick a period in the last fifty years.* (6) *Clearly, the quality of movies has declined since the late 1940s for a number of reasons.*

(7) *First, film studios and producers have little control over what will happen to their movies.* (8) *As a result of a Supreme Court decision, studios can no longer own chains of movie theaters and can no longer guarantee a certain number of rentals and showings for a particular film.* (9) *Consequently, any given movie can easily sink into the market without a trace.* (10) *The money spent on such a movie is a total loss.* (11) *As a result, producers, who are naturally more concerned with making money than with making art, have become less willing to invest in any project that does not promise to be financially worthwhile.* (12) *The result is fear of the new.* (13) *More than ever, the successful films that are pro-duced are turned into formulas and are copied until the public becomes bored with the model.* (14) *The result is a pattern that does little to raise the quality of new films.*

(15) *One might think that the decline of the studios has been a boon to independent filmmakers.* (16) *Independent artists are faced with monumental difficulties in raising money for a project.* (17) *Unless an "indie" film has a successful director or a popular star, the project can be stalled forever by timid financial backers.*

(18) *The decline in good films is especially unfortunate.* (19) *Probably more people than ever before want to make movies and have the background and skills.* (20) *Yet, such talent rarely finds its way into the theater.* (21) *Still, people keep on going to the movies and they are seeing worse and worse films each year.*

39. Which of the following is the best revision of sentence 1?

(A) Different periods have been singled out by movie buffs as "Golden Age of Films."

(B) Movie buffs single out different periods as the "Golden Age of Films."

(C) Different periods, known as "Golden Age of Films" have been singled out by movie buffs.

(D) Periods called the *Golden Age of Films* being singled out by movie buffs.

(E) Different periods, known as the *Golden Age of Films*, have been singled out by movie buffs.

40. To improve the coherence of paragraph 1, which of the following sentences should be deleted?

(A) Sentence 2
(B) Sentence 3
(C) Sentence 4
(D) Sentence 5
(E) Sentence 6

41. Which sentence contains the thesis statement?

(A) Sentence 1
(B) Sentence 2
(C) Sentence 4
(D) Sentence 5
(E) Sentence 6

42. What is the best way to combine these sentences from paragraph 2?

Consequently, any given movie can easily sink into the market without a trace. The money spent on such a movie is a total loss.

(A) Any given movie can sink into the market, and it becomes a total loss.

(B) Consequently any movie becomes a total loss when it sinks into the market.

(C) Becoming a total loss, movies sink into the market.

(D) Given a movie that sinks into the market, you have a total loss.

(E) Consequently, any movie can sink into the market, becoming a total loss.

43. Which of the following revisions of sentence 16 provides the smoothest ordering of supporting information in paragraph 3?

(A) However, independent artists are also faced with monumental difficulties in raising money for a project.

(B) Independent artists are also faced with monumental difficulties in raising money for a project.

(C) Independent artists are faced with monumental difficulties in raising money for a project, however.

(D) Raising money for a film project is monumental for independent artists like it is for studios and mainstream producers.

(E) In addition, independent artists are often faced with monumental difficulties in raising money for a project.

44. Considering the essay as a whole, which of the following best describes the function of paragraph 4?

(A) To lend further support to the essay's thesis

(B) To present an opposing argument and present a counterargument

(C) To present some objective data in support of an alternate opinion

(D) To state the thesis

(E) To summarize the support and bring the essay to a satisfactory close

Questions 45 through 50 are based on the following first draft of an essay, which is a response to an assignment discussing summer jobs.

(1) *Some people would identify a good summer job as one that takes little effort and pays well.* (2) *Others would choose an exotic location like Maui, the Rocky Mountains, or the Florida Keys.* (3) *Among the best summer jobs are those that offer advantages in both the present and the future by training the person to work hard and deal with all kinds of people.* (4) *Working as a waiter is one such job.* (5) *Being a waiter teaches valuable skills for working efficiently and relating to others.*

(6) *A good waiter learns to work efficiently in order to survive a truly demanding job.* (7) *A waiter may be responsible for as many as twenty-five customers at a time.* (8) *To provide good service, he or she must learn to be many things at once.* (9) *Menus are distributed, water is poured, and then the waiter takes orders.*

(10) *A waiter can learn an even more valuable skill—the ability to relate to people—through serving all kinds of customers.* (11) *A certain behavior must be mastered if a waiter is to please customers and make good tips: confidence with strangers, politeness, friendliness, patience, and calmness.* (12)

Waiting on tables also enables a person to learn to cope with all sorts of difficult people, such as talkers, complainers, and tricksters. (13) *Most of all, in pressured situations a waiter must learn how to handle people and stay in control.* (14) *If a server can learn to remain courteous when customers are rude and when everything goes wrong, that person will have acquired skills that will be beneficial throughout life.*

(15) *Waiting on tables is an experience a person should not miss because it teaches efficiency and coping with others.* (16) *One benefit of waiting tables is definite, however.* (17) *A server will find chemistry, English, or another job easier after having learned to serve seventy dinners a night to demanding adults and wriggling children.* (18) *In addition to these advantages, a restaurant may overlook the beach, a forest, or city lights.*

45. With regard to the essay as a whole, which of the following best describes the writer's intent in paragraph 1?

(A) To present the purpose of the essay

(B) To establish comparisons among summer jobs

(C) To initiate support for the thesis

(D) To establish the organization of the essay

(E) To amuse the reader

46. Considering the context of paragraph 1, which of the following is the best combination of sentences 4 and 5?

(A) Working as a waiter is one such job and it teaches valuable skills for working efficiently and relating to others.

(B) Working as a waiter is one such job because you learn valuable skills for working efficiently and relating to others.

(C) Working as a waiter is one such job because it teaches valuable skills for working efficiently and relating to others.

(D) Working as a waiter, teaches valuable skills for working efficiently and relating to others.

(E) Working as a waiter or waiting on tables, teaches valuable skills for working efficiently and relating to others.

47. Which of the following revisions of sentence 8 improves the sense of the sentence?

(A) He or she must learn to do many things at once to provide good service.

(B) To provide good service, they must be many things at once.

(C) To provide good service, he or she must of learned to do many things at once.

(D) One must do many things at once to provide good service.

(E) To provide good service, a waiter must learn to do many things at once.

48. With regard to the writing style of the essay, which of the following revisions of sentence 8 is best?

(A) Water is poured, menus are distributed, and then the waiter takes orders.

(B) First pouring the water and then distributing menus, then taking orders.

(C) The waiter distributes the menus and then takes orders pouring water.

(D) First you must pass out menus, then you distribute menus, next you take orders.

(E) Menus are distributed, water is poured, and orders are taken.

49. Which of the following revisions of sentence 10 provides the smoothest transition between paragraphs 2 and 3?

(A) Second, a waiter can learn a valuable skill—the ability to relate to people—through serving all kinds of customers.

(B) In addition a waiter can learn an even more valuable skill—the ability to relate to people—through serving all kinds of customers.

(C) What a waiter can learn, also, is a even more valuable skill—the ability to relate to people—through serving all kinds of customers.

(D) A waiter can learn an even more valuable skill—the ability to relate to people—through serving all kinds of customers.

(E) The ability to relate to people—through serving all kinds of customers—is a valuable skill to have.

50. Which of the following changes would most improve the coherence of paragraph 4?

(A) Move sentence 15 to the end of the paragraph

(B) Switch 16 and 17 with 18

(C) Reverse 16 and 17

(D) Reverse 18 and 16

(E) Delete 15

Practice Exercise Set 2

ANSWERS AND EXPLANATIONS

SELF-EVALUATION RUBRIC

	6	5	4	3	2	1
Overall Impression	Demonstrates excellent command of the conventions of English; outstanding writing competence; thorough and effective; incisive	Demonstrates good command of the conventions of English; good writing competence; less thorough and incisive than the highest essays	Demonstrates adequate command of the conventions of English; competent writing	Demonstrates fair command of the conventions of English; some writing competency	Demonstrates little command of the conventions of English; poor writing skills; unacceptably brief; fails to respond to the question	Lacking skill and competence
Thesis and Purpose	Exhibits excellent perception and clarity; original, interesting, or unique approach; includes apt and specific references, facts, and/or examples	Exhibits good perception and clarity; engaging approach; includes specific references, facts, and/or examples	Clear and perceptive; somewhat interesting; includes references, facts, and/or examples	Somewhat clear but exhibits incomplete or confused thinking; dull, mechanical, overgeneralized	Very little clarity; confusing; flawed logic	Very confusing or completely off the topic
Organization and Development	Meticulously organized and thoroughly developed; coherent and unified	Well organized and developed; coherent and unified	Reasonably organized and developed; generally coherent and unified	Moderately organized and developed; some incoherence and lack of unity	Little or no organization and development; incoherent and void of unity	No apparent organization or development; incoherent
Use of Sentences	Effectively varied and engaging; virtually error free	Varied and interesting; a few errors	Adequately varied; some errors	Moderately varied and marginally interesting; one or more major errors	Little or no variation; dull and uninteresting; some major errors	Numerous major errors
Word Choice	Interesting and effective; virtually error free	Generally interesting and effective; a few errors	Occasionally interesting and effective; several errors	Moderately dull and ordinary; some errors in diction	Mostly dull and conventional; numerous errors	Numerous major errors; extremely immature
Grammar and Usage	Virtually error free	Occasional minor errors	Some minor errors	Some major errors	Severely flawed; frequent major errors	Extremely flawed

Instructions: Rate yourself in each of the categories on the rubric. Circle the description in each category that most accurately reflects your performance. Enter the numbers on the lines below. Then, calculate the average of the six numbers to determine your final score. On the SAT I, at least two readers will rate your essay on a scale of 1 to 6, with 6 being the highest. Because it is difficult to score yourself objectively, you may wish to ask a respected friend or teacher to assess your writing to reflect more accurately its effectiveness.

SELF-EVALUATION

Each category is rated 6 (high) to 1 (low)

Overall Impression	_____
Thesis and Purpose	_____
Organization and Development	_____
Use of Sentences	_____
Word Choice	_____
Grammar and Usage	_____
TOTAL	_____
Divide by 6 for final score	_____

OBJECTIVE EVALUATION

Each category is rated 6 (high) to 1 (low)

Overall Impression	_____
Thesis and Purpose	_____
Organization and Development	_____
Use of Sentences	_____
Word Choice	_____
Grammar and Usage	_____
TOTAL	_____
Divide by 6 for final score	_____

Quick-Score Answers

1.	C	11.	C	21.	C	31.	C	41.	E
2.	A	12.	E	22.	C	32.	C	42.	E
3.	C	13.	D	23.	C	33.	C	43.	A
4.	C	14.	A	24.	C	34.	C	44.	E
5.	B	15.	B	25.	D	35.	C	45.	A
6.	E	16.	C	26.	D	36.	D	46.	C
7.	C	17.	D	27.	A	37.	E	47.	E
8.	D	18.	C	28.	C	38.	D	48.	E
9.	A	19.	B	29.	B	39.	B	49.	B
10.	A	20.	E	30.	E	40.	C	50.	B

MULTIPLE-CHOICE SELF-EVALUATION

SCORING

	Number Correct	Number Incorrect
Identifying Sentence Errors, Questions 1–20		
Improving Sentences, Questions 21–38		
Improving Paragraphs, Questions 39–50		
Subtotal		
Penalty Points	N/A	.25 × number incorrect =

Total Score

Number Correct _____

Subtract Penalty Points _____

Equals _____

Where do you need to improve? _____

_____

Spend more time working on that area. See Chapters 7 through 9 for help with grammar, mechanics, punctuation, usage, and sentence and paragraph structure.

PRACTICE EXERCISE SET 2

ANSWERS AND EXPLANATIONS

IDENTIFYING SENTENCE ERRORS

1. **The correct answer is (C.)** The subject, *tent and bag*, is plural but the verb *is* is singular. Use *are*.

2. **The correct answer is (A)**. Do no use *outside of* to mean *besides* or *except*.

3. **The correct answer is (C)**. The past participle of *to become* is *become*.

4. **The correct answer is (C)**. Use *as well as*.

5. **The correct answer is (B)**. The past participle of *drink* is *drunk*. See Chapter 7 for more on irregular verbs.

6. **The correct answer is (E)**. All elements—subject-verb agreement, tenses, and modifiers—are correct.

7. **The correct answer is (C)**. The pronoun *he* has an ambiguous antecedent. The sentence would be clearer if it read "his father said he . . ."

8. **The correct answer is (D)**. The verb *returned* should be present tense.

9. **The correct answer is (A)**. Use *may* instead of *can* to mean *likely to*.

10. **The correct answer is (A)**. Replace the double negative with *had but*.

11. **The correct answer is (C)**. The word *immigrated* is used improperly. Use *emigrated*. *Emigrate* means "leave a country for a new residence."

12. **The correct answer is (E)**.

13. **The correct answer is (D)**. The pronoun *them* is too distant from its antecedent *pockets* to be clear. The phrase should read *in her pockets*.

14. **The correct answer is (A)**. The objective case *me* should be used because the word is the object of the preposition *between*.

15. **The correct answer is (B)**. The sentence incorrectly uses an adverb *badly* in place of a predicate adjective *bad*. *Felt* is a linking verb, and connecting verbs are modified by predicate adjectives, not adverbs.

16. **The correct answer is (C).** The sentence makes an unbalanced comparison. The sentence should compare similar ideas. It should read ". . . than the damage caused by the hurricane last year that destroyed downtown Laguna Beach."

17. **The correct answer is (D).** The word *alright* is nonstandard English. Use *all right*.

18. **The correct answer is (C).** The sentence contains an illogical comparison. When comparing one of a group with the rest of the group, a sentence must contain the words *other* or *else*.

19. **The correct answer is (B).** The sentence contains nonparallel phrasing. Use *your friends from work*.

20. **The correct answer is (E).**

IMPROVING SENTENCES

Note: Although some choices may have more than one error, only one error is listed for each incorrect response.

21. **The correct answer is (C).**

   Choice (A)   Active voice is preferable to passive voice.
   Choice (B)   Active voice is preferable to passive voice.
   Choice (D)   The choice is wordy compared to choice (C).
   Choice (E)   The use of a dash should be avoided.

22. **The correct answer is (C).**

   Choice (A)   The tense of the verb makes this choice incomprehensible.
   Choice (B)   The thought is incomplete.
   Choice (D)   The pronoun *that* should be used.
   Choice (E)   The tense of the verb is incorrect.

23. **The correct answer is (C).**

   Choice (A)   The modifying phrase *where it had been placed many evenings ago* is misplaced. It should modify *cloth,* not *cage*.
   Choice (B)   The modifier *many evenings ago* is misplaced.
   Choice (D)   The phrase *placed there* is indefinite. It is not clear if the reference is to the *cage* or to the *cloth*.
   Choice (E)   The tense of the verb *had been hanging* is incorrect.

24. The correct answer is (C).

Choice (A)   The tense of the verb *is hovering* is incorrect. It should be past tense.

Choice (B)   The tense of the verb *is hovering* is incorrect. It should be past tense.

Choice (D)   The pronoun *that* is preferred to *which*.

Choice (E)   Active voice is preferable to passive voice.

25. The correct answer is (D).

Use a colon to introduce a sentence that summarizes or explains the sentence before it.

Choice (A)   Active voice is preferable to passive voice.

Choice (B)   The choice is a run-on sentence with a comma splice.

Choice (C)   The sentence is passive and a run-on.

Choice (E)   The word after the colon needs to be capitalized.

26. The correct answer is (D).

Choice (A)   The passive voice is too weak for an imperative sentence.

Choice (B)   Although the sentence is grammatically correct, an implied subject is more effective in an imperative sentence.

Choice (C)   *Yarns* is a nonstandard plural.

Choice (E)   The verb tense is incorrect.

27. The correct answer is (A).

Choice (B)   The common idiom is *featured a cast*.

Choice (C)   The thought is incomplete without including *of characters*.

Choice (D)   The modifiers are misplaced.

Choice (E)   The choice is a sentence fragment.

28. The correct answer is (C).

Choice (A)   The construction is not parallel.

Choice (B)   The pronoun *we*, not *us*, should be used.

Choice (D)   The pronoun *we*, not *us*, should be used.

Choice (E)   The conditional tense *are being* should be used.

29. The correct answer is (B).

Choice (A)   The antecedent of the pronoun *them* is the singular *general*. The correct pronoun is *him*.

Choice (C)   The *general's* staff is *his*.

Choice (D)   The wording is not clear.

Choice (E)   The thought is incomplete.

30. **The correct answer is (E).**
Remember that *who's* means *who is.*
Choice (A)	The nominative *who,* not the objective pronoun *whom,* should be used.
Choice (B)	The possessive *whose,* not the contraction *who's,* should be used.
Choice (C)	The error is the same as in choice (A).
Choice (D)	Two nominative pronouns, not two objective pronouns, should be used.

31. **The correct answer is (C).**
Choice (A)	The subordinate clause must be in the past tense, not the present.
Choice (B)	The sentence is a fragment.
Choice (D)	A comma setting off the nonessential adjective clause is necessary.
Choice (E)	The verb tense is incorrect.

32. **The correct answer is (C).**
Choice (A)	The construction is not parallel.
Choice (B)	The construction is not parallel.
Choice (D)	This choice changes the meaning of the sentence.
Choice (E)	The choice is wordy compared to choice (C).

33. **The correct answer is (C).**
Choice (A)	The choice contains a comma splice.
Choice (B)	The choice is awkward and contains an incorrect semicolon.
Choice (D)	The pronoun is ambiguous.
Choice (E)	This choice changes the meaning of the sentence.

34. **The correct answer is (C).**
Choice (A)	The pronoun *it* is unclear.
Choice (B)	The pronoun *it* is unclear.
Choice (D)	The pronoun *it* is unclear.
Choice (E)	*His* refers to a character in the book, not to the *author.*

35. **The correct answer is (C).**
Choice (A)	The sentence contains a dangling modifier.
Choice (B)	The sentence contains a dangling participle. The subject *I* was not diving for prey.
Choice (D)	The wording is awkward.
Choice (E)	The sentence is a fragment.

36. **The correct answer is (D).**

    Choice (A)   The coordination is faulty.

    Choice (B)   The wording is awkward.

    Choice (C)   The use of subordination is illogical.

    Choice (E)   The choice is a run-on sentence.

37. **The correct answer is (E).**
See Chapter 7 for more about superlative and comparative forms of adjectives.

    Choice (A)   *Fearfulest* is a nonstandard superlative.

    Choice (B)   The superlative is incorrect. The adjective should be *scariest.*

    Choice (C)   The superlative is incorrect and nonstandard.

    Choice (D)   The sentence is redundant.

38. **The correct answer is (D).**

    Choice (A)   The verb form is incorrect. It should read *wrung.*

    Choice (B)   The verb tense agreement is incorrect.

    Choice (C)   The participle is used incorrectly, changing the meaning of the sentence.

    Choice (E)   The prepositional phrase is improperly placed.

IMPROVING PARAGRAPHS

39. **The correct answer is (B).** It is written in the active voice and is correct in all aspects of grammar and mechanics.

    Choice (A)   Active voice is preferable to passive voice.

    Choice (C)   Active voice is preferable to passive voice.

    Choice (D)   The sentence is incomplete.

    Choice (E)   The use of italics is improper.

40. **The correct answer is (C).** The sentence contains information that expands on sentence 3 but is not necessary to support the thesis.

    Choice (A)   This sentence leads the reader to the thesis statement.

    Choice (B)   This sentence leads the reader to the thesis statement.

    Choice (D)   This sentence leads the reader to the thesis statement.

    Choice (E)   This sentence is the thesis statement.

41. **The correct answer is (E).** It states the thesis.

    Choice (A)   The sentence leads the reader to the thesis statement.

    Choice (B)   The sentence leads the reader to the thesis statement.

    Choice (C)   The sentence is irrelevant.

    Choice (D)   The sentence leads the reader to the thesis statement.

42. **The correct answer is (E).** It retains the correct meaning of the sentences while using a participle to add variety to the sentence structures in the paragraph.

    Choice (A)   The sentence contains an ambiguous pronoun.

    Choice (B)   The meaning of the sentence is changed.

    Choice (C)   The sense of the sentence is reversed.

    Choice (D)   The sentence is confusing. The use of *you* changes the tone.

43. **The correct answer is (A).** It is the clearest use of transitions and is grammatically correct. Transitions establish relationships and clarify order.

    Choice (B)   Although the sentence is good, the two transitions in choice (A), *however* and *also*, work better.

    Choice (C)   Although the sentence is good, the transitions in choice (A), *however* and *also*, work better.

    Choice (D)   The use of *like* is incorrect.

    Choice (E)   The sentence contains a transitional phrase *in addition* that indicates addition, whereas the sentence requires one indicating contrast. The use of *often* changes the meaning.

44. **The correct answer is (E).** Paragraph 4 summarizes and concludes the essay.

    Choice (A)   The paragraph summarizes and concludes the essay.

    Choice (B)   There is no argument or counterargument.

    Choice (C)   The choice contains no objective data.

    Choice (D)   The thesis statement is in paragraph 1.

45. **The correct answer is (A).** Paragraph 1 presents the purpose of the essay.

    Choice (B)   The essay does not compare summer jobs.

    Choice (C)   Support is found in the body paragraphs.

    Choice (D)   The thesis does establish an order for support, but the purpose of paragraph 1 is broader.

    Choice (E)   The choice is completely wrong.

46. **The correct answer is (C).** All punctuation and grammar are correct.

  Choice (A)   A comma between two independent clauses joined by a conjunction is required.

  Choice (B)   The pronoun *you* is incorrect. It should be third person singular *he* or *she*.

  Choice (D)   The comma is incorrectly placed in the subject.

  Choice (E)   This choice lacks a smooth transition from sentence 2 to sentence 3.

47. **The correct answer is (E).** All the answers except choice (E) contain awkward phrasing.

  Choice (A)   The wording is awkward.

  Choice (B)   This choice contains an ambiguous pronoun reference.

  Choice (C)   The preposition *of* is used in place of the helping verb *have*.

  Choice (D)   This choice contains the extremely formal pronoun *one* instead of the common *he or she*.

48. **The correct answer is (E).** It is the only choice that is a complete sentence with correct constructions.

  Choice (A)   The construction is not parallel.

  Choice (B)   The sentence is incomplete.

  Choice (C)   The sentence contains a dangling participle.

  Choice (D)   The choice is a run-on sentence with a pronoun shift to *you*.

49. **The correct answer is (B).** It uses the transition *in addition*. See Chapter 3 for transitional phrases that indicate order of importance.

  Choice (A)   The sentence has a transition indicating chronological order when the organization of the essay indicates order of importance.

  Choice (C)   The sentence contains no transitions.

  Choice (D)   The sentence contains no transitions.

  Choice (E)   The sentence contains no transitions.

50.   **The correct answer is (B).** This rearrangement uses sentences 16 and 17 to support and reinforce sentence 18.

    Choice (A)   Sentence 15 is a reminder of the thesis. It is better placed at the beginning of the conclusion.

    Choice (C)   This choice is illogical and makes the paragraph more confusing.

    Choice (D)   This choice is also illogical.

    Choice (E)   This choice suggests eliminating the reminder of the thesis statement, which is not acceptable.

Practice Exercise Set 3

PRACTICAL ADVICE

Before you begin this Practice Set, review the

- Timing guide for writing the essay
- Top 10 rules of effective writing
- System for working the multiple-choice test questions
- Strategies for answering the different types of multiple-choice questions

You will find these reviews compiled for you in a handy Quick Reference Guide on pages 372–373.

Answers and Explanations are provided immediately after the set of practice exercises, but do not look at them until you have finished all the exercises in the set. Time this Practice Set as though it were the real test; that means allotting 20 minutes to write the essay and 25 minutes to answer the multiple-choice questions.

WRITING THE ESSAY

Directions: Think carefully about the issue described in the excerpt below and about the assignment that follows it.

In choosing a college to attend, the location of a college is more important than its size or its extracurricular sports and activities.

Assignment: What is your opinion of the idea that location is a more critical factor in choosing a college than either size or extracurricular sports and activities? Plan and write an essay that develops your point of view on the issue. Support your opinion with reasoning and examples from your reading, your personal experience, or your observations.

Write your essay on separate sheets of paper or go to www.petersons.com/satessayedge.

ANSWER SHEET:
PRACTICE EXERCISE SET 3

1 Ⓐ Ⓑ Ⓒ Ⓓ Ⓔ	21 Ⓐ Ⓑ Ⓒ Ⓓ Ⓔ	41 Ⓐ Ⓑ Ⓒ Ⓓ Ⓔ
2 Ⓐ Ⓑ Ⓒ Ⓓ Ⓔ	22 Ⓐ Ⓑ Ⓒ Ⓓ Ⓔ	42 Ⓐ Ⓑ Ⓒ Ⓓ Ⓔ
3 Ⓐ Ⓑ Ⓒ Ⓓ Ⓔ	23 Ⓐ Ⓑ Ⓒ Ⓓ Ⓔ	43 Ⓐ Ⓑ Ⓒ Ⓓ Ⓔ
4 Ⓐ Ⓑ Ⓒ Ⓓ Ⓔ	24 Ⓐ Ⓑ Ⓒ Ⓓ Ⓔ	44 Ⓐ Ⓑ Ⓒ Ⓓ Ⓔ
5 Ⓐ Ⓑ Ⓒ Ⓓ Ⓔ	25 Ⓐ Ⓑ Ⓒ Ⓓ Ⓔ	45 Ⓐ Ⓑ Ⓒ Ⓓ Ⓔ
6 Ⓐ Ⓑ Ⓒ Ⓓ Ⓔ	26 Ⓐ Ⓑ Ⓒ Ⓓ Ⓔ	46 Ⓐ Ⓑ Ⓒ Ⓓ Ⓔ
7 Ⓐ Ⓑ Ⓒ Ⓓ Ⓔ	27 Ⓐ Ⓑ Ⓒ Ⓓ Ⓔ	47 Ⓐ Ⓑ Ⓒ Ⓓ Ⓔ
8 Ⓐ Ⓑ Ⓒ Ⓓ Ⓔ	28 Ⓐ Ⓑ Ⓒ Ⓓ Ⓔ	48 Ⓐ Ⓑ Ⓒ Ⓓ Ⓔ
9 Ⓐ Ⓑ Ⓒ Ⓓ Ⓔ	29 Ⓐ Ⓑ Ⓒ Ⓓ Ⓔ	49 Ⓐ Ⓑ Ⓒ Ⓓ Ⓔ
10 Ⓐ Ⓑ Ⓒ Ⓓ Ⓔ	30 Ⓐ Ⓑ Ⓒ Ⓓ Ⓔ	50 Ⓐ Ⓑ Ⓒ Ⓓ Ⓔ
11 Ⓐ Ⓑ Ⓒ Ⓓ Ⓔ	31 Ⓐ Ⓑ Ⓒ Ⓓ Ⓔ	
12 Ⓐ Ⓑ Ⓒ Ⓓ Ⓔ	32 Ⓐ Ⓑ Ⓒ Ⓓ Ⓔ	
13 Ⓐ Ⓑ Ⓒ Ⓓ Ⓔ	33 Ⓐ Ⓑ Ⓒ Ⓓ Ⓔ	
14 Ⓐ Ⓑ Ⓒ Ⓓ Ⓔ	34 Ⓐ Ⓑ Ⓒ Ⓓ Ⓔ	
15 Ⓐ Ⓑ Ⓒ Ⓓ Ⓔ	35 Ⓐ Ⓑ Ⓒ Ⓓ Ⓔ	
16 Ⓐ Ⓑ Ⓒ Ⓓ Ⓔ	36 Ⓐ Ⓑ Ⓒ Ⓓ Ⓔ	
17 Ⓐ Ⓑ Ⓒ Ⓓ Ⓔ	37 Ⓐ Ⓑ Ⓒ Ⓓ Ⓔ	
18 Ⓐ Ⓑ Ⓒ Ⓓ Ⓔ	38 Ⓐ Ⓑ Ⓒ Ⓓ Ⓔ	
19 Ⓐ Ⓑ Ⓒ Ⓓ Ⓔ	39 Ⓐ Ⓑ Ⓒ Ⓓ Ⓔ	
20 Ⓐ Ⓑ Ⓒ Ⓓ Ⓔ	40 Ⓐ Ⓑ Ⓒ Ⓓ Ⓔ	

IDENTIFYING SENTENCE ERRORS

Instructions: The sentences in this section test your knowledge of grammar, usage, diction (choice of words), and idiom.

Some sentences are correct.

No sentence contains more than one error.

The underlined and lettered parts of each sentence below may contain an error in grammar, usage, word choice, or expression. Read each sentence carefully, and identify the item that contains the error according to standard written English.

Indicate your choice by filling in the corresponding oval on your answer sheet. Only the underlined parts contain errors. Assume that the balance of the sentence is correct. No sentence contains more than one error.

Some sentences may contain no error. In those cases, the correct answer will always be No error Ⓔ.

SAMPLE QUESTION

The meteor showers <u>attracted</u>
                          A
astronomers from all over the world, <u>for</u>
                                          B
there <u>had never been</u> such a brilliant <u>one</u>
              C   D
in recent times. <u>No error</u>
                      E

SAMPLE ANSWER

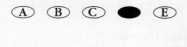

---

1. The seamen <u>pulled on</u> <u>his</u> parka and <u>went</u>
                     A   B   C
    on the deck <u>to see the island.</u> <u>No error</u>
                       D   E

2. Tom and Frank <u>returned</u> home <u>faster than</u>
                       A   B
    expected<u>;</u> and they quickly changed into
             C
    <u>their</u> soccer uniforms. <u>No error</u>
        D   E

3. The honor guard <u>came to attention,</u> <u>and</u>
                          A   B
    the audience <u>saluted</u> the flag as
                      C
    it <u>was risen</u> over the courthouse building.
           D
    <u>No error</u>
        E

4. The <u>shortcomings</u> of the United States
             A
    Constitution <u>was</u> quickly <u>rectified</u> by the
                     B   C
    framers <u>with the Bill of Rights.</u> <u>No error</u>
                     D   E

5. While Danny and Keisha <u>were vacationing</u>
                                 A
    in the Caribbean, <u>they went scuba</u>
                            B
    <u>diving</u> and <u>came face to face</u> with a lemon
        C   D
    shark. <u>No error</u>
                E

6. The sights and smells of the holiday
    season are <u>beautiful,</u> <u>but</u> <u>more wonderful</u>
                   A   B   C
    <u>of all</u> is the gala sound you hear. <u>No error</u>
        D   E

7. Moving quick, the Navy Seal Team
         A
    came on shore to secure the landing zone
         B   C
    for the troops that followed. No error
         D   E

8. Each member of the prom committee
         A
    started to report to the group on their
         B   C
    area of responsibility, but time ran out
         D
    before the last person spoke. No error
                 E

9. To the horror of all those who were
         A   B
    watching, the spacecraft raised up and
         C   D
    flew away. No error
           E

10. Disdain of his constituents was the reason
         A   B
    that Congressman Jameson
         C
    was not reelected. No error
         D   E

11. The police began to solve the crime by
            A
    taking fingerprints, canvassing the
         B   C
    neighborhood for witnesses, and to talk
                   D
    with the victims. No error
           E

12. The tropical sun had just dipped below
           A
    the western horizon as the small sailboat,
         B
    framed by the azure sea and scarlet sky,
         C
    came into view. No error
         D   E

13. Jason is considered the best of the two
         A   B
    guards on the team, so he throws the ball
             C
    in from out of bounds. No error
         D   E

14. At Eileen's Dress Shop, the dresses are
         A   B
    similar to department stores, except they
         C
    are more expensive and have more sizes.
                 D
    No error
     E

15. The play was in three acts; the first two
         A   B
    acts were boring but the last act was filled
         C   D
    with action. No error
           E

16. The football game was so exciting that
         A
    hardly nobody left the stands until the last
         B   C   D
    play. No error
         E

17. As young puppies, the dog owner
         A
    tried to instill discipline in Jasper and
         B
    Murphy, but their youthful exuberance
         C
    prevented long training sessions. No error
         D   E

18. In many business organizations the movers
         A
    and shakers are not the people which
         B   C
    have the titles. No error
         D   E

19. When Hari and Tamiko returned from
              A
    their vacation, they quickly found
         B
    themselves back in the day-to-day grind.
         C   D
    No error
     E

20. Todd and Laurie were both candidates for
         A
    class president, but neither were the one
             B
    who was finally elected. No error
     C D   E

IMPROVING SENTENCES

Instructions: The underlined sections of the sentences below may contain errors in standard written English, including awkward or ambiguous expressions, poor word choice, incorrect sentence structure, or faulty grammar, usage, and punctuation. In some items, the entire sentence may be underlined.

Read each sentence carefully. Identify which of the five alternative choices is most effective in correctly conveying the meaning of the original statement. Choice (A) always repeats the original. Select (A) if none of the other choices improves the original sentence.

Indicate your choice by filling in the corresponding oval on the answer sheet. Your choice should make the most effective sentence—clear and precise, with no ambiguity or awkwardness.

SAMPLE QUESTION

Ansel Adams photographed landscapes <u>and they communicate</u> the essence of Yosemite and other mountainous regions.

(A) and they communicate
(B) landscapes, they communicate
(C) landscapes, and communicating
(D) which communicate
(E) that communicate

SAMPLE ANSWER

21. Pilots in all branches of the military must be highly skilled, but Naval aviators are the ones <u>that must complete night carrier landings.</u>

(A) that must complete night carrier landings.
(B) that must complete their night carrier landings.
(C) who must complete night carrier landings.
(D) which must complete night carrier landings.
(E) that have to complete night carrier landings.

22. Paul quickly went to the grocery store <u>and selected the items on his mother's list, which he carelessly threw</u> into the cart before rushing to the checkout counter.

(A) and selected the items on his mother's list, which he carelessly threw
(B) and, with his mother's list in hand, he carelessly threw the items that he selected
(C) and, using his mother's list of items, he was carelessly throwing them
(D) and with his mother's list of items he was carelessly throwing them
(E) and throwing his mother's list of items carelessly

www.petersons.com

23. The man who cleaned the pool was a diligent worker, <u>and he was enjoyable to be around because he was always whistling.</u>

    (A) and he was enjoyable to be around because he was always whistling.
    (B) it was enjoyable to be around him because he was always whistling.
    (C) being around him was always enjoyable because he was always whistling.
    (D) and he was enjoyable to be around because he always was whistling.
    (E) to be around him would be enjoyable because he always whistled.

24. In winter <u>the number of workers absent from their jobs with illness were</u> very high.

    (A) the number of workers absent from their jobs with illness were
    (B) absenteeism with illness was
    (C) illness that created job absenteeism were
    (D) the numbers of workers absent from their jobs with illness were
    (E) the number of workers absent from their jobs with illness was

25. In order to get into the college of your choice, <u>one needs to take several steps,</u> including the submission of a complete application.

    (A) one needs to take several steps
    (B) you need to take several steps
    (C) one will need to take several steps
    (D) taking several steps by you
    (E) several steps should be taken by one

26. I was horrified <u>to hear her terrible language, to feel her extreme animosity, and also seeing her horrible manners.</u>

    (A) to hear her terrible language, to feel her extreme animosity, and also seeing her horrible manners.
    (B) to hear her terrible language, to feel her extreme animosity, and also to see her horrible manners.
    (C) to hear her terrible language, feeling her extreme animosity, and also seeing her horrible manners.
    (D) to hear her terrible language, to feel her extreme animosity, and seeing her horrible manners.
    (E) to hear her terrible language, seeing her horrible manners, and also to feel her extreme animosity.

27. The fastest eaters in the entire high school <u>were Tom and him.</u>

    (A) were Tom and him.
    (B) was Tom and him.
    (C) were Tom and he.
    (D) were him and Tom.
    (E) was he and Tom.

28. After his accident and the emergency surgery, <u>Larry looked awful.</u>

    (A) Larry looked awful.
    (B) Larry looked awfully.
    (C) Larry appeared awful.
    (D) Larry looked pale and tired.
    (E) Larry appeared awful pale and tired.

29. Will you please bring my Yorkshire terrier to the veterinarian about noon?

    (A) Will you please bring my Yorkshire terrier to the veterinarian about noon?
    (B) Will you please take my Yorkshire terrier to the veterinarian about noon?
    (C) Please, will you please bring my Yorkshire terrier to the veterinarian about noon?
    (D) Please, will you bring my yorkshire terrier to the veterinarian about noon?
    (E) How about taking my yorkshire terrier to the veterinarian about noon?

30. This electric automobile may travel as fast as 60 miles per hour.

    (A) This electric automobile may travel
    (B) A electric automobile can travel
    (C) That electric automobile may travel
    (D) An electric automobile may travel
    (E) This electric automobile can travel

31. By noon I will have been planting over two hundred marigolds.

    (A) I will have been planting
    (B) I will have planting
    (C) us will have been planted
    (D) I will have planting
    (E) I will have planted

32. Of all the swimmers in the Life Guard training program, Ahmad was the faster swimmer.

    (A) the Life Guard training program, Ahmad was the faster swimmer.
    (B) the life guard training program, Ahmad were the faster swimmer.
    (C) the life guard training program, Ahmad was the fastest swimmer.
    (D) the Life Guard training program, Ahmad was the fastest swimmer.
    (E) the Life Guard training program, Ahmad swam faster.

33. Those criteria for choosing the winner are unfair.

    (A) Those criteria for choosing the winner are unfair.
    (B) That criteria for choosing the winner is unfair.
    (C) That criteria for choosing the winner are unfair.
    (D) Those criteria for choosing the winner is unfair.
    (E) The criteria for choosing the winner is unfair.

34. Senior citizens from all over the nation has come to Los Angeles to protest cuts in social security.

    (A) has come to Los Angeles to protest cuts in social security.
    (B) has come to Los Angeles to protest cuts in Social Security.
    (C) has come to L.A. to protest cuts in social security.
    (D) has angrily come to Los Angeles to protest cuts in social security.
    (E) have come to Los Angeles to protest cuts in Social Security.

35. Due to the fact that he was undernourished, he was extremely thin.

    (A) Due to the fact that he was undernourished,
    (B) Due to the fact that he were undernourished,
    (C) Since he were undernourished
    (D) Because he was undernourished,
    (E) Because of the fact that he was undernourished,

36. <u>Nobody in the company believes they will lose their jobs.</u>

  (A) Nobody in the company believes they will lose their jobs.
  (B) Nobody in the company believe they will lose their jobs.
  (C) Nobody in the company believes he can lose their jobs.
  (D) Nobody in the company believes one will lose their job.
  (E) Nobody in the company believes she will lose her job.

37. When you are a sales associate at the store where Carmen works, <u>you must follow a strict dress code.</u>

  (A) you must follow a strict dress code.
  (B) one must follow a strict dress code.
  (C) I must follow a strict dress code.
  (D) people must follow a strict dress code.
  (E) one may follow a strict dress code.

38. <u>Jasper enjoys a very unique position in our family.</u>

  (A) Jasper enjoys a very unique position in our family.
  (B) Jasper enjoys a unique position in our family.
  (C) Jasper enjoys an extremely unique position in the family.
  (D) Jasper is a very unique member of our family.
  (E) A very unique position in our family is enjoyed by Jasper.

IMPROVING PARAGRAPHS

> **Instructions:** The selections below are unedited drafts of students' essays. Carefully read each essay. Sections of each essay need to be rewritten to make the meaning clearer and more precise.
>
> Each essay is followed by a series of questions about changes that might improve all or part of its organization, development, sentence structure, language usage (diction), audience focus, or use of the conventions of standard written English.
>
> Choose the answer that most clearly and effectively expresses the writer's intended meaning. Indicate your choice by filling in the appropriate oval on the answer sheet.

Questions 39 through 44 are based on the following first draft of an essay presenting arguments for self-employment.

(1) *For many people the thought of part-time work can create images of flipping hamburgers and mopping floors. (2) On the other hand it is possible to find part-time work where you can be your own boss. (3) Jobs like gardening, baby-sitting, or tutoring students provide the opportunity to control your own destiny since you are your own boss.*

(4) *You may present the argument that working for oneself can be harder than working for someone else. (5) You may find it necessary to go and search for customers; a requirement not found when you are an employee of a company. (6) Planning for your own business is also a complexity that you don't come across as a company worker. (7) These challenges, however, can be overcome.*

(8) *The hurdles you have to overcome are all within your power to control, and yet the benefits of self-employment are those that are making life more fulfilling. (9) It is not unexpected that you will need to turn over some rocks to find customers, but newspaper advertising, handbills, and word of mouth can get the message around that you are a service provider. (10) In some cases you may find it* necessary to acquire tools to perform your work. (11) *That can be done by purchasing secondhand equipment, and in some situations you may find that the supplier will help you finance the acquisition until you can pay it off.*

(12) *There are benefits besides the money that accrue to you from starting your own business. (13) First, as your own boss you can control the time and place of your work. (14) Certainly, you have to take care of your customers, but none the less you are the one in control. (15) Secondly, you are providing a service to society. (16) How do you know that? (17) Who in their right mind would pay you if you weren't providing something useful? (18) The bottom line is your own company is good for you and good for others.*

39. Which of the following is the best revision of sentence 4 in the second paragraph?

(A) Some may have presented the argument that working for yourself can be harder than working for someone else.

(B) You may present the argument that working for yourself can be harder than working for someone else.

(C) Presenting your argument of a difficulty with self-employment.

(D) There are some people who can present the argument that working for themselves can be harder than working for others.

(E) People find that working on their own is more difficult than working for others.

40. Which of the following is the best revision of the underlined portion of sentence 8?

The hurdles you have to overcome are all within your power to control, and yet the benefits of self-employment are those that are making life more fulfilling.

(A) making life more fulfilling.

(B) fulfilling.

(C) those that make life more fulfilling.

(D) fulfilling to one's life.

(E) the one's that are more fulfilling for your life.

41. Which of the following is the best revision of the underlined portion of sentence 11?

That can be done by purchasing second-hand equipment, and in some situations you may find that the supplier will help you finance the acquisition until you can pay it off.

(A) Purchasing secondhand equipment can do that

(B) The purchase of secondhand equipment is a means

(C) Secondhand equipment has been available

(D) To accomplish this goal one only need to purchase secondhand equipment

(E) Purchasing secondhand equipment can be done

42. Which of the following is the best revision of sentence 15?

(A) Secondly, you can provide a service to society.

(B) Second, you are providing a societal service.

(C) Second, you will be providing a service to society.

(D) In the second place you are providing a service to society.

(E) Second, you are providing a service to society.

43. With regard to coherence, style, and tone, which of the following sentences should be deleted?

(A) Sentences 14 and 15

(B) Sentences 13 and 17

(C) Sentences 15 and 18

(D) Sentences 16 and 17

(E) Sentences 16 and 18

44. Considering the essay in its entirety, which of the following statements best describes the purpose of the last paragraph?

  (A) An argument against working for other people.

  (B) A statement of the condition of various employment methods.

  (C) Examples of how people view the work.

  (D) A summary of the benefits of self-employment.

  (E) An assessment of the validity of the position that the author takes toward work.

Questions 45 through 50 are based on the following first draft of an essay, which is a response to an assignment discussing destructive types of weather.

(1) *Someone once said that the most talked about subject is the weather.* (2) *When people talk about the weather, it is often an element of idle chitchat.* (3) *On the other hand sometimes the discussion can turn more serious, such as when a destructive storm has played havoc in the area.* (4) *One weather condition that rarely, if ever, becomes the topic of a positive conversation is hail.*

(5) *The problem with hail is its destructive nature.* (6) *Hailstones can range from pea-sized objects to grapefruit-like chunks of ice.* (7) *When they fall from the sky, they can reach speeds of over 100 miles per hour.* (8) *The largest stones weighing over two pounds, you can imagine the impact when these missiles hit the ground with that kind of force.*

(9) *For example, in Fort Worth, Texas, hailstones destroyed roofs on homes and buildings and they looked like cannon balls when they hit the water in swimming pools.* (10) *Damage to vehicles and structures can be awesome.* (11) *It has been reported that people were reported killed by hail in India.* (12) *In*

1977 there was a plane crash in Georgia that was likely caused by hail.

(13) *The greatest destruction from hail, however, is to crops.* (14) *The impact of hail on the grain fields in the Midwest can be devastating.* (15) *Elsewhere, high-value crops such as fruits and vegetables can be wiped out by one untimely hailstorm.*

(16) *The friendly banter about weather between people doesn't contemplate the horrific problems that can be caused by hail.* (17) *This nasty type of weather can bring financial disaster.* (18) *However, even worse severe hail storms can cause enormous suffering to many people.*

45. Which of the following is the best revision of the underlined section of sentence 3?

On the other hand sometimes the discussion can turn more serious, such as when a destructive storm has played havoc in the area.

  (A) serious; such as when a destructive storm plays havoc in the area.

  (B) serious, the subject being destructive storms have played havoc in the area.

  (C) serious, to a destructive storm has wreaked havoc in the area.

  (D) serious: since destructive storms can wreak havoc in the area.

  (E) serious, to a destructive storm that has wreaked havoc in the area.

46. What is the purpose of sentence 5 in paragraph 2?

  (A) It is the topic sentence of a paragraph presenting support for the main idea.

  (B) It is the thesis statement of the essay.

  (C) It presents a fact as supporting evidence.

  (D) It serves as a transition from paragraph 1.

  (E) It introduces spatial order for development.

47. With regard to style and tone, which of the following is the best revision of sentence 8?

    (A) You can imagine the impact and that kind of force when these missiles hit the ground.

    (B) The impact of the largest two-pound missiles when these missiles hit the ground with that kind of force is unimaginable.

    (C) You can imagine the impact when these largest of missiles hit the ground weighing over two pounds with that kind of force.

    (D) You can imagine the impact when these two-pound missiles hit the ground with that kind of force.

    (E) Imagine the impact of these missiles, which can weigh over two pounds, when they hit the ground!

48. To improve the coherence of paragraph 3, how should the paragraph be revised?

    (A) Sentence 9 should be moved to the end of the paragraph.

    (B) Sentences 10 and 11 should be switched.

    (C) Sentence 10 should begin the paragraph.

    (D) Sentence 12 should be the first sentence of the paragraph.

    (E) Sentences 10 and 12 should be switched.

49. In terms of style, which of the following is the best revision of sentence 14 in paragraph 4?

    (A) The impact of hail on the grain fields in the Midwest is devastating.

    (B) Grain fields in the Midwest have been devastated by hail.

    (C) Hail has impacted the devastated grain fields of the Midwest.

    (D) Hail has devastated grain fields in the Midwest.

    (E) Devastated grain fields exist in the Midwest because of hail.

50. Which of the following is the best revision of sentence 16?

    (A) The friendly banter between people about weather doesn't contemplate the horrific problems that can be caused by hail.

    (B) The friendly banter among people about weather does not negate the horrific problems that can be caused by hail.

    (C) The friendly banter among people about weather does not contemplate the horrific problems that can be caused by hail.

    (D) When people engage in friendly banter about weather, that doesn't negate the horrific problems that can be caused by hail.

    (E) The friendly weather banter between people does not negate the horrific problems that can be caused by hail.

Practice Exercise Set 3

ANSWERS AND EXPLANATIONS

SELF-EVALUATION RUBRIC

	6	5	4	3	2	1
Overall Impression	Demonstrates excellent command of the conventions of English; outstanding writing competence; thorough and effective; incisive	Demonstrates good command of the conventions of English; good writing competence; less thorough and incisive than the highest essays	Demonstrates adequate command of the conventions of English; competent writing	Demonstrates fair command of the conventions of English; some writing competency	Demonstrates little command of the conventions of English; poor writing skills; unacceptably brief; fails to respond to the question	Lacking skill and competence
Thesis and Purpose	Exhibits excellent perception and clarity; original, interesting, or unique approach; includes apt and specific references, facts, and/or examples	Exhibits good perception and clarity; engaging approach; includes specific references, facts, and/or examples	Clear and perceptive; somewhat interesting; includes references, facts, and/or examples	Somewhat clear but exhibits incomplete or confused thinking; dull, mechanical, overgeneralized	Very little clarity; confusing; flawed logic	Very confusing or completely off the topic
Organization and Development	Meticulously organized and thoroughly developed; coherent and unified	Well organized and developed; coherent and unified	Reasonably organized and developed; generally coherent and unified	Moderately organized and developed; some incoherence and lack of unity	Little or no organization and development; incoherent and void of unity	No apparent organization or development; incoherent
Use of Sentences	Effectively varied and engaging; virtually error free	Varied and interesting; a few errors	Adequately varied; some errors	Moderately varied and marginally interesting; one or more major errors	Little or no variation; dull and uninteresting; some major errors	Numerous major errors
Word Choice	Interesting and effective; virtually error free	Generally interesting and effective; a few errors	Occasionally interesting and effective; several errors	Moderately dull and ordinary; some errors in diction	Mostly dull and conventional; numerous errors	Numerous major errors; extremely immature
Grammar and Usage	Virtually error free	Occasional minor errors	Some minor errors	Some major errors	Severely flawed; frequent major errors	Extremely flawed

Instructions: Rate yourself in each of the categories on the rubric. Circle the description in each category that most accurately reflects your performance. Enter the numbers on the lines below. Then, calculate the average of the six numbers to determine your final score. On the SAT I, at least two readers will rate your essay on a scale of 1 to 6, with 6 being the highest. Because it is difficult to score yourself objectively, you may wish to ask a respected friend or teacher to assess your writing to reflect more accurately its effectiveness.

SELF-EVALUATION

Each category is rated 6 (high) to 1 (low)
Overall Impression _____
Thesis and Purpose _____
Organization and Development _____
Use of Sentences _____
Word Choice _____
Grammar and Usage _____

TOTAL _____
    Divide by 6 for final score _____

OBJECTIVE EVALUATION

Each category is rated 6 (high) to 1 (low)
Overall Impression _____
Thesis and Purpose _____
Organization and Development _____
Use of Sentences _____
Word Choice _____
Grammar and Usage _____

TOTAL _____
    Divide by 6 for final score _____

Quick-Score Answers

1.	B	11.	D	21.	C	31.	E	41.	A
2.	C	12.	E	22.	B	32.	C	42.	E
3.	D	13.	B	23.	A	33.	A	43.	D
4.	B	14.	C	24.	E	34.	E	44.	D
5.	E	15.	D	25.	B	35.	D	45.	E
6.	C	16.	B	26.	B	36.	E	46.	A
7.	A	17.	A	27.	C	37.	A	47.	E
8.	C	18.	C	28.	D	38.	B	48.	C
9.	D	19.	E	29.	B	39.	B	49.	D
10.	A	20.	B	30.	E	40.	C	50.	B

MULTIPLE-CHOICE SELF-EVALUATION

Scoring

	Number Correct	Number Incorrect
Identifying Sentence Errors, Questions 1–20		
Improving Sentences, Questions 21–38		
Improving Paragraphs, Questions 39–50		
Subtotal		
Penalty Points	N/A	.25 × number incorrect =

Total Score

Number Correct _____

Subtract Penalty Points _____

Equals _____

Where do you need to improve? _____

_____

Spend more time working on that area. See Chapters 7 through 9 for help with grammar, mechanics, punctuation, usage, and sentence and paragraph structure.

ANSWERS AND EXPLANATIONS

IDENTIFYING SENTENCE ERRORS

1. **The correct answer is (B).** The noun *seamen* is plural; therefore, the phrase *his parka* should be the plural *their parkas*.

2. **The correct answer is (C).** A comma is required to separate two independent clauses joined by a conjunction.

3. **The correct answer is (D).** The correct tense of the verb is the past tense *rose*.

4. **The correct answer is (B).** The subject of the sentence *shortcomings* is plural, so the verb should be the plural *were*.

5. **The correct answer is (E).** All elements of the sentence—verb tenses, pronoun antecedents, and punctuation—are correct.

6. **The correct answer is (C).** The comparison is of three elements, so the superlative form of the adverb *most* is needed.

7. **The correct answer is (A).** The adverb *quickly* should be used to modify the verb *moving*.

8. **The correct answer is (C).** The antecedent of the pronoun *their* is the singular *each*. The singular pronouns *his* or *her* should be used.

9. **The correct answer is (D).** The past tense of the verb *rise* is *rose*.

10. **The correct answer is (A).** The common idiom is *disdain for*.

11. **The correct answer is (D).** The sentence lacks parallel construction. Use the verb form *talking*. Correct a sentence containing faulty parallelism by reworking it so that each parallel idea is expressed by the same grammatical construction.

12. **The correct answer is (E).** All elements are correct. The word *western* is not capitalized because it refers to a direction, not to a specific geographic region.

13. **The correct answer is (B).** When comparing two elements, use *better*, not *best*.

14. **The correct answer is (C).** The statement contains an illogical comparison. Use the phrase *similar to those at*.

15. **The correct answer is (D).** A comma is needed to separate independent clauses joined by a conjunction.

16. **The correct answer is (B).** Use *anybody* to avoid a double negative.

17. **The correct answer is (A).** The phrase *as young puppies* is a misplaced modifier. It should be placed after the words it modifies, *Jasper and Murphy*.

18. **The correct answer is (C).** The pronoun *who* should be used when referring to people. *Which* and *that* should be used to refer to things and *who* to people.

19. **The correct answer is (E).** All elements are correct, including the hyphenation of the unit modifier *day-to-day*.

20. **The correct answer is (B).** The pronoun *neither* is singular. Use the singular verb *was*.

IMPROVING SENTENCES

Note: Although some choices may have more than one error, only one error is listed for each incorrect response.

21. **The correct answer is (C).**

Choice (A)	The pronoun *that* should not be used to refer to people. Use *who* instead.
Choice (B)	The use of *their* adds nothing to the sentence.
Choice (D)	The pronoun *which* should not be used to refer to people. Use *who* instead.
Choice (E)	The change in the verb does not alter the incorrect use of the pronoun *that*.

22. **The correct answer is (B).**

Choice (A)	The modifier *which he carelessly threw* is misplaced. It should modify *items,* not *list*.
Choice (C)	The tense of the verb *was throwing* is incorrect.
Choice (D)	The tense of the verb *was throwing* is incorrect.
Choice (E)	The sentence incorrectly states that he was *throwing his mother's list of items carelessly*. The sentence remains incomplete.

23. **The correct answer is (A).**

Choice (B)	Active voice is preferable to passive voice.
Choice (C)	Active voice is preferable to passive voice.
Choice (D)	The adverb *always* should be placed to modify *whistling*.
Choice (E)	The phrasing *to be around him* is awkward.

24. The correct answer is (E).

Choice (A) The subject of the sentence *number* is singular. The verb should be the singular *was*.

Choice (B) *Absenteeism* is *due to* illness.

Choice (C) The subject of the sentence *illness* is singular. The verb should be the singular *was*.

Choice (D) *Numbers of* is an incorrect idiom.

25. The correct answer is (B).

Choice (A) The subject should be the second person pronoun *you*.

Choice (C) The verb should be present tense, not future tense.

Choice (D) The phrase is a sentence fragment.

Choice (E) The active voice is preferable to the passive voice.

26. The correct answer is (B).

Choice (A) The sentence has a predicate structure that is not parallel—two infinitives and a present participle.

Choice (C) This choice has a predicate structure that is not parallel—two present participles and an infinitive.

Choice (D) This sentence has the same error as choice (A).

Choice (E) This sentence has the same error as choice (A).

27. The correct answer is (C).

Choice (A) There is an error in pronoun choice. A linking verb requires the nominative case *he*.

Choice (B) This choice contains the same pronoun choice error and an error in subject-verb agreement.

Choice (D) This choice contains the same error as choice (A), and it is preferable to place a proper noun before a pronoun.

Choice (E) The wording is grammatically correct, but it is preferable to place a proper noun before a pronoun.

28. The correct answer is (D).

Choice (A) The clause contains an informal expression *awful*.

Choice (B) This choice includes an adverb modifying *Larry* instead of an adjective.

Choice (C) The clause contains an informal expression *awful*.

Choice (E) The clause needs the adverb *awfully* to modify *pale*. Use adverbs to modify adjectives.

29.   The correct answer is (B).

Choice (A)	The sentence uses *bring* incorrectly. It means "to carry from a distant place to a nearer one." The correct word is *take*, which means "to carry from a nearer place to a farther one."
Choice (C)	This choice has the same error as choice (A).
Choice (D)	The sentence has an error in capitalization as well as the error in verb choice.
Choice (E)	This choice is very informal and has an error in capitalization.

30.   The correct answer is (E).

Choice (A)	The clause has an error in verb choice. *May* means "to have permission to," not "to have the ability to," which is the meaning of *can*.
Choice (B)	The wording contains an error in article use. *A* should be *An*.
Choice (C)	This choice has the same error as choice (A).
Choice (D)	This choice has the same error as choice (A).

31.   The correct answer is (E).

Choice (A)	The clause contains a verb tense error.
Choice (B)	The clause contains a verb tense error and a verb form error.
Choice (C)	The clause contains a subject error as well as a verb tense error.
Choice (D)	The clause contains a verb form error.

32.   The correct answer is (C). This is a tricky question. If the official title of the program were Life Guard Training Program, then none of the choices would be correct. But since the original statement does not capitalize the words *training program,* the reader has to assume that is not the official title; thus, capitalizing *Life Guard* is incorrect.

Choice (A)	This choice contains a comparative adjective instead of a superlative.
Choice (B)	This choice contains a comparative adjective instead of a superlative and errors in verb tense and capitalization.
Choice (D)	This choice contains an error in capitalization.
Choice (E)	This choice contains an error in capitalization as well as a comparative adverb instead of a superlative.

33. The correct answer is (A).

Data is another word that people often think is singular when it is the plural form of *datum,* a single piece of information.

Choice (B)   There is an error in subject-verb agreement. *Criteria* is plural.

Choice (C)   This has the same error as choice (B) as well as an error in pronoun-adjective agreement.

Choice (D)   This has the same error as choice (B). The singular of *criteria* is *criterion.*

Choice (E)   This contains the same error as choice (B).

34. The correct answer is (E).

Choice (A)   The sentence contains an error in subject-verb agreement and an error in capitalization.

Choice (B)   This choice contains an error in subject-verb agreement.

Choice (C)   This choice contains an error in subject-verb agreement, an error in capitalization, and an informal term, *L.A.*

Choice (D)   This choice contains errors in subject-verb agreement and capitalization.

35. The correct answer is (D).

Choice (A)   This choice is wordy.

Choice (B)   This choice is wordy and contains an error in subject-verb agreement.

Choice (C)   This choice contains an error in subject-verb agreement.

Choice (E)   This choice is wordy.

36. The correct answer is (E).

Choice (A)   The sentence contains an error in pronoun antecedent agreement.

Choice (B)   The sentence contains the same error as choice (A) and an error in subject-verb agreement.

Choice (C)   The sentence contains an error in subject-verb agreement.

Choice (D)   The sentence contains an error in pronoun antecedent agreement.

37. The correct answer is (A).

Choice (B)   This choice contains an error in pronoun agreement.

Choice (C)   This choice contains an error in pronoun agreement.

Choice (D)   This choice contains an error in pronoun agreement.

Choice (E)   This choice contains an error in pronoun agreement.

38. **The correct answer is (B).**

Choice (A)   The sentence is illogical. *Unique* means "one of a kind," so there is no point in adding *very*.

Choice (C)   This choice contains the same error as choice (A).

Choice (D)   This choice changes the meaning of the sentence.

Choice (E)   This choice not only contains the same error as choice (A) but is also awkwardly worded in the passive voice.

IMPROVING PARAGRAPHS

39. **The correct answer is (B).** It corrects the pronoun antecedent problem.

Choice (A)   The antecedent of the pronoun *yourself* is the third person *some*.

Choice (C)   This is a sentence fragment.

Choice (D)   This sentence is in the third person. The essay is from the point of view of second person.

Choice (E)   The sentence is a declaration of fact. That is not the intent of the author.

40. **The correct answer is (C).** It uses the proper form of the verb.

Choice (A)   The tense of the verb is incorrect.

Choice (B)   There is a misplaced modifier. *Life*, not *benefits*, is more fulfilling.

Choice (D)   The wording is a shift from second to third person.

Choice (E)   The possessive case is incorrect.

41. **The correct answer is (A).** This choice has the best sentence structure.

Choice (B)   The thought is incomplete.

Choice (C)   The clause does not apply to the sentence.

Choice (D)   The phrasing is awkward.

Choice (E)   The clause does not apply to the sentence.

42. **The correct answer is (E).** It has parallel structure and uses a common idiom. Only use *can* to mean "to have the ability to or be able to."

Choice (A)   The use of *can* alters the author's meaning.

Choice (B)   The phrase *societal service* is not a common idiom.

Choice (C)   The tense of the verb should be present, not future.

Choice (D)   The sentence lacks parallel construction. *In the second place* is not parallel with *first*.

43. **The correct answer is (D).** These sentences are not necessary to the point of the paragraph.

Choice (A)   Sentences 14 and 15 restate important points made in the essay.

Choice (B)   Sentence 13 restates an important point.

Choice (C)   Sentence 15 restates an important point, and 18 reminds readers of the thesis.

Choice (E)   Sentence 18 reminds readers of the thesis.

44. **The correct answer is (D).** The last paragraph summarizes the benefits of self-employment. No other answer contains this thought.

45. **The correct answer is (E).** It has correct punctuation and standard English wording.

Choice (A)   The clause is dependent; therefore, a comma should separate it, not a semicolon.

Choice (B)   Active voice is preferable to passive voice.

Choice (C)   The wording is incoherent.

Choice (D)   The clause is dependent; therefore, a comma should separate it, not a colon.

46. **The correct answer is (A).** It identifies the topic of the paragraph.

Choice (B)   The thesis statement is contained in the first paragraph.

Choice (C)   It is a statement containing an idea, not a presentation of supporting fact.

Choice (D)   Although it does provide a transition from the first paragraph, that is not its primary purpose.

Choice (E)   It does not provide spatial order.

47. **The correct answer is (E).** All the answers except choice (E) contain awkward phrasing. Each of the incorrect choices uses the phrase *that kind*, wording that is unimpressive at best.

48. **The correct answer is (C).** It is the topic sentence; therefore, it should be the first sentence. Sentence 10 is the best topic sentence for the paragraph. It also provides a transition from the preceding paragraph. Sentences 9, 11, and 12 present facts in support of the topic sentence.

49. The correct answer is (D). The wording and structure are direct and to the point.

Choice (A) This choice is wordy compared to the more direct statement in choice (D).

Choice (B) The active voice is preferable to the passive voice.

Choice (C) The active voice is preferable to the passive voice.

Choice (E) The wording is awkward.

50. The correct answer is (B). The wording and structure are direct and to the point.

Choice (A) This is an error in the choice of verb and/or an error in diction. *Banter* means "lively chat"; it can't contemplate anything.

Choice (C) The verb *contemplate* does not properly express the author's thought that hail can be devastating.

Choice (D) The thought is poorly developed. People talking don't have the ability to negate an act of nature.

Choice (E) The thought is poorly developed. People talking don't have the ability to negate an act of nature.

Practice Exercise Set 4

PRACTICAL ADVICE

Before you begin this Practice Set, review the

- Timing guide for writing the essay

- Top 10 rules of effective writing

- System for working the multiple-choice test questions

- Strategies for answering the different types of multiple-choice questions

You will find these reviews compiled for you in a handy Quick Reference Guide on pages 372–373.

Answers and Explanations are provided immediately after the set of practice exercises, but do not look at them until you have finished all the exercises in the set. Time this Practice Set as though it were the real test; that means allotting 20 minutes to write the essay and 25 minutes to answer the multiple-choice questions.

WRITING THE ESSAY

Directions: Think carefully about the issue described in the excerpt below and about the assignment that follows it.

It is not winning that counts, but how you play the game.

Assignment: What is your opinion of the idea that how you live your life is more important than winning—being successful? Plan and write an essay that develops your point of view on the issue. Support your opinion with reasoning and examples from your reading, your personal experiences, and your observations.

Write your essay on separate sheets of paper or go to www.petersons.com/satessayedge.

ANSWER SHEET:
PRACTICE EXERCISE SET 4

1 Ⓐ Ⓑ Ⓒ Ⓓ Ⓔ	21 Ⓐ Ⓑ Ⓒ Ⓓ Ⓔ	41 Ⓐ Ⓑ Ⓒ Ⓓ Ⓔ
2 Ⓐ Ⓑ Ⓒ Ⓓ Ⓔ	22 Ⓐ Ⓑ Ⓒ Ⓓ Ⓔ	42 Ⓐ Ⓑ Ⓒ Ⓓ Ⓔ
3 Ⓐ Ⓑ Ⓒ Ⓓ Ⓔ	23 Ⓐ Ⓑ Ⓒ Ⓓ Ⓔ	43 Ⓐ Ⓑ Ⓒ Ⓓ Ⓔ
4 Ⓐ Ⓑ Ⓒ Ⓓ Ⓔ	24 Ⓐ Ⓑ Ⓒ Ⓓ Ⓔ	44 Ⓐ Ⓑ Ⓒ Ⓓ Ⓔ
5 Ⓐ Ⓑ Ⓒ Ⓓ Ⓔ	25 Ⓐ Ⓑ Ⓒ Ⓓ Ⓔ	45 Ⓐ Ⓑ Ⓒ Ⓓ Ⓔ
6 Ⓐ Ⓑ Ⓒ Ⓓ Ⓔ	26 Ⓐ Ⓑ Ⓒ Ⓓ Ⓔ	46 Ⓐ Ⓑ Ⓒ Ⓓ Ⓔ
7 Ⓐ Ⓑ Ⓒ Ⓓ Ⓔ	27 Ⓐ Ⓑ Ⓒ Ⓓ Ⓔ	47 Ⓐ Ⓑ Ⓒ Ⓓ Ⓔ
8 Ⓐ Ⓑ Ⓒ Ⓓ Ⓔ	28 Ⓐ Ⓑ Ⓒ Ⓓ Ⓔ	48 Ⓐ Ⓑ Ⓒ Ⓓ Ⓔ
9 Ⓐ Ⓑ Ⓒ Ⓓ Ⓔ	29 Ⓐ Ⓑ Ⓒ Ⓓ Ⓔ	49 Ⓐ Ⓑ Ⓒ Ⓓ Ⓔ
10 Ⓐ Ⓑ Ⓒ Ⓓ Ⓔ	30 Ⓐ Ⓑ Ⓒ Ⓓ Ⓔ	50 Ⓐ Ⓑ Ⓒ Ⓓ Ⓔ
11 Ⓐ Ⓑ Ⓒ Ⓓ Ⓔ	31 Ⓐ Ⓑ Ⓒ Ⓓ Ⓔ	
12 Ⓐ Ⓑ Ⓒ Ⓓ Ⓔ	32 Ⓐ Ⓑ Ⓒ Ⓓ Ⓔ	
13 Ⓐ Ⓑ Ⓒ Ⓓ Ⓔ	33 Ⓐ Ⓑ Ⓒ Ⓓ Ⓔ	
14 Ⓐ Ⓑ Ⓒ Ⓓ Ⓔ	34 Ⓐ Ⓑ Ⓒ Ⓓ Ⓔ	
15 Ⓐ Ⓑ Ⓒ Ⓓ Ⓔ	35 Ⓐ Ⓑ Ⓒ Ⓓ Ⓔ	
16 Ⓐ Ⓑ Ⓒ Ⓓ Ⓔ	36 Ⓐ Ⓑ Ⓒ Ⓓ Ⓔ	
17 Ⓐ Ⓑ Ⓒ Ⓓ Ⓔ	37 Ⓐ Ⓑ Ⓒ Ⓓ Ⓔ	
18 Ⓐ Ⓑ Ⓒ Ⓓ Ⓔ	38 Ⓐ Ⓑ Ⓒ Ⓓ Ⓔ	
19 Ⓐ Ⓑ Ⓒ Ⓓ Ⓔ	39 Ⓐ Ⓑ Ⓒ Ⓓ Ⓔ	
20 Ⓐ Ⓑ Ⓒ Ⓓ Ⓔ	40 Ⓐ Ⓑ Ⓒ Ⓓ Ⓔ	

IDENTIFYING SENTENCE ERRORS

1. Although Ali had worked hard to perfect
                    A   B
    her artistic skills, she wondered what all
              C
    her work had proven. No error
              D   E

2. As the thirty-three-car field roared away

    from the starting line, it was clear that the
                    A
    blue roadster was the faster competitor
                    B
    when it left the other vehicles in its dust.
     C   D
    No error
      E

3. Keisha is a girl who loves to perform; and
                            A
    she uses her skills at dancing as an outlet
            B   C
    for her considerable energy. No error
            D   E

4. Helene and Jamie have been accepted to
                         A
    the colleges of their choice, but its a
               B   C
    wonder that they made it considering all
    the crazy things that they did in high
                           D
    school. No error
          E

5. The football coach told his team that the

    keys to winning were playing with desire,
                   A   B

PART III: PUTTING IT ALL TOGETHER

never giving up, and to tackle with a
          C   D
vengeance. No error
          E

6. In the artist's community, many of the
          A
members had a lot of disdain about some
                B
painters' making money from commercial
  C   D
portraits. No error
        E

7. While fishing the longlines in the North

Atlantic, the small fishing boat encoun-
      A
tered an unexpected hurricane, but it was
            B
able to survive due to the courageous
       C   D
work of the crew. No error
          E

8. My sister is highly skilled at many creative
         A
things, including decorating, writing, and
          B
story telling, but I think I might be able
             C
to beat her at volleyball. No error
   D   E

9. The problems that confront most of us in
          A
life is secondary to those challenges that
  B   C
people who are facing life-threatening
        D
diseases must overcome. No error
          E

10. Tomas thought that his job will always be
          A
there for him, but he took steps to insure
     B   C   D
financial security for his family. No error
           E

11. Sean, Jaimie, and Ramesh were leaving for
          A
their new jobs, but on the way his car
    B   C
broke down, and they were late. No error
       D   E

12. Although Jerry was known as a fast
          A
runner, his time for running a mile
      B
was much worse than Lois. No error
    C   D   E

13. The thief ran from the police as

fast as he could, but he couldn't barely
   A   B
crawl over the brick wall because he was
               C   D
so fat. No error
       E

14. The volcanoes that form the

Hawaiian islands have been spewing lava
         A   B
for millions of years, but the

ocean, wind, and rain keep wearing
         C
these mountains down. No error
     D   E

15. When the New Year's celebration is
          A
over and people return to a normal
     B
schedule, one wonders if there will be
        C   D
anything that has changed from the prior

year. No error
    E

16. While studying for an examination, you
       A
rarely get a chance to focus on activities
        B   C
that are entertaining. No error
 D   E

17. People of all ages admire Tiger Woods'

skill at golf alot, and many feel his success
       A
at such a young age puts him
  B   C   D
at the forefront of athletes in all forms of
       D
sports. No error
     E

18. Of the two responsibilities that my parents

gave me, the <u>most difficult</u> was taking
   A   B

care of my baby brother <u>who</u>
                              C

<u>constantly cried.</u> <u>No error</u>
     D   E

19. Upon entering the art <u>museum,</u> Paul and
                          A

Laura <u>came</u> across a <u>most unique</u> replica
      B   C

of an ancient Roman artifact <u>made</u> out of
                             D

gold and silver. <u>No error</u>
                 E

20. I came home <u>after playing</u> tennis feeling
                  A

that I <u>let</u> my sister down because our
      B

opponents <u>beat</u> us <u>soundly.</u> <u>No error</u>
         C   D   E

IMPROVING SENTENCES

Instructions: The underlined sections of the sentences below may contain errors in standard written English, including awkward or ambiguous expressions, poor word choice, incorrect sentence structure, or faulty grammar, usage, and punctuation. In some items, the entire sentence may be underlined.

Read each sentence carefully. Identify which of the five alternative choices is most effective in correctly conveying the meaning of the original statement. Choice (A) always repeats the original. Select (A) if none of the other choices improves the original sentence.

Indicate your choice by filling in the corresponding oval on the answer sheet. Your choice should make the most effective sentence—clear and precise, with no ambiguity or awkwardness.

SAMPLE QUESTION

Ansel Adams photographed landscapes <u>and they communicate</u> the essence of Yosemite and other mountainous regions.

(A) and they communicate
(B) landscapes, they communicate
(C) landscapes, and communicating
(D) which communicate
(E) that communicate

SAMPLE ANSWER

 Ⓐ Ⓑ Ⓒ Ⓓ ⬤

---

21. Many emeralds, once they are placed in a setting, are <u>as beautiful in their appearance as diamonds.</u>

(A) as beautiful in their appearance as
(B) as beautiful in its appearance as
(C) as beautiful in their appearance like
(D) as beautiful as
(E) beautiful in appearance as

22. Band members spend a great deal of time <u>marching they also must practice playing</u> their instruments on their own time.

(A) marching they also must practice playing
(B) marching; they also must practice playing
(C) marching, they also must practice playing
(D) marching: they also must practice playing
(E) marching and they also must practice playing

23. The speed and beauty of the new roadster <u>accounts for its popularity</u> with car enthusiasts.

    (A)   accounts for its popularity
    (B)   accounts for one's popularity
    (C)   account for its popularity
    (D)   is the reason why it is popular
    (E)   is accounting for the popularity

24. The newspaper said that during the final match Martina <u>was trying to overcome</u> the pain from her sprained ankle, but she could not do so.

    (A)   was trying to overcome
    (B)   having tried to overcome
    (C)   would try to overcome
    (D)   will try to overcome
    (E)   tried to overcome

25. <u>The amount of energy produced by the chemical reactions was enormous</u>, according to the scientists.

    (A)   The amount of energy produced by the chemical reactions was enormous
    (B)   The amounts of energy produced by the chemical reactions was enormous
    (C)   The amount of energy produced by the chemical reactions were enormous
    (D)   The amount of energy that was being produced by the chemical reactions was enormous
    (E)   The amount of energy that had been produced by the chemical reactions were enormous

26. The substitute teacher <u>said quietly but with firmness that discipline would be maintained in her classroom.</u>

    (A)   said quietly but with firmness that discipline would be maintained in her classroom.
    (B)   said quietly but with firmness that discipline should be maintained in her classroom.
    (C)   said that discipline would be maintained quietly but with firmness in her classroom.
    (D)   said quietly but firmly that discipline would be maintained in her classroom.
    (E)   said quietly but with firmness discipline will be maintained in my classroom.

27. <u>At the age of 10 years old, Sonya's parents took her to Disneyland for the very first time.</u>

    (A)   At the age of 10 years old, Sonya's parents took her to Disneyland for the very first time.
    (B)   For the very first time at the age of 10, Sonya's parents took her to Disneyland.
    (C)   When Sonya was 10, her parents took her on her first trip to Disneyland.
    (D)   Sonya's parents took Sonya to Disneyland for her first trip at age 10.
    (E)   For her first trip to Disneyland Sonya was taken by her parents at age 10.

28. The search for better transportation methods is <u>a financial issue with the more costly solution usually the best.</u>

 (A) a financial issue with the more costly solution usually the best.
 (B) a financial issue with the most costly solution usually the best.
 (C) financial with the more costly solution usually the best.
 (D) the more costly solution usually the best in financial issues.
 (E) a financial issue with the more costly solution usually the better.

29. <u>No one but Janet and me know</u> who won the election for class president.

 (A) No one but Janet and me know
 (B) No one but Janet and I know
 (C) Nobody but Janet and I know
 (D) No one but Janet and me knows
 (E) No one but Janet and me will know

30. The sport of sailing not only challenges a person's physical stamina <u>but it tests one's ability to judge speed and distance over water.</u>

 (A) but it tests one's ability to judge speed and distance over water
 (B) but it tests their ability to judge speed and distance over water
 (C) but also it tests one's ability to judge speed and distance over water
 (D) but also they test one's ability to judge speed and distance over water
 (E) but also it can test one's ability to judge speed and distance over water

31. The development of new feed grains that <u>can grow quickly, be harvested easily, and they are planted anywhere</u> is the goal of many agricultural scientists.

 (A) can grow quickly, be harvested easily, and they are planted anywhere
 (B) can grow quickly, be harvested easily, and it is planted anywhere
 (C) can grow quickly be harvested easily and they are planted anywhere
 (D) can grow quickly, be harvested easily, and can be planted anywhere
 (E) are grown quickly, can be harvested easily, and they are planted anywhere

32. <u>While traveling to London from Paris, John encountered a truly remarkable person.</u>

 (A) While traveling to London from Paris, John encountered a truly remarkable person.
 (B) While John was traveling to London from Paris, John encountered a truly remarkable person.
 (C) While traveling to London from Paris John encountered a truly remarkable person.
 (D) While he traveled to London from Paris, John encountered a truly remarkable person.
 (E) While traveling to London from Paris, John encountered a person of some remark.

33. The world's center for cinema, <u>visitors come in large numbers to Los Angeles each year.</u>

(A) visitors come in large numbers to Los Angeles each year.

(B) visitors have come in large numbers to Los Angeles each year.

(C) Los Angeles has a large number of visitors each year.

(D) visitors to Los Angeles come in large numbers each year.

(E) Los Angeles has visitors in a large number each year.

34. <u>Baseball players, especially those of an earlier day, are superstitious;</u> even now some players make sure that they never have bats that lay crossed near the bat rack.

(A) Baseball players, especially those of an earlier day, are superstitious;

(B) Baseball players, especially those of an earlier day, are superstitious,

(C) Baseball players are superstitious, especially those of an earlier day;

(D) Baseball players especially those of an earlier day are superstitious;

(E) Baseball players, especially those of an earlier day, are superstitious and

35. I was very pleased with the results of the detailing that <u>I did on my car, although not completing it in the time I had allotted.</u>

(A) I did on my car, although not completing it in the time I had allotted.

(B) I did on my car although not completing it in the time I had allotted.

(C) I did on my car, although not having had it completed in the time I had allotted.

(D) I did on my car, although not completing it in the time I had allotted to do it in.

(E) I did on my car, although I did not complete it in the time allotted.

36. A strong back and <u>a strong desire for success was all that was needed to complete</u> the task of building the brick wall.

(A) a strong desire for success was all that was needed to complete

(B) a strong desire for success were all that were needed to complete

(C) a strong desire for success were all that was needed to complete

(D) a strong desire for success was all that were needed to complete

(E) a strong desire for success was all that one needed to complete

37. <u>The main point of Johnson's article in the newspaper was his belief</u> that the corrupt politicians would never be prosecuted for their misdeeds.

   (A) The main point of Johnson's article in the newspaper was his belief

   (B) The main point of Johnson's article in the newspaper is his belief

   (C) Johnson's main point in the article in the newspaper was his belief

   (D) The main point of the article in the paper was Johnson's belief

   (E) The main point of Johnson's article in the paper was Johnson's belief

38. Although my parents were well intentioned, <u>the advice that they gave me was not well received by me; I argued with them at every turn</u>.

   (A) the advice that they gave me was not well received by me; I argued with them at every turn

   (B) the advice that they gave me was not well received by me; I argued with them at every turning

   (C) the advice that they gave me was not well received; I argued with them at every turn

   (D) the advice that they gave me was not well received; I was arguing with them at every turn

   (E) the advice that they gave me was not well received, and I argued with them at every turn

IMPROVING PARAGRAPHS

Questions 39 through 44 are based on the following first draft of an essay, which is a response to an assignment discussing the reasons people travel by airplane.

(1) *Not everyone is an advocate of flying.* (2) *In fact, many people go to a good deal of effort to avoid flying.* (3) *Opposition to air travel is difficult for the seasoned traveler to understand, however, the confirmed nonflier can cite dates and locations of airline disasters.* (4) *In spite of the concerns of many, air transport continues to offer a combination of convenience, speed, and safety that is unmatchable by any other means of transportation.*

(5) *Air travel is inconvenient.* (6) *An argument that is often made by the nonfliers.* (7) *Their contention is that passengers may have to wait for hours to receive their luggage.* (8) *Statistics, however, do not support one's argument to that effect.* (9) *Luggage is rarely delayed or lost.*

(10) *On the other hand, there is one convenience with air travel that is often overlooked.* (11) *Parking at airports is designed for long-term stays; whereas, parking at bus and train depots usually is only for the short-term user.*

(12) *Despite the obvious speed and convenience of air travel, there are some who remain convinced that flying in a commercial aircraft is very dangerous.* (13) *Once again, the*

statistics do not support this concern. (14) *Airline accidents are very rare, and, when compared with other transportation systems, the loss of life is significantly less.*

(15) *By all objective criteria, air travel is fast, safe and convenient.* (16) *Those opposing this fact should study the evidence.*

39. Which of the following is the best revision of the underlined portion of sentence 3 in paragraph 1?

Opposition to air travel is difficult for the seasoned traveler to understand, however, the confirmed nonflier can cite dates and locations of airline disasters.

(A) to understand, however, the confirmed nonflier can cite airline disasters by dates and locations
(B) to understand; however, the dates and locations of airline disasters can be cited by the confirmed nonflier
(C) to understand; however, the confirmed nonflier can cite dates and locations of airline disasters
(D) to understand, and the confirmed nonflier can cite dates and locations of airline disasters
(E) to understand; however, the confirmed nonflier will be able to cite dates and locations of airline disasters

40. Which of the following is the best revision of sentence 4 in paragraph 1?

(A) In spite of the concerns of many, air transportation offers an unmatched combination of convenience, speed, and safety.

(B) In spite of the concerns of many, air transport continues to offer a combination of convenience, speed, and safety that is unmatched by any other means of transportation.

(C) Air transport continues to offer a combination of convenience, speed, and safety that is unmatchable by any other means of transportation, despite the concerns of many.

(D) In spite of the concerns of many, air transport has continued to offer a combination of convenience, speed, and safety that is unmatchable by any other means of transportation.

(E) In spite of the concerns of many, air transport continues to offer a combination of convenience, speed, and safety, and it is unmatched by any other means of transportation.

41. Keeping in mind the context of sentences 5 and 6 in paragraph 2, which of the following is the best revision of those sentences?

(A) Air travel is inconvenient; an argument that is often made by the nonfliers.

(B) Nonfliers will often make an argument that air travel wasn't convenient.

(C) The inconvenience of air travel that is an argument that is often made by nonfliers.

(D) Nonfliers often argue that air travel is inconvenient.

(E) It is often argued by nonfliers that air travel can be inconvenient.

42. Which of the following is the best revision of line 8 in paragraph 2?

(A) However, statistics do not support one's argument to that effect.

(B) Statistics, however, do not support their argument.

(C) Statistics, however, do not support one's argument.

(D) There is no support for their argument in statistics.

(E) Their argument to that effect is not supported by statistics.

43. Which of the following is the best revision of the underlined portion of sentence 12 in paragraph 4?

Despite the obvious speed and convenience of air travel, there are some who remain convinced that flying in a commercial aircraft is very dangerous.

(A) there are some who remain convinced that flying in a commercial aircraft is very dangerous

(B) flying in a commercial aircraft is very dangerous according to some people

(C) there are some who have remained convinced that flying in a commercial aircraft is very dangerous

(D) there are some that remain convinced that flying in a commercial aircraft is very dangerous

(E) some people are convinced that flying in a commercial aircraft might be very dangerous

44. Which of the following is the best choice to close the last paragraph of the essay?

(A) Doing so will make them like flying.

(B) If they study the evidence, they will surely enjoy flying.

(C) When you do, you will probably like to go flying.

(D) Flying can be helpful to everyone, having looked at all of the available data.

(E) After analyzing the facts, many nonfliers may be convinced to fly.

Questions 45 through 50 are based on the following first draft of an essay, which is a response to an assignment discussing sports.

(1) *There is no doubt that the sport of golf has a lot to offer.* (2) *Players exercise in a beautiful green environment.* (3) *Players can feel the satisfaction of improving their score.* (4) *Players can take up golf at almost any age and play into their golden years.* (5) *However, for beginning golfers the problems and annoyances of the game taxes their patience and challenge their resolve.* (6) *Learning to play golf is tantalizing but frustrating because success and enjoyment are just out of reach.*

(7) *The first annoying aspect for new players is the golf course itself.* (8) *The distance from the tee to the hole can be over 500 yards.* (9) *Many holes are located so that the green is impossible to been seen by the players.* (10) *The rough is the unmowed area that borders the fairways.* (11) *It can pose problems for beginners.* (12) *Not only can golfers lose their ball but also trees and rocks pose hazards preventing a straight drive to the green.* (13) *Ponds and streams add tranquillity to the course's ambiance until a ball sinks below the surface.*

(14) *Usually golfers play in groups of three or four.* (15) *When experienced golfers team with beginners, the new golfer feels pressure to perform.* (16) *Friendly, well-intentioned advice flusters a beginning golfer, adding to his or her frustration.* (17) *Impatient players may want to play through which causes beginners to wait or to rush their play.* (18) *This tension causes new golfers to play worse.*

(19) *Inconsistency frustrates beginners the most.* (20) *Multitudinous ways exist for new golfers to make mistakes.* (21) *Hitting poor shots can make beginning players feel unskilled, foolish, and ineffective.* (22) *Hitting some good shots and some bad shots, however, can be worse.* (23) *Wasting a good drive with several bad putts can make players furious with themselves.*

(24) *Many new golfers would agree that golf is the most frustrating game in the world.* (25) *Just as a golfer decides to quit, a solid swing sends the ball rocketing to the green.* (26) *The game fascinates once more.* (27) *Golf is frustrating.* (28) *However, it is a challenge as well.*

45. Which of the following is the best revision of sentence 5?

(A) For beginning golfers the problems and annoyances of the game taxes their patience and challenges their resolve.

(B) However, for beginning golfers the problems and annoyances of the game tax their patience and challenge their resolve.

(C) But for beginning golfers the problems and annoyances of the game tax their patience and challenge their resolve.

(D) For beginning golfers, however, the problems and annoyances of the game taxes their patience and challenges their resolve.

(E) However the problems and annoyances of the game taxes the patience of beginning golfers and challenges their resolve.

46. Which of the following is the best revision of sentence 9?

(A) Many holes have locations that make it impossible for players to see the green.

(B) Many holes are located so the green is impossible to be seen by the players.

(C) The location of a great many holes causes the green to be difficult, if not impossible, to be seen by the players.

(D) The hole and the green are sometimes located so that it is impossible to be seen by the players.

(E) Many holes, located on the green, are impossible to be seen by the players.

47. Which is the most effective way to combine sentences 10 and 11?

(A) The rough is the unmowed area that borders the fairways and can pose problems for beginners.

(B) The rough can pose problems for beginners because it is the unmowed area that borders the fairways.

(C) Known as the rough, the unmowed areas bordering the fairways pose problems for beginners.

(D) The unmowed area that borders the fairways is called the rough, it can pose problems for beginners.

(E) The rough, the unmowed area, that borders the fairways, so it can pose problems for beginners.

48. Considering the sentences that precede sentence 17, which of the following is the best revision of sentence 17?

(A) Impatient players sometimes want to play through, which causes beginners to wait or to rush their play.

(B) Also, impatient players may want to play through, which causes beginners to wait or to rush their play.

(C) Impatient players may want to play through and that causes beginners to wait or to rush their play.

(D) Next, impatient players may want to play through, which causes beginners to wait or to rush their play.

(E) Impatient players will play through; causing beginners to wait or to rush their play.

49. To improve the coherence of the essay, which of the following is the best revision of sentence 19?

(A) The most frustrating thing for beginners is inconsistency.

(B) Of all the annoyances beginning players will experience during their golfing years, it is inconsistency that frustrates beginners the most.

(C) Nevertheless, inconsistency frustrates beginners the most.

(D) Inconsistency is totally frustrating to beginners.

(E) However, of all the frustrations experienced by beginners, inconsistency upsets them the most.

50. What is the purpose of sentence 24?

(A) The sentence repeats the idea expressed in the thesis statement.

(B) The sentence begins an interesting final comment.

(C) The sentence adds interesting detail.

(D) The sentence establishes the tone.

(E) The sentence is the clincher.

Practice Exercise Set 4

ANSWERS AND EXPLANATIONS

SELF-EVALUATION RUBRIC

	6	5	4	3	2	1
Overall Impression	Demonstrates excellent command of the conventions of English; outstanding writing competence; thorough and effective; incisive	Demonstrates good command of the conventions of English; good writing competence; less thorough and incisive than the highest essays	Demonstrates adequate command of the conventions of English; competent writing	Demonstrates fair command of the conventions of English; some writing competency	Demonstrates little command of the conventions of English; poor writing skills; unacceptably brief; fails to respond to the question	Lacking skill and competence
Thesis and Purpose	Exhibits excellent perception and clarity; original, interesting, or unique approach; includes apt and specific references, facts, and/or examples	Exhibits good perception and clarity; engaging approach; includes specific references, facts, and/or examples	Clear and perceptive; somewhat interesting; includes references, facts, and/or examples	Somewhat clear but exhibits incomplete or confused thinking; dull, mechanical, overgeneralized	Very little clarity; confusing; flawed logic	Very confusing or completely off the topic
Organization and Development	Meticulously organized and thoroughly developed; coherent and unified	Well organized and developed; coherent and unified	Reasonably organized and developed; generally coherent and unified	Moderately organized and developed; some incoherence and lack of unity	Little or no organization and development; incoherent and void of unity	No apparent organization or development; incoherent
Use of Sentences	Effectively varied and engaging; virtually error free	Varied and interesting; a few errors	Adequately varied; some errors	Moderately varied and marginally interesting; one or more major errors	Little or no variation; dull and uninteresting; some major errors	Numerous major errors
Word Choice	Interesting and effective; virtually error free	Generally interesting and effective; a few errors	Occasionally interesting and effective; several errors	Moderately dull and ordinary; some errors in diction	Mostly dull and conventional; numerous errors	Numerous major errors; extremely immature
Grammar and Usage	Virtually error free	Occasional minor errors	Some minor errors	Some major errors	Severely flawed; frequent major errors	Extremely flawed

Instructions: Rate yourself in each of the categories on the rubric. Circle the description in each category that most accurately reflects your performance. Enter the numbers on the lines below. Then, calculate the average of the six numbers to determine your final score. On the SAT I, at least two readers will rate your essay on a scale of 1 to 6, with 6 being the highest. Because it is difficult to score yourself objectively, you may wish to ask a respected friend or teacher to assess your writing to reflect more accurately its effectiveness.

SELF-EVALUATION

Each category is rated 6 (high) to 1 (low)

Overall Impression   _____

Thesis and Purpose   _____

Organization and Development   _____

Use of Sentences   _____

Word Choice   _____

Grammar and Usage   _____

TOTAL   _____

Divide by 6 for final score   _____

OBJECTIVE EVALUATION

Each category is rated 6 (high) to 1 (low)

Overall Impression   _____

Thesis and Purpose   _____

Organization and Development   _____

Use of Sentences   _____

Word Choice   _____

Grammar and Usage   _____

TOTAL   _____

Divide by 6 for final score   _____

Quick-Score Answers

1. D	11. C	21. D	31. D	41. D
2. B	12. D	22. B	32. A	42. B
3. A	13. B	23. C	33. C	43. A
4. C	14. A	24. E	34. A	44. E
5. D	15. E	25. A	35. E	45. B
6. B	16. E	26. D	36. B	46. A
7. D	17. A	27. C	37. D	47. C
8. E	18. B	28. B	38. C	48. B
9. B	19. C	29. D	39. C	49. E
10. A	20. E	30. C	40. A	50. A

MULTIPLE-CHOICE SELF-EVALUATION

SCORING

	Number Correct	Number Incorrect
Identifying Sentence Errors, Questions 1–20		
Improving Sentences, Questions 21–38		
Improving Paragraphs, Questions 39–50		
Subtotal		
Penalty Points	N/A	.25 × number incorrect =

Total Score

Number Correct _____

Subtract Penalty Points _____

Equals _____

Where do you need to improve? _____

_____

Spend more time working on that area. See Chapters 7 through 9 for help with grammar, mechanics, punctuation, usage, and sentence and paragraph structure.

ANSWERS AND EXPLANATIONS

IDENTIFYING SENTENCE ERRORS

1. **The correct answer is (D).** The form of the verb is incorrect. *Proved* is preferred, not *proven*.

2. **The correct answer is (B).** The superlative form of the adjective should be used when comparing more than two elements. Use *fastest*.

3. **The correct answer is (A).** A comma should be used to separate two independent clauses joined by the conjunction *and*.

4. **The correct answer is (C).** The contraction *it's*, not the possessive pronoun *its*, is correct. If you can substitute *it is* in the sentence, then *it's* is correct. If the substitution does not make sense, then *its* is correct.

5. **The correct answer is (D).** The word *tackling* should be used in order to maintain parallel construction.

6. **The correct answer is (B).** The proper idiom is *disdain for*.

7. **The correct answer is (D).** Use *due to* as an adjective modifying a noun, not as a preposition. The correct form would be *because of the courageous work*.

8. **The correct answer is (E).** You might think that *highly skilled* is incorrect, but adverbs modifying adjectives are never hyphenated.

9. **The correct answer is (B).** The subject *problems* is plural; therefore, the verb must be the plural *are*.

10. **The correct answer is (A).** The past tense *would* should be used.

11. **The correct answer is (C).** The possessive pronoun *his* could refer to any of the three. Using the possessive form of one of the subject nouns would make this clearer, such as *Ramesh's car*.

12. **The correct answer is (D).** The comparison is not parallel. Use *Lois's time* or *Lois's*.

13. **The correct answer is (B).** The use of *barely* creates a double negative.

14. **The correct answer is (A).** The word *islands*, in this case, is a proper noun, so the initial *i* should be capitalized.

15. **The correct answer is (E).** Although the use of *one* may seem stilted, the sentence is correct. The clue is the third person singular verb.

16. **The correct answer is (E).** Don't be confused by the participle *studying.* It is not a dangling participle because it modifies the subject of the independent clause *you.*

17. **The correct answer is (A).** The word *alot* is nonstandard spelling; it should be *a lot. Alot* is a common spelling, but it is incorrect.

18. **The correct answer is (B).** The comparative form *more* should be used.

19. **The correct answer is (C).** The word *unique* means "one of a kind" and cannot be modified by *most.*

20. **The correct answer is (E).** *Let* is one of those verbs whose present and past tenses are the same. The sentence calls for simple past tense. Don't confuse *leave* and *let. Leave* means "to go;" it doesn't mean "to allow or permit."

IMPROVING SENTENCES

Note: Although many choices contain more than one error, only one error is identified.

21. **The correct answer is (D).** The redundant phrase *in their appearance* is removed.

    Choice (A) The phrase *in their appearance* is redundant.
    Choice (B) The pronoun *its* is incorrect.
    Choice (C) The word *like* is incorrect.
    Choice (E) The wording is awkward.

22. **The correct answer is (B).** A semicolon is required to separate two independent clauses. Do not use a semicolon to separate independent clauses already joined by a conjunction.

    Choice (A) A semicolon is required to separate two independent clauses.
    Choice (C) A semicolon is required to separate two independent clauses.
    Choice (D) A semicolon is required to separate two independent clauses.
    Choice (E) A comma is required to separate two independent clauses joined by the conjunction *and.*

23. **The correct answer is (C).** The verb *account* properly relates to the plural subject.

    Choice (A)   The verb *appeals* does not agree with the plural subject.

    Choice (B)   The possessive pronoun *one's* refers to a person, not a car.

    Choice (D)   The wording is awkward.

    Choice (E)   The wording is awkward.

24. **The correct answer is (E).** The past tense *tried* is correct.

    Choice (A)   The tense of the verb is incorrect. Use the past tense *tried.*

    Choice (B)   The tense of the verb is incorrect. Use the past tense *tried.*

    Choice (C)   The tense of the verb is incorrect. Use the past tense *tried.*

    Choice (D)   The tense of the verb is incorrect. Use the past tense *tried.*

25. **The correct answer is (A).** The verb is singular, and the tense is correct. For more on verb tenses and subject-verb agreement, see Chapter 7.

    Choice (B)   The plural *amounts* is incorrect.

    Choice (C)   The noun *amount* is singular; therefore, the verb should be singular.

    Choice (D)   The tense of the verb *was being produced* is incorrect.

    Choice (E)   The noun *amount* is singular; therefore, the verb should be singular.

26. **The correct answer is (D).** This choice has parallel construction and proper word choice.

    Choice (A)   The phrase *with firmness* is not parallel in construction with *quietly.*

    Choice (B)   The shift in the verb to *should* is incorrect.

    Choice (C)   The modifier *quietly but with firmness* is misplaced.

    Choice (E)   The shift to a direct quotation requires appropriate punctuation.

27. **The correct answer is (C).** The sentence does not have a misplaced modifier nor is it wordy.

   Choice (A)   This choice is very wordy and has a misplaced modifier.

   Choice (B)   The modifiers are misplaced, leaving the meaning ambiguous.

   Choice (D)   The sentence is wordy, and the placement of modifiers is awkward.

   Choice (E)   The use of passive voice is not desirable.

28. **The correct answer is (B).** The superlative *most* is correct.

   Choice (A)   The comparative *more* is incorrect.

   Choice (C)   The comparative *more* is incorrect.

   Choice (D)   The modifiers are misplaced.

   Choice (E)   There are more than two items being compared, so *better* is incorrect.

29. **The correct answer is (D).** The subject of the sentence is the singular *no one*, so the verb must be singular, *knows.*

   Choice (A)   The subject *no one* is singular; therefore, the verb must be the singular *knows.*

   Choice (B)   The objective pronoun *me* should be used. Don't be confused by the placement of *me*. It is part of the compound object of the preposition *but. But* can be used in place of the preposition *except* as it is being used here.

   Choice (C)   The objective pronoun *me* should be used.

   Choice (E)   The tense of the verb is incorrect.

30. **The correct answer is (C).** The use of the phrase *but also* gives the sentence parallel construction.

   Choice (A)   The conjunction *not only* needs to be paired with *but also.*

   Choice (B)   The pronoun *their* is incorrect.

   Choice (D)   The pronoun *they* is incorrect.

   Choice (E)   The verb *can* is not necessary to convey the meaning of the sentence.

31. **The correct answer is (D).** The verb construction is parallel in all three parts.

   Choice (A)   The wording lacks parallel construction.

   Choice (B)   The pronoun *it* is incorrect.

   Choice (C)   Commas are needed to separate items in a series.

   Choice (E)   The verb selection improperly changes the meaning of the sentence.

32. **The correct answer is (A).** The wording is direct and to the point.

   Choice (B)   The wording is redundant.
   Choice (C)   A comma is required to set off the introductory phrase.
   Choice (D)   The wording is redundant.
   Choice (E)   The wording is awkward.

33. **The correct answer is (C).** The wording is simple and to the point.

   Choice (A)   The modifier *world's center* is misplaced.
   Choice (B)   The tense of the verb is incorrect.
   Choice (D)   The modifier *world's center* is misplaced.
   Choice (E)   The wording is awkward.

34. **The correct answer is (A).** The punctuation and wording are correct.

   Choice (B)   A semicolon, not a comma, is needed to separate two independent clauses.
   Choice (C)   The placement of the modifier *especially those of an earlier day* is not clear and direct.
   Choice (D)   Commas are required to set off parenthetical comments.
   Choice (E)   A comma is required before the conjunction *and*.

35. **The correct answer is (E).** The sentence is direct and has parallel construction.

   Choice (A)   The verb *completing* is not parallel with *was pleased*.
   Choice (B)   A comma is required after *car*.
   Choice (C)   The tense of the verb is incorrect.
   Choice (D)   The wording is awkward.

36. **The correct answer is (B).** The plural *were* is properly used here because the subject is compound.

   Choice (A)   The verb *was* should be replaced by the plural *were* in both locations.
   Choice (C)   The verb *was* should be replaced by the plural *were*.
   Choice (D)   The verb *was* should be replaced by the plural *were*.
   Choice (E)   The inclusion of *one* is superfluous.

37. **The correct answer is (D).** This choice eliminates the improper use of *his* and avoids redundancy.

 Choice (A) The possessive pronoun *his* cannot refer to the possessive proper noun *Johnson's.*

 Choice (B) The verb tense is incorrect.

 Choice (C) The possessive pronoun *his* cannot refer to the possessive proper noun *Johnson's.*

 Choice (E) The wording contains a redundancy.

38. **The correct answer is (C).** The unnecessary *by me* is removed, and the punctuation is correct.

 Choice (A) The phrase *by me* is redundant.

 Choice (B) The proper idiom is *at every turn.*

 Choice (D) The tense of the verb *was arguing* is incorrect.

 Choice (E) The conjunction *and* is unnecessary.

Improving Paragraphs

39. **The correct answer is (C).** The punctuation and voice are correct.

 Choice (A) A semicolon is needed to separate two independent clauses.

 Choice (B) It is preferable to use the active voice.

 Choice (D) The conjunction *and* alters the meaning of the selection.

 Choice (E) The tense of the verb is incorrect.

40. **The correct answer is (A).** This choice is succinct and avoids improper diction.

 Choice (B) This choice is unnecessarily wordy.

 Choice (C) The phrase *despite the concerns of many* is misplaced.

 Choice (D) The word *unmatchable* is improper diction. The proper word is *unmatched.*

 Choice (E) This choice is unnecessarily wordy.

41. **The correct answer is (D).** This choice is direct and to the point. The shortest answer is often the best. It must still convey the writer's thought, but the brief answer will avoid errors that are contained in the longer choices.

 Choice (A) The second clause is not independent; therefore, the semicolon is incorrect.

 Choice (B) The past tense *wasn't* is incorrect.

 Choice (C) The wording is a sentence fragment.

 Choice (E) The active voice is preferable to the passive voice.

42. The correct answer is (B). The pronoun *their* is correct, and the wording is direct.

Choice (A) The possessive pronoun *one's* is incorrect.

Choice (C) The possessive pronoun *one's* is incorrect.

Choice (D) The phrase *in statistics* incorrectly modifies *argument*.

Choice (E) The phrase *to that effect* is unnecessary.

43. The correct answer is (A). All elements of the sentence are correct.

Choice (B) In context, the noun *people,* not *flying,* should be the subject of the sentence.

Choice (C) The tense of the verb *have remained* is incorrect.

Choice (D) Don't be confused by the use of *some* to refer to people. The relative pronoun *who* is still correct, so *that* is incorrect.

Choice (E) The change in the verb to *might* alters the tone of the sentence.

44. The correct answer is (E). This choice contains a good statement of theme, transition, and summary.

Choice (A) The choice is too firm in its assessment of the nonfliers' *liking* flying.

Choice (B) The choice is too firm in its assessment of the nonfliers' *enjoying* flying.

Choice (C) The choice incorrectly shifts to second person.

Choice (D) The phrase *having looked at all of the available data* is a misplaced participle.

45. The correct answer is (B). The sentence corrects the error in subject-verb agreement.

Choice (A) The choice contains singular verbs that do not agree with the plural subject *problems* and *annoyances.*

Choice (C) The choice corrects the agreement error, but the sentence begins with a conjunction *but.*

Choice (D) The choice does not correct the subject-verb problem.

Choice (E) The sentence is missing a comma after the transition *however* and does not correct the subject-verb error.

46. **The correct answer is (A).** The sentence is in the preferred active voice.

    Choice (B)   The choice contains two awkwardly worded clauses written in the passive voice.

    Choice (C)   The sentence is overwritten.

    Choice (D)   Besides the use of the passive voice, this sentence includes a pronoun-agreement error.

    Choice (E)   This passive sentence changes the meaning of the original.

47. **The correct answer is (C).** The choice is succinct and adds sentence variety to the essay.

    Choice (A)   This choice makes equal two clauses of unequal weight. Being the unmowed area and being able to pose problems are not equal qualities, but in this choice, being joined by *and* makes them seem equal.

    Choice (B)   The choice is illogical.

    Choice (D)   The choice contains a comma splice.

    Choice (E)   The sentence is incomplete.

48. **The correct answer is (B).** The sentence contains a necessary transition. See page 37 for a chart showing transitions for different types of writing organization.

    Choice (A)   The choice does not have a transition.

    Choice (C)   The sentence requires a comma to separate the two independent clauses.

    Choice (D)   While the sentence does have a transition, *next* is used for chronological or spatial development.

    Choice (E)   The choice uses the semicolon incorrectly. A comma would be correct.

49. **The correct answer is (E).** The use of transitional words makes the essay's development by order of importance easy to follow.

    Choice (A)   The paragraph requires transition, but this choice has none.

    Choice (B)   This choice is wordy.

    Choice (C)   *Nevertheless* is an inappropriate transition for order-of-importance development.

    Choice (D)   The sentence contains nonstandard English—the slang word *totally*.

50. **The correct answer is (A).** The sentence repeats the idea expressed in sentence 6, the thesis statement.

Choice (B)   Sentence 25 begins an interesting final comment.

Choice (C)   Sentence 26 continues the final comment.

Choice (D)   Sentence 27, along with the final sentence, is the clincher.

Choice (E)   Sentence 28 completes the clincher.

QUICK REFERENCE GUIDE

PACING GUIDE FOR WRITING THE ESSAY

5 minutes	Step 1	Read the question carefully.
	Step 2	Restate to yourself what the question is asking. Underline the key words.
	Step 3	Make a list by brainstorming all the ideas that come to mind. Write down your ideas.
	Step 4	Create a thesis from the ideas you have brainstormed.
	Step 5	Turn your brainstorm into an informal working plan by numbering the items that you want include in your essay in the order in which you want to include them. Cross out ideas that no longer fit now that you have a thesis statement.
4 minutes	Step 6	Begin writing your introduction by stating your thesis clearly.
	Step 7	Read your first paragraph to be sure that your ideas follow each other logically and support your thesis.
10 minutes	Step 8	Check your quick list of ideas. Choose the next idea and write a transition into your second paragraph. Keep writing until you use all the RELEVANT ideas on your quick list.
4 minutes	Step 9	Write a solid conclusion using one of the following techniques: (a) rephrasing your thesis, (b) summarizing your main points, (c) referring in some way back to your introductory paragraph.
2 minutes	Step 10	Proofread and revise neatly.

TOP 10 RULES OF EFFECTIVE WRITING

Rule 1: Use Action Verbs and the Active Voice
Rule 2: Use Precise Words
Rule 3: Say What You Mean
Rule 4: Maintain Your Tone
Rule 5: Use Direct Language
Rule 6: Use Concise Language
Rule 7: Improve Sentences
Rule 8: Develop Sentence Variety
Rule 9: Use Standard Rules of English for Capitalization
Rule 10: Use Standard Rules of English for Punctuation

STRATEGIES FOR ANSWERING MULTIPLE-CHOICE QUESTIONS

- Carefully read the entire sentence, NOT just the underlined phrases. The underlined words may seem correct unless you read the whole statement.

- As you read, listen for any words or phrases that do not "sound" right to you. Anything that sounds awkward or strange may be a mistake.

- Always substitute into the sentence the choices for the part that you think is incorrect.

- Do not spend time to read choice (A), because it repeats the original sentence.

- Find the best answer, not one that is simply correct. More than one choice may be correct, but only one best fits the context.

- If the sentence sounds correct to your ear, the correct choice is probably (A).

- Answer the easy questions first.
  NOTE: Be sure to skip the answer ovals for the questions you skip.

- Look for errors according to difficulty:

  1. Capitalization and punctuation errors

  2. Grammar and syntax errors

  3. Usage, sequence of tenses, parallel structure, redundancy, and then other errors

- Read a sentence or passage through twice before making any decision about an answer.

- Identify the subject and the predicate of each sentence to help you find errors in usage, redundancy, and relevance.